Job Search

Job Search

Marketing Your Military Experience

5th Edition

David G. Henderson

STACKPOLE
BOOKS

Published by
STACKPOLE BOOKS
5067 Ritter Road
Mechanicsburg, PA 17055
www.stackpolebooks.com

Printed in the United States of America

10 9 8 7 6 5 4 3 2 1

Cover design by Tessa J. Sweigert

We gratefully acknowledge the cooperation of Herb Schwab for use of the *Army Career and Alumni Program* home page.

Library of Congress Cataloging-in-Publication Data

Henderson, David G., 1939–
    Job search : marketing your military experience / David G. Henderson.—
5th ed.
        p. cm.
    Includes index.
    ISBN-13: 978-0-8117-3590-2
    ISBN-10: 0-8117-3590-7
    1. Job hunting—United States. 2. Risumis (Employment) 3. Retired
military personnel—Employment—United States. 4. Career changes—
United States. I. Title.
    HF5382.75.U6H46 2009
    650.14086'970973—dc22
                                    2009016448

CONTENTS

ACKNOWLEDGMENTS

Special thanks are due to those who provided comments, suggested additions, and offered encouragement on this fifth edition, including Col. Joe Breen, USAF (Ret.); Sgt.Major Mark Hornung, USMC (Ret.); Susan Rubel, Robert Moran, and Jane Symionow of the Air Force Association; Bill Gaul, former President of The Destiny Group; and all of the former clients who graciously allowed me to use their resumes in this edition of the book.

I would also like to thank my wife, Debbie, for her graphic design work for the illustrations and charts. Lastly, I would like to thank my editor, Mark Allison, and his able assistant, Janelle Steen, for their patience and support in getting the fifth edition to press, and all the sales staff who have worked with me to ensure that *Job Search* continues to remain the top career transition book for retiring and separating military personnel as it has been for the past nineteen years.

INTRODUCTION

He who is not prepared today will be less so tomorrow.
—Ovid

Welcome to CIVWORLD! If you are completing military service in the near future, you will soon find yourself competing in an environment very different from that to which you have previously been exposed. This new environment, with a set of rules all its own, is called the civilian job market. It has no training manuals, field exercises, or operational readiness inspections to prepare you for its often puzzling and exasperating ways, where at times the only enemy turns out to be an empty mailbox, snail mail or e-mail, or a phone that doesn't ring.

Despite your previous military career experiences and your rapid ability to adapt to new jobs and responsibilities, you will still be faced with some tough choices as you approach the end of your active service. In the past, a set of orders provided you with all the information you needed to move on to the next duty station and start your new assignment. Once you have made the decision to leave active duty, however, there will be no set of orders, and the new assignment will be up to you. Where you choose to settle and what you elect to do will be critical to you and your family given a fluctuating economy and a job market that is constantly reinventing itself. So, now the real adventure begins!

Whether you are leaving the service after four years or twenty-plus years, you will be taking with you a wealth of experience, training, and specialized skills in a variety of occupational fields, or possibly just one occupational field. As you start your job search, you will find that a number of these occupational fields correspond directly to occupations or professions in the civilian workforce. In fact, if the majority of your service has been in one of these directly relatable civilian occupations, you will be able to identify a crossover occupational field without any problem. If, however, you are uncertain about how to use your military skills in the civilian marketplace, this book is for you. It was specifically designed to address this issue, as well as others facing those who fall into what is commonly called "the generalist category," which accommodates those who served in more than one occupational specialty during the course of their military career.

When should you start your job search? Is a professional resume necessary before you begin the hunt for a new job? Where do you first look for a job? How long will it take to land that first job? Should you post your resume on the Internet? What sort of Internet job banks, bulletin boards, and job search engines will be available to assist you in your job search as you exit the service? How should you prepare for your first interview? What salary should you expect to be offered for your new job? These are some of the more common questions separating and retiring members ask once they decide to leave the military. This book answers these questions and many more.

Each chapter of *Job Search* represents a major investment of time, especially if you do the required research in unfamiliar areas and then systematically file employment-related information for future use. As you prepare for your own job search, it is best to start twelve to eighteen months in advance of your separation or retirement date. Assess your interests, skills, experience, and lifestyle; set career goals; research the job market for the area where you plan to settle after leaving the military; prepare a marketable resume to support your desired area of work; circulate your resume in the marketplace and on the Internet (selectively); and learn all you can about the interview process, including salary negotiation and the principal components of a compensation package. Follow this advice and the other job search information in this book, and you could easily be on your way to achieving another successful rite of passage—from military servicemember to productive civilian employee.

If you have already made the transition to the civilian workforce, but you have decided a job change is in order, this book will be an excellent reference as you tackle the job search process once again. You may even find current job market information that wasn't available during your first job search.

Another added attraction of this book is the collection of sample resumes prepared for former servicemembers who, like yourself, were also transitioning for the first time, or possibly changing jobs for the second time since their initial transition. Although resume formats have not changed all that much over the years, there are a few new wrinkles in the main categories that make up the resume. The addition of a Computer Skills section (i.e., identifying one's proficiency in standard Microsoft operating systems and software, as well as any military systems), an Awards and Achievements section, a Special Achievements/Accomplishments or Special Qualifications section, the inclusion of a current government security clearance, and the emphasis on a ten-year window of career experience, rather than summarizing all of your work experience since you started in the military, have quietly moved to the forefront in the preparation of a new millennium resume.

One-page resumes, while acceptable under some conditions, tend to slight the individuals who complete a full twenty- or thirty-year career. Staying at a page and a half to two pages should keep you in the competitive range and not cause a prospective employer to overlook you. The resumes provided in appendix A have been arranged by those occupational specialties that tend to match up best with careers in CIVLANT. There should be a specialty and a format, or possibly even several specialties, that you can identify with in this appendix, which in turn should help you design a top-notch resume for pursuing your own job search.

The Internet section of the Converging Technologies chapter in this edition has been updated to reflect the latest changes to the Department of Defense career transition process. In addition, valuable information has been incorporated from several of the better job search books that cover twenty-first century workplace terms, job hunting websites, and suggested procedures for job searching in a downsized and rapidly changing job market. Also identified is an updated list of the best military-related job search and resume-posting sites since the last edition of the book. The improvements in the military-related job search assistance websites are extremely impressive, with the Military Officers Association of America (formerly TROA) leading the way with its monthly jobs bulletin board that boasts no fewer than 1,500 job postings at any given time. Learning how to traverse the labyrinth of the Internet and selectively use the job search tools available on the various job search websites, job banks, job search engines, and job search agents will make your career transition that much easier and rewarding over the duration of your job search campaign.

Since the last issue of this book, there have been a number of words added to the job search vocabulary, mostly as a result of advances in Internet technology. Words such as *branding, offshoring, blogging, competitive intelligence, electronic reading devices, Google, Linkedin.com, Jibber.Jobber.com, user groups*, and a number of others are now an integral part of the job search process. In addition to the advances in the desktop PC and laptop computer, we now have the use of handheld BlackBerrys, iPhones, Palm Pres, and other multimedia devices, as well as job hunting guides available in all the major occupational fields, both in hardcover and as part of an electronic reading library of books.

Whatever your particular situation, the information and advice offered in this book can make your job search an extremely worthwhile endeavor. When the techniques and strategies for the job search campaign are employed in the manner recommended, you will find yourself a more confident and better prepared candidate as you seek rewarding employment in a highly competitive civilian job market. Draw selectively from the armory of tools, technology, and advice within the covers of this book, and then hit the second career battlefield armed for success. "To the Victor goes the Job."

CHAPTER 1

DEFINING YOUR OCCUPATIONAL INTERESTS, SKILLS, AND LIFESTYLE

*A man must know his destiny . . . if he does not recognize it,
then he is lost. . . . if he has the imagination, he will turn
around and fate will point out to him what fork in the road
he should take, it he has the guts, he will take it.*
— *General George S. Patton, U.S. Army*

ASSESSMENT

Having made the decision to leave the military and seek employment in the civilian world, you are ready for the first step in the career transition process—making an assessment of your occupational interests, skills, and lifestyle. Start this evaluation twelve to eighteen months prior to separation or retirement with a written list of what is important to you in the following categories:

- Occupational interests and career fields with most opportunity for growth and job security
- Personal work values or ethics
- Skills, abilities, and any special qualifications
- Preferred lifestyle after military service
- Geographic regions of interest

The information you record for each of these areas will serve as an excellent starting point for developing a meaningful job search campaign. It will also allow counselors and friends to support your job search efforts with sound advice and recommendations.

As you start to investigate possible career fields for life after the military, make sure that job opportunities in these fields actually exist and are not just pipe dreams. Keep in mind that the best chance for obtaining a good job will be in an occupation where your military service, career-based skills, and military occupational specialty (MOS) training provide a bridge that leads to a relatable civilian position.

If you decide to pursue a line of work in civilian life that does not draw on your previous military experience, you should assess the impact of this decision in relation to your time left in service to prepare for it. Budget the time remaining in such a way that you can take advantage of service-offered courses that may fall in the area of second career interests. Whatever your specific needs, make a point of determining course availability at least eighteen to twenty-four months before leaving the military. Almost every U.S. and overseas military installation has an education office staffed by highly qualified personnel who can assist you in applying for off-duty education programs or courses that can improve your potential for landing desirable jobs in second career fields, or in occupational specialties best suited for your professional training and qualifications.

If you have already retired, you may still be able to take advantage of many of the same educational and specialized testing services that are available to active-duty members. Check with your own service, or the military installation nearest you, to see if the education office, career transition center, or Family Services Center can be of assistance.

Whether you select a career that mirrors your military service or an area unrelated to that experience, your next step is to determine your primary occupational interests and how they relate to similar career fields in the civilian workforce.

Occupational Interests and Career Fields

As you consider the wide range of civilian career fields, you will need to determine which civilian occupation corresponds best to your service experience and, just as important, where your occupational interests lie. To assist you in this analysis, answer the following questions: What occupational work areas do you feel most typify your career experiences? Do the formal military training and any civilian training you received while in the military have any direct applicability to a specific civilian occupational field? (The answer would be yes if you had a job such as air controller, computer programmer or operator, truck fleet dispatcher, pilot, or logistician.) When you have answered these questions, use this information to define your skills and abilities and identify potential career fields.

To identify a prospective career field where your MOS, skills, and experience may be best applied, a trip to the nearest public or military library is recommended. Several helpful books and reference guides have been included in appendix E, "Recommended Reading." One that is useful to start with is the current edition of the *Occupational Outlook Handbook*, followed by *The Encyclopedia of Careers and Vocational Guidance* (fourteenth or current edition).

If you are unable to identify a civilian career field that matches up with your previous military experience, you may want to consider a brief session with a career counselor. The counselor may recommend a standardized assessment inventory to ensure that you do not select a career field unsuited to your background, interests, and temperament. Taking advantage of several of the standard assessment instruments currently available would give you a better idea of who you are, which in turn could provide added benefits as you progress through this book.

Vocational Assessment Inventories

The actual process of assessing one's interest and abilities for potential employment in the civilian workforce upon transition is not easily found in the majority of job search books available in today's marketplace. For some unknown reason, most job search authors make the assumption that you have already decided on what it is you want to do or what you are most qualified for, so they start their primers at this particular on-ramp in the job search highway. So, with this as a given, just what types of vocational assessment inventories are available to you, and what might be the best one for you to take in an effort to firm up your particular desires and match them with your assessed and proven skills and capabilities?

Vocational assessment inventories are broken down into two basic groups: self-directed or requiring interpretive assistance. Self-directed refers mainly to those assessments you take on your own, and the results are normally provided in some measurable format that should assist in your decision-making process. The latter type requires the assistance of a trained counselor or a person qualified to interpret the various assessments and provide you with the results. Both types may be found for free on the Internet or from your Family Support Center, or through fee-based organizations online or through the mail. Based on a review of the recommended assessment websites, it would appear that free assessment tools are readily available, more than adequate, and able to provide you with the basic information with which to base a reasonable occupational decision. In addition to the self-directed and assistance-required assessments, there are personality and type indicators and interest inventories. The latter two types will be discussed in the next section.

Now that you have the basic fundamentals of what makes up the vocational assessment inventories, you need to go the Riley Guide (*www.rileyguide.com/assess.html*) for a more detailed breakdown of their self-assessment resources. When you have finished reading through the Riley Guide, proceed to the Quintessential Careers website (*www.quintcareers.com/career_assessment.html*) for a breakout of the various assessment tools that are either free or fee based.

Career assessment inventories are useful for military members who have made the decision to change careers and embark on a new stage in their lives. Departing military personnel have found these instruments to be helpful in narrowing their career search to specific civilian occupational fields matching their interests, skills, and personality types.

Five commonly used assessment instruments are the Myers-Briggs Type Indicator (MBTI), the Strong-Campbell Vocational Interest Blank (SVIB), the Holland Self-Directed Search (SDS), the Work Readiness Profile (WRP), and the Work Preference Inventory (WPI). The first two are published by Consulting Psychologists Press of California, and the SDS and WRP are published by Psychological Assessment Resources (PAR). You can access the WPI from the Quintessential Careers website.

The Myers-Briggs Type Indicator is widely used in business and education for career counseling, management development, and identification of leadership styles. The MBTI measures personality preferences and categorizes your personality characteristics, based on your selection of opposing preferences from four personality areas: extrovertive or introvertive (E-I), sensing or intuiting (S-N), thinking or feeling (T-F), and judging or perceiving (J-P). A skilled career counselor can help match your personality type with compatible job titles in various occupational career fields.

The MBTI is often used in combination with more specific vocational assessment instruments such as the SVIB or the SDS to provide an in-depth look at personality makeup and vocational interests that neither of the inventories could provide on its own.

The Strong-Campbell Vocational Interest Blank helps individuals make effective career decisions regardless of sex or ethnic background. It is continually updated to reflect changes in the labor force and job market. No other inventory matches its sophisticated interpretive techniques or breadth of data reported.

The SVIB is designed to identify and compare your interest patterns with those of successful people who have worked for at least ten years in each of a number of occupations. Interest patterns are identified in terms of six general occupational themes-realistic, investigative, artistic, social, enterprising, and conventional. The general line of questioning relates to academic and social interests, leisure activities, and specific fields of work. The creators of this instrument are quick to point out that the instrument is not designed to measure overall abilities or skills, but rather interactions on a daily basis with the world you live in, including likes and dislikes.

According to Psychological Assessment Resources, the Holland Self-Directed Search is the most widely administered career interest inventory in the world, having been used by more than sixteen million people. It is a self-administered instrument that helps individuals identify occupations that best suit their interests and abilities. The SDS provides immediate feedback on the vocational areas and occupations that would be a good match, all in about thirty to forty-five minutes.

The Work Readiness Profile is an excellent tool for those who may be separating with a service-connected disability. It assesses an individual's readiness to work by identifying abilities, supports, and empowerments rather than dwelling on the disability level. It assumes that with appropriate support mechanisms, adaptive skills, and behavior the individual can contribute to the workforce. The WRP should be taken in conjunction with one or the other three instruments in order to give a more meaningful picture of the opportunities available to the individual.

The Work Preference Inventory (WPI) is a twenty-five-question, fifteen-minute test designed to assess the types of work tasks with which you prefer to work. It assesses individual differences based on intrinsic and extrinsic motivational orientations. Intrinsic motivation includes self-determination, competence, task involvement, curiosity, enjoyment, and interest. Extrinsic motivation includes concerns with competition, evaluation, recognition, salary or other tangible incentives, and authority interaction. The importance of taking the WPI lies in its ability to help you better clarify what you value in terms of work style based on behavioral measures of motivation, as well as on personality characteristics and attitudes.

It is wise to take the MBTI along with either the SVIB or the SDS, since these tests tend to complement one another. Address any questions you may have concerning the availability and cost of taking these instruments to your nearest military base education office, career transition office, Family Service Center, or local community college. Costs are minimal.

Job Characteristics—Work Values and Ethic

Upon leaving the military, you are going to be in total control of your destiny, at least for a short while, and maybe longer if you decide to go into business for yourself. Reflect back on the numerous experiences of your service career in order to determine what elements you find desirable in a work environment. Determine your preferences in the following areas:

- Structured or unstructured environment (telecommuting allowed)
- Workplace proximity to your home (commuting time)
- Rigid or flexible hours and/or telecommuting
- Supervise large or small numbers of people (or none at all)
- Opportunities for advancement on regular basis
- Travel, minimal travel, or no travel
- High stress or moderate to no stress
- Short-term projects or those that require years
- Indoors or outdoors
- Physically demanding or office-oriented
- Salary based on incentives with cost-of-living raises, or fixed income and either cost-of-living raises or merit increases
- Tuition assistance or no additional training required for position
- More people-oriented than data- or object-oriented

The job characteristics you select from the above list will reveal the type of work environment you should seek once you leave the military. For example, you may not be comfortable unless you return to a structured environment with a "corporate ladder" where salaries and promotions are driven by performance and achievement. Or, you may not want a highly structured existence again, and instead will choose to pursue or create an opportunity where you can be your own boss.

Whatever your choices from the above list may be, they should be useful in helping you identify a career field with job positions that offer the type of environment and structure you desire. Before matching your list to potentially desirable career fields, review your skills and abilities to ensure that they, too, will be compatible with whatever occupation you decide to pursue.

Skills and Abilities

During your military service you had an opportunity to supervise various numbers of personnel, to manage budgets, and in many cases to be responsible for expensive equipment. Sidney Fine, in the now

FREQUENTLY USED SERVICE SKILLS

ORGANIZATIONAL/ MANAGEMENT	FUNCTIONAL	FINANCIAL
Interviewing	Computer Applications	Purchasing
Screening	Operating (equipment and vehicles)	Budgeting
Recruiting	Flying	Controlling
Training	Navigating (ships and aircraft)	Disbursing
Assigning	Communicating	Obligating
Supervising	Researching	Reprogramming
Organizing	Programming	Contracting
Planning	Processing	Accounting
Directing	Designing	
Counseling	Testing	
Evaluating	Procuring	
Promoting	Packaging	
Disciplining	Storing	
Transferring	Transporting	
	Distributing	
	Maintaining	
	Repairing	
	Upgrading	

superseded *Dictionary of Occupational Titles*, breaks down this experience into skills that deal with three groups-people, data, and things.

Many of the skills and abilities acquired in the military coincide with Fine's three primary groups: organizational or management skills (people), functional skills (things), and financial skills (data). Depending on your particular military specialty, you probably used more skills from one subgroup than from the others.

In reviewing the accompanying chart, you should be able to identify a number of skills in all three subgroups. In some cases you may think of others that are not shown that would perhaps apply only to your particular occupational specialty. Be sure to jot these down; they will come in handy later when you construct a worksheet profile for relating your military experience to a specific civilian occupational field.

Once you have recorded the information relating to your skills, determine which occupational specialties within the chosen career field would make the best use of these skills. Zero in on your predominant skills and identify those that relate to comparable civilian fields such as medicine, data processing, music, aviation, computers, or transportation.

Lifestyle after the Service

The lifestyle you select after the service is up to you. There may be certain military benefits that you will want to take advantage of because they have been earned as a result of service, while other elements of military life will be gladly left behind. How and where you socialize may change once you are free of the restrictions associated with base living. Friendships made in the service will either last or slowly fade away, and new ones will come along to take their place. Whatever the case, the lifestyle characteristics that are most important to you, such as where you live, climate, and proximity to places of interest, should be considered.

Geographic Area of Interest

Where you live after you leave the service is a major piece of the puzzle in your job search. Naturally you and your spouse may have had some discussions about where you'd like to live, but no decisions were made. What it comes down to is whether your best of all worlds can include as many of the following as possible: good year-round weather; closeness to relatives, friends, and job opportunities; schools for your kids; possible work opportunities for your spouse; and availability of recreational activities, sports facilities, parks, beaches, and the mountains. Somewhere in the laundry list of preferences is a combination that will suit the needs of you and your family. Unfortunately, bountiful job opportunities are not always found in your chosen geographic region. Be smart, and carefully check out an area's job market before you decide to either relocate or return to your hometown.

DEFINING GOALS FOR A SECOND CAREER

Unlike the military, where like clockwork you were eligible for promotion to the next higher rank after so many years in grade, or moved to the next duty station for a new assignment, the civilian world is not quite as highly structured. Whether you seek employment in a corporation, as a franchisee, as an independent businessperson, or with the county, state, or federal government, you will need to set reasonable short- and long-term goals. Properly defined, these goals will provide you and your family with a comfortable lifestyle and the means for attaining a decent retirement income.

Short-Term Goals

Short-term goals need to be realistic and attainable. They might include getting a job in a particular field, resettling the family in another geographic area, acquiring additional funds to cover a college education for your children, purchasing a new family car, establishing a sound financial planning program for the future, and ensuring that your estate is adequately insured to cover the major bills your spouse might be faced with should you die early in your new career.

This is also a good time to rethink your investment and insurance plans and do a little financial planning on your own or with the help of a certified financial planner. A sound financial plan is really the cornerstone in ensuring a less stressful entry into the civilian workplace, especially if there is a gap of several months between exiting the military and starting your first job.

Once you have decided on your short-term goals, set a reasonable time frame for accomplishing them. Think in terms of trying to fulfill these goals within six months to a year from the time you start working on them. This will allow for any unforeseen changes or reasonable adjustments associated with new employment and a possible change in lifestyle.

Long-Term Goals

Your long-term goals need to be reasonable and attainable rather than hard and fast. Allow yourself some degree of flexibility, since this may be your first time at trying to set goals that will have a major impact on your future.

Examples of long-term goals are achieving a certain position or status within your new company, working toward attaining a second retirement (if you have recently retired from the military), developing second career expertise that will be marketable in the event career opportunities with your current company do not meet your expectations, and looking for ways to improve the segment of the company in which you perform the majority of your work.

As part of your personal development plan, your new company will assist you in setting reasonable long-term goals to meet your own professional needs while satisfying corporate expectations for your overall growth within the company. These expectations are normally built into your position description and/or your annual performance review.

If you choose the self-employment route, your long-term goals will be slightly different. Promotions and status really don't matter, and you will already have a profession that is probably marketable in the workplace. You will be more concerned with building a client base and marketing your goods or skills at a rate at which you can satisfy consumer or customer demand, with an ultimate long-term goal of maintaining a strong client base.

Career Goal Trade-offs

Meeting your second career goals will take a combination of motivation, self-determination, and dedication—all three of which most military professionals have in abundance. Job satisfaction, income, and insurance and healthcare are major factors that will play a role in any decision you make about accepting a particular position. Other factors influencing your decision might include your personality, health, family considerations, and the job market in the geographic area where you intend to settle.

Attaining career goals may require some trade-offs along the way (see the "Career Goal Trade-offs" diagram). The best example of this is job satisfaction. In order to have job satisfaction, you may have to give up a chance at a higher entry salary and possibly a promotion. Then again, you can accept higher pay and benefits and with them the attendant promotions, risks, and stress. Wherever you end up and whatever occupation you decide to pursue, be prepared to make whatever trade-offs are necessary to ensure a healthy, personally rewarding, and comfortably prosperous career.

CAREER GOAL TRADE-OFFS

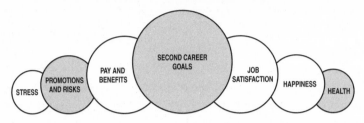

If you would like to pursue a structured career, you may want to consider putting together a career pattern that parallels the one you followed while in the service. For an example of how to map out your future in a given field, refer to the table on page 13.

The sample second career patterns matrix is designed to take the place of your present career pattern in the military. This new career matrix depicts selected professional and trade organization (technician) positions and traces typical career paths in several occupations, based on the age of the servicemember at the time of exit from the military.

After reviewing these sample career paths, be aware that the succession of positions shown for the different categories will vary by industry; they are benchmarks to measure your progress in the specialty you elect to pursue. You should also keep in mind that, unlike the military, the civilian sector changes its organization to match market shifts or modifications to corporate philosophy. Like the military, there may be passovers and possibly slower-than-normal promotional opportunities.

If you're not interested in a structured career pattern and would prefer to be unencumbered by bureaucracy and the company line, you may decide that working for yourself is the route to follow. Remember that even as your own boss, you will face some of the same career trade-offs experienced by those who enter the corporate world.

Preseparation Assistance Guide

As part of Operation Transition, the Department of Defense has published four editions of its *Preseparation Guide* (see appendix E), the latest being February 2007, to assist all servicemembers and their families in preparing for either the expiration of active service or retirement. This comprehensive guide helps you to maneuver through

SAMPLE SECOND CAREER PATTERNS

Age	YEARS AFTER LEAVING MILITARY		
	1–2 Years	3–5 Years	6–10 Years
20–37	Tradesman Technician Jr. Analyst Jr. Associate Jr. Engineer	Job Supervisor/Foreman Sr. Technician Analyst Associate Engineer	Site/Line Supervisor Sr. Technician Sr. Analyst Sr. Associate Sr. Engineer
38–45	Sr. Technician Sr. Analyst Sr. Associate Sr. Engineer Program Manager	Chief Technician Sr. Principal Analyst Partner Project Engineer Group Manager	Chief Technician Chief Analyst Partner Director of Engineering Division Director
46–52	Sr. Principal Analyst Program Manager Sr. Associate Sr. Engineer Consultant	Chief Analyst Division Director Partner Chief Engineer Consultant	Systems Director Vice President Sr. Partner Dir. for Engineering Ops. Sr. Consultant
53–60	Project Director Division Director Dir. for Engineering Ops. Partner Sr. Consultant	VP for Systems Mgt. Division Director VP Engineering Sr. Partner Sr. Consultant	Group Vice President Sr. Vice President President Managing Partner Retire

the intricacies of the separation process while taking advantage of all the military resources available. The guide is given to each separating servicemember six months prior to leaving the service.

The table of contents for the guide is also repeated on DD Form 2648 (see form on page 15), which each servicemember is directed to fill out in the presence of his or her transition counselor. The sections of the checklist that are most relevant to job searches are "Introduction to Transition Assistance" (chapter 1), "Effects of a Career Change" (chapter 2), and "Employment Assistance" (chapter 3). The remaining chapters deal with benefits programs, entrepreneurship/business ownership, education and training, financial considerations, possible reserve affiliations, employment restrictions after leaving the military, and VA disability benefits.

The Individual Transition Plan in chapter 1 of the guide is similar to the steps outlined in this chapter of Job Search. The guide recommends a seven-phase approach as follows:

Phase One: Assessment (Who are you?)

Phase Two: Exploration (What do you want to do?)

Phase Three: Skills Development (Are my current skills relatable to those required in the civilian world?)

Phase Four: Trial Career Programs (internships, volunteering, and temporary jobs)

Phase Five: The Job Search (similar to the procedures in this book)

Phase Six: Selection (accepting the right job)

Phase Seven: Support (family, relocation, and coping with stress)

The next step is following a suggested timeline of recommended actions starting at the six-month point of the preseparation period and winding down to the last thirty days prior to separation. This timeline contains a number of similar actions shown in the job search milestone schedule in chapter 4 of this book, which starts at the twelve- to eighteen-month preseparation point in the career transition process.

Chapter 2 of the *Preseparation Guide* deals mainly with the stress and grieving associated with separation from the military and where to go to seek help. Chapter 3 discusses several of the recommended approaches and tools for maneuvering through the career transition process found in chapters 3, 4, and 5 of *Job Search*. Areas of similarity will be addressed in each of these chapters.

**PRESEPARATION COUNSELING CHECKLIST
FOR ACTIVE COMPONENT SERVICE MEMBERS**
(Please read Privacy Act Statement below before completing this form.)

SECTION I - PRIVACY ACT STATEMENT

AUTHORITY: 10 USC 1142, E.O. 9397.
PRINCIPAL PURPOSE(S): To record preseparation services and benefits requested by and provided to Service members; to identify preseparation counseling areas of interest as a basis for development of an Individual Transition Plan (ITP). The signed preseparation counseling checklist will be maintained in the Service member's official personnel file. Title 10, USC 1142, requires that not later than 90 days before the date of separation, preseparation counseling for Service members be made available.
ROUTINE USE(S): None.
DISCLOSURE: Voluntary; however, it will not be possible to initiate preseparation services or develop an Individual Transition Plan (ITP) for a Service member if the information is not provided.

SECTION II - PERSONAL INFORMATION *(To be filled out by all applicants)*

1. NAME *(Last, First, Middle Initial)*		2. SSN	3. GRADE

4. SERVICE *(X one)*		5. DUTY STATION	6. ANTICIPATED DATE OF SEPARATION *(YYYYMMDD)*	I am *(X one)*
ARMY	AIR FORCE			Retiring
MARINE CORPS	COAST GUARD			Separating Voluntarily
NAVY				Separating Involuntarily

7. DATE CHECKLIST PREPARED *(YYYYMMDD)*	7.a. Place an X in this box ONLY if you have less than 90 days remaining on active duty before separation or retirement. Please read the following instructions: If voluntarily separating or retiring and you have less than 90 days remaining on active duty before your separation or retirement, why was your preseparation counseling not conducted earlier? Please go to Section V - REMARKS and check the response that best describes the reason why preseparation counseling was not conducted earlier.

SECTION III. ALL TRANSITIONING SERVICE MEMBERS MUST READ INSTRUCTIONS, SIGN AND DATE.

a. Items checked "YES" are mandatory for Service member to receive further information or counseling, or attend additional workshops, briefings, classes, etc. Service members that check "YES" in Item 11.a. will be released by Commanders to attend the appropriate workshop, briefing, etc. in its entirety.

b. Shaded Areas: Areas that are shaded mean (1) the information is not applicable or (2) the information is referring to a Web site address and the URL requires no explanation. For example: 11.b. is shaded under SPOUSE because DD Form 2586 does not apply to spouses. Items 11.f.(1) and (2) are shaded because they refer to Web site addresses and they require no explanation.

c. POST GOVERNMENT (MILITARY) SERVICE EMPLOYMENT RESTRICTION COUNSELING (Item 19): Service members cannot decline this counseling. It is required prior to separation. Therefore, no blocks exist to allow Service members the option of checking "YES", "NO", or "NA". Transition/Command Career Counselors shall refer separating and retiring Service members to an installation legal office (Staff Judge Advocate or Counsel's Office) to ensure they receive a post government (military) employment restrictions briefing or counseling from an ethics official.

d. I was offered preseparation counseling on the above date (Item 7) on my transition benefits and services as appropriate. I understand that this preseparation counseling is provided to assist my transition process as required by Title 10, USC, Chapter 58, Section 1142.

e. I have checked those items where I desire further information or counseling. I have also been advised where to obtain assistance in developing an Individual Transition Plan (ITP).

f. I ☐ accept ☐ decline *(X appropriate block)* preseparation counseling. *(If you check the "decline" box, you are declining preseparation counseling only on those items on this checklist where you have the option of declining.)* Sign and date the checklist.

8a. SERVICE MEMBER SIGNATURE	b. DATE *(YYYYMMDD)*	9a. TRANSITION COUNSELOR SIGNATURE	b. DATE *(YYYYMMDD)*

SECTION IV. Please indicate *(by checking YES or NO)* whether you *(or your spouse if applicable)* desire counseling for the following services and benefits. All benefits and services checked YES should be used in developing your ITP. The following services and benefits are available to all Service members, unless otherwise specified:

	SERVICE MEMBER			SPOUSE			REFERRED TO
	YES	NO	N/A	YES	NO	N/A	
10. EFFECTS OF A CAREER CHANGE							
11. EMPLOYMENT ASSISTANCE							
a. Dept. of Labor sponsored Transition Assistance Workshops and Service sponsored Transition Seminars/Workshops							
b. Use of DD Form 2586 (Verification of Military Experience and Training)							
(1) Do you want a copy of your Verification of Military Experience and Training (VMET) Document? If yes, go to http://www.dmdc.osd.mil/vmet to print your VMET document and cover letter.							
c. DoD Job Search Web site http://www.dod.jobsearch.org							
d. Transition Bulletin Board (TBB) and Public and Community Service Opportunities http://www.dmdc.osd.mil/ot/							
e. Teacher and Teacher's Aide Opportunities/Troops to Teachers http://www.proudtoserveagain.com							
f. Federal Employment Opportunities							
(1) http://www.usajobs.com							
(2) http://www.go-defense.com							
g. Hiring Preference in Non-Appropriated Fund (NAF) jobs (Eligible Involuntary Separatees)							

DD FORM 2648, JUN 2005 PREVIOUS EDITION IS OBSOLETE.

PRESEPARATION COUNSELING CHECKLIST FOR ACTIVE COMPONENT SERVICE MEMBERS	NAME *(Last, First, Middle Initial)*						SSN	
SECTION IV *(Continued)*		SERVICE MEMBER			SPOUSE			REFERRED TO
		YES	NO	N/A	YES	NO	N/A	
11. EMPLOYMENT ASSISTANCE *(Continued)*								
h. State Employment Agencies/America's Job Bank								
(1) http://www.ajb.org								
i. Career One Stop http://www.careeronestop.org								
12. RELOCATION ASSISTANCE *NOTE: Status of Forces Agreement limitations apply for overseas Service members.*								
a. Permissive (TDY/TAD) and Excess leave								
*b. Travel and transportation allowances								
13. EDUCATION/TRAINING								
a. Education benefits (Montgomery GI Bill, Veterans Educational Assistance Program, Vietnam-era, etc.)								
(1) http://www.gibill.va.gov								
b. Workforce Investment Act (WIA)								
c. Additional education or training options								
(1) Small Business Administration http://www.sba.gov								
d. Licensing, Certification and Apprenticeship Information								
(1) Department of Labor http://www.acinet.org								
(2) U.S. Army https://www.cool.army.mil								
(3) U.S. Military Apprenticeship Program https://www.cnet.navy.mil/usmap/								
(4) DANTES http://www.dantes.doded.mil/dantes_web/danteshome.asp								
e. Defense Activity for Non-Traditional Educational Support http://www.dantes.doded.mil/dantes_web/danteshome.asp								
14. HEALTH AND LIFE INSURANCE								
a. Transitional Health Care Benefit - for Eligibility Criteria and additional information go to: http://www.tricare.osd.mil or http://www.tricare.osd.mil/Factsheets/viewfactsheet.cfm								
b. Option to purchase 18-month conversion health insurance. Concurrent pre-existing condition coverage with purchase of conversion health insurance. http://www.tricare.osd.mil/chcbp								
c. Veterans' Group Life Insurance (VGLI) http://www.insurance.va.gov								
d. Veterans Centers http://www.va.gov/rcs								
15. FINANCES								
a. Financial Management (TSP, Retirement, SBP)								
b. Separation pay (Eligible Involuntary Separatees)								
c. Unemployment compensation								
d. Other financial assistance (VA Loans, SBA Loans, and other government grants and loans)								
16. RESERVE AFFILIATION								
17. VETERANS BENEFITS BRIEFING								
18. DISABLED VETERANS BENEFITS								
a. Disabled Transition Assistance Program (DTAP)								
b. VA Disability Benefits http:www.va.gov								

19. POST GOVERNMENT (MILITARY) SERVICE EMPLOYMENT RESTRICTION COUNSELING
Information on post government (military) employment counseling (restrictions on employment, imposed by statute and regulation) shall be conducted by Services as appropriate. Transition/Command Career Counselors shall refer separating and retiring Service members to an installation legal office (Staff Judge Advocate or Counselor's Office) to ensure they receive a post government (military) employment restrictions briefing or counseling from an ethics official.

20. INDIVIDUAL TRANSITION PLAN (ITP)

a. As a separating Service member, after receiving basic preseparation counseling information and completing this checklist, you and your spouse (if applicable) are entitled to receive assistance in developing an Individual Transition Plan (ITP) based on the areas of interest you have identified on this checklist. The preseparation counseling checklist addresses a variety of transition services and benefits to which you may be entitled. Each individual is strongly encouraged to take advantage of the opportunity to develop an ITP. The purpose of the ITP is to identify educational, training, and employment objectives and to develop a plan to help you achieve these objectives. It is the Military Department's responsibility to offer Service members the opportunity and assistance to develop an ITP. It is the Service member's responsibility to develop an ITP based on his/her specific objectives and the objectives of his or her spouse, if appropriate.

	SERVICE MEMBER			SPOUSE		
	YES	NO	N/A	YES	NO	N/A
b. Based upon information received during Preseparation Counseling, do you desire assistance in developing your ITP? If yes, the Transition staff/Command Career Counselor is available to assist you.						

DD FORM 2648, JUN 2005

PRESEPARATION COUNSELING CHECKLIST FOR ACTIVE COMPONENT SERVICE MEMBERS	NAME *(Last, First, Middle Initial)*	SSN

SECTION V - REMARKS *(Attach additional pages if necessary)*

Complete the following ONLY if you placed an X in Item 7a. See page 1, Section II, Item 7a.

21. My counseling was conducted 89 days or less before my separation or retirement because: *(X one)*

- [ ] MISSION REQUIREMENTS
- [ ] PERSONAL REASONS
- [ ] MEDICAL SEPARATION
- [ ] LEGAL SEPARATION
- [ ] CHANGE IN CAREER DECISION
- [ ] OTHER *(Please provide a brief explanation)*

KEY POINTS

- As you prepare to leave the military, the first step in your job search will be to perform an individual assessment or self-evaluation of your skills, work preferences, personality/type indicators, and possible career choices.
- Review your occupational experience as part of the assessment, and in order to make the best use of your service skills and training, select a civilian occupational field that most closely matches your military experience.
- Take advantage of reference books and guides available at your local military or public library to give you better insight into career fields and occupational specialties. (See appendix E for recommended reading.)
- Review the two major assessment websites—the Riley Guide and Quintessential Careers—for assistance in validating your interests and occupation
- When you determine additional schooling is necessary in order to achieve a position in a new occupation, use whatever service benefits are available to assist you in this area. The new GI Bill is one such benefit that you should utilize during or after you separate or retire from active service.
- Select a work environment that will complement your work style and personal preferences.
- Remember: Skills used in the military normally fall into three principal areas—organizational or managerial, functional, and financial.
- Identify the skills and abilities that best typify your military experience as they relate to people, things, and data and to the skills required by your preferred civilian occupational field.
- Select a lifestyle that not only provides personal satisfaction but also complements the work values in your new position.
- Be sure the geographic area you select to settle in has job opportunities that match your qualifications. Failing to research the job market could have disastrous results.
- Define short- and long-term career goals and set a timetable for achieving them. Be sure to keep them flexible enough to adapt to the chosen business environment.

- Be aware of career goal trade-offs that may have to be made in order to find a job that has the values, opportunities, and income necessary for you to be happy.
- If you desire structure in your second career, consider the career matrix for a typical position in a profession as tracked in the "Sample Second Career Patterns" chart in this chapter.
- Use the "Preseparation Counseling Checklist" (DD Form 2648) found in this chapter and in the DOD *Preseparation Guide* as a cornerstone for your Individual Transition Plan.

CHAPTER 2

THE JOB MARKET

The Department of Labor's biennial *Occupational Outlook Handbook* bulletin, 2008–09 edition, provides an employment forecast as well as the projected occupational structure of the workforce from 2006 to 2016. In the accompanying chart, the eight major occupational groups shown represent the types of occupations that people leaving the military currently serve in and reflect the projected changes in total employment by percent from 2006 to 2016. The accompanying table from the U.S. Bureau of Labor Statistics further amplifies the projections (2006 to 2016) of the fastest growing occupations, along with the levels of education and training they currently require.

Percent change in total employment by major occupational group, projected 2006–16

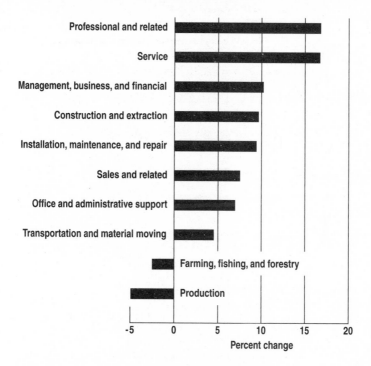

Source: "Tomorrow's Jobs." *Occupational Outlook Handbook 2008–09.*

In the "Tomorrow's Jobs" segment of the *Occupational Outlook Handbook 2008–09*, several factors are worth noting relative to industry employment growth in the service-producing industries for the period 2006 to 2016:

- Professional, scientific, and technical services will grow by 28.8 percent and add 2.1 million jobs by 2016. Computer systems design and related services (network administrators, network engineers, database managers, etc.) will grow by 38.3 percent and add nearly one-quarter of all the new jobs in the professional, scientific, and technical services occupations.
- Healthcare services will continue to increase due to an aging population with longer life expectancies and will grow by 25.4

Percent change in employment in occupations projected to grow fastest, 2006–16

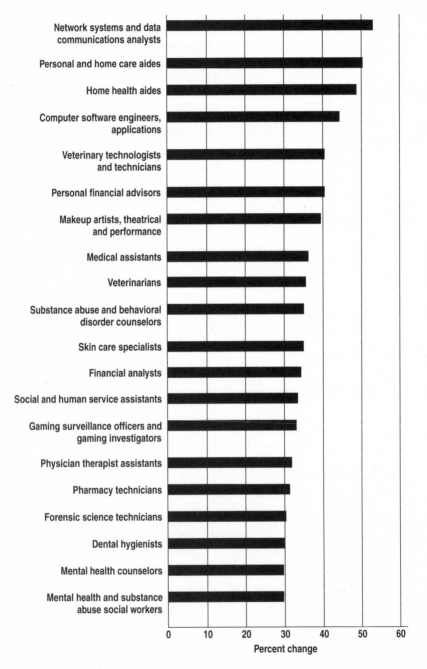

Source: "Tomorrow's Jobs." *Occupational Outlook Handbook 2008–09.*

Fastest-Growing Occupations, 2006–16

(Numbers in thousands)

| 2006 National Employment Matrix code and title | | Employment | | Change | | Quartile rank by 2006 median annual earnings[1] | Most significant source of postsecondary education or training[2] |
Title	Code	2006	2016	Percent	Numeric		
Network systems and data communications analysts	15-1081	262	402	53.4	140	VH	Bachelor's degree
Personal and home care aides	39-9021	767	1,156	50.6	389	VL	Short-term on-the-job training
Home health aides	31-1011	787	1,171	48.7	384	VL	Short-term on-the-job training
Computer software engineers, applications	15-1031	507	733	44.6	226	VH	Bachelor's degree
Veterinary technologists and technicians	29-2056	71	100	41.0	29	L	Associate degree
Personal financial advisors	13-2052	176	248	41.0	72	VH	Bachelor's degree
Makeup artists, theatrical and performance	39-5091	2	3	39.8	1	H	Postsecondary vocational award
Medical assistants	31-9092	417	565	35.4	148	L	Moderate-term on-the-job training
Veterinarians	29-1131	62	84	35.0	22	VH	First professional degree
Substance abuse and behavioral disorder counselors	21-1011	83	112	34.3	29	H	Bachelor's degree
Skin care specialists	39-5094	38	51	34.3	13	L	Postsecondary vocational award
Financial analysts	13-2051	221	295	33.8	75	VH	Bachelor's degree
Social and human service assistants	21-1093	339	453	33.6	114	L	Moderate-term on-the-job training
Gaming surveillance officers and gaming investigators	33-9031	9	12	33.6	3	L	Moderate-term on-the-job training
Physical therapist assistants	31-2021	60	80	32.4	20	H	Associate degree
Pharmacy technicians	29-2052	285	376	32.0	91	L	Moderate-term on-the-job training
Forensic science technicians	19-4092	13	17	30.7	4	H	Bachelor's degree
Dental hygienists	29-2021	167	217	30.1	50	VH	Associate degree
Mental health counselors	21-1014	100	130	30.0	30	H	Master's degree
Mental health and substance abuse social workers	21-1023	122	159	29.9	37	H	Master's degree

Fastest-Growing Occupations, 2006–16 continued

(Numbers in thousands)

2006 National Employment Matrix code and title		Employment		Change		Quartile rank by 2006 median annual earnings[1]	Most significant source of postsecondary education or training[2]
Title	Code	2006	2016	Percent	Numeric		
Marriage and family therapists	21-1013	25	32	29.8	7	H	Master's degree
Dental assistants	31-9091	280	362	29.2	82	L	Moderate-term on-the-job training
Computer systems analysts	15-1051	504	650	29.0	146	VH	Bachelor's degree
Database administrators	15-1061	119	154	28.6	34	VH	Bachelor's degree
Computer software engineers, systems software	15-1032	350	449	28.2	99	VH	Bachelor's degree
Gaming and sports book writers and runners	39-3012	18	24	28.0	5	VL	Short-term on-the-job training
Environmental science and protection technicians, including health	19-4091	36	47	28.0	10	H	Associate degree
Manicurists and pedicurists	39-5092	78	100	27.6	22	VL	Postsecondary vocational award
Physical therapists	29-1123	173	220	27.1	47	VH	Master's degree
Physician assistants	29-1071	66	83	27.0	18	VH	Master's degree

[1] The quartile rankings of Occupational Employment Statistics Survey annual wages data are presented in the following categories: VH = very high ($46,360 or more), H = high ($30,630 to $46,300), L = low ($21,260 to $30,560), and VL = very low (up to $21,220). The rankings were based on quartiles, with one-fourth of total employment defining each quartile. Wages are for wage and salary workers.

[2] An occupation is placed into 1 of 11 categories that best describes the postsecondary education or training needed by most workers to become fully qualified in that occupation. For more information about the categories, see Occupational Projections and Training Data, 2006–07 edition, Bulletin 2602 (Bureau of Labor Statistics, February 2006) and Occupational Projections and Training Data, 2008–09 edition (Bureau of Labor Statistics, forthcoming)

Source: Bureau of Labor Statistics

percent and account for 4 million new jobs, the second highest numerical increase of any industry by 2016. Registered nurses and home healthcare aides will lead the increase in jobs for the healthcare sector.

- Educational services are projected to increase by 18.8 percent and add nearly 5.5 million more jobs by 2016. Most jobs will be for teachers, who are projected to account for 1.3 million jobs.

- The information technology industry is expected to increase by 6.9 percent and add 212,000 jobs by 2016. Information-related industries such as software publishing, Internet publishing and broadcasting, and wireless telecommunications carriers are expected to grow by 32 percent, 44.1 percent, and 40 percent, respectively. Increased demand for telecommunication services (such as cell phone service providers incorporating the Internet capabilities of Blackberries, iPhones, and other devices), high-speed Internet connectivity, and software will lead the growth among these industries.

The occupational makeup of each industry will continue to undergo low to moderate change as it approaches the year 2016, adjusting workforce composition based on the skills and training necessary to meet new requirements in the production and services areas. Fortunately, the skills and training you received while serving in the military will hold you in good stead as you prepare to enter the workforce in 2009 through 2016 and beyond.

WORKFORCE TRENDS

According to "Tomorrow's Jobs" segment, there are several trends developing in the area of employment opportunities that could affect those leaving military service within the next ten years.

- The median age of the workforce by the year 2016 will be forty-two. This is good news for two reasons. First, if you leave the military with fewer than twenty years of service, you will automatically fall into the prime age category (twenty-five to fifty-four) which represents 64.6 percent of the American workforce, a 5 percent decrease since the last edition of this book. Second, if you stay in the military for twenty years, you will, in most cases be at or near the average worker's age of forty-two and in the prime age category where the majority of job opportunities can be found.

- Baby boomers (ages fifty-five to sixty-four) will increase by 30.3 percent more than any other age group. The thirty-five to forty-four age group will decrease by 5.5 percent. This should afford the age thirty-eight to fifty-five military servicemembers an added benefit of fewer contenders for fewer jobs in a recovering marketplace.

- The pool of young workers (sixteen to twenty-four) entering the workplace will decline by 1.1 percent over the 2006 to 2016 period. If you will be leaving the military after completing your initial enlistment or reserve officer obligation, this reduction in competition should provide a slight advantage, since your skills and training will definitely be in demand at the technician or middle management levels of the workforce.

- Women are projected to represent a slightly greater portion (46.6 percent) of the labor force by 2016. As the number of women graduating from college and graduate schools increases, they will continue to compete on a more favorable basis for managerial and professional jobs traditionally held by men. These statistics should also support the job aspirations of women currently in the military who have educational credentials that supplement their leadership and experience in the occupational fields that will be in demand in 2009 and beyond. This would be especially true over the past ten years with the increased number of occupational fields within all the military services that are now open to women.

JOB OPPORTUNITIES

The April 2007 issue of *Money* magazine carried an excellent article on the "Best Jobs in America" (*www.cnnmoney.com/bestjobs2007*). Compiled in conjunction with Salary.com, the article covered four segments of the population most interested in what they called "second act" careers, or more specifically, those who fell into the following four categories: early to mid career changers, parents returning to work, retiring military, and workers over fifty. Interestingly enough, the term "second act" career in the article relates well to the "second career" military retiree or even those separating with fewer than twenty years' service. The section on the retiring military showcased twenty occupations in which a transitioning servicemember could best find follow-on or crossover employment upon leaving active duty. Sixteen of these occupations are shown below. The other four occupations not included were areas in which the servicemember would be least apt to seek employment.

- Operations or Intelligence Analyst
- Network Systems Manager
- Field Service Engineer
- Operations Manager for Logistics
- Sr. Trainer/Training Manager
- Comptroller
- Construction Manager
- Contracts Administrator III
- Engineering Manager
- Human Resources Manager
- Instructor, Military College
- Recruiting Manager
- Security Manager
- Traffic Manager (vehicle or vessel)
- Warehouse Supervisor

Each occupation listed addressed salary information, job growth, stability, ease of transition, and the education or training required for the position. The accompanying chart (Best Jobs in America for Transitioning Military) shows associated job data and ten-year growth projections. While most cite an undergraduate degree as a prerequisite, there is a high probability for some of these occupations, such as a Security or Recruiting Manager, that previous military service experience in the field in multiples of five or ten years, or two or more assignments, should be an acceptable equivalent for hiring purposes.

The following paragraphs highlight those occupations where a former military AFSC, MOS, or Designator has some direct crossover relevance to the occupation being showcased. O*Net identification numbers or SOCs are provided for most of the positions under the main occupational category.

Best Jobs in America for Transitioning Military

Ocupation title	Median Salary	10-Year Job Growth	Growth in Jobs 2007–16	Education/Experience
Operations or Intelligence Analyst	$ 68,900	36%	17,402 – 204,500	BS + 4–7 years in field
Network Systems Manager	$ 73,600	38%	106,868 – 261,500	BS + 5 years in field
Field Service Engineer	$ 74,900	10%	7,047 – 22,939	BS + 6–8 years in field
Logistics Operations Manager	$ 82,500	36%	29,660 – 203,600	BS + 8 years in field
Sr. Trainer/Training Manager	$ 83,500	26%	54,632 – 94,000	BS +4-7 years in field
Comptroller	$ 69,800	15%	78,156 – 153,867	BS + 5 years in field
Construction Manager	$ 102,800	11%	44,641 – 122,682	BS + 7 years in field
Contracts Administrator III	$ 67,800	7%	5,207 – 21,444	BS + 7 years in field
Engineering Manager	$ 109,600	13%	27,757 – 62,671	BSE + 8 years in field
Human Resources Manager	$ 78,400	20%	31,859 – 58,319	BS + 7 years in field
Instructor Military College	$ 40,200	32%	524,444 – 892,101	BS/MS +2–4 years in Service
Instrumentation/Calibration Technician III	$ 57,800	10%	17,730 – 55,758	HS Grad – Military Service Tech School
Recruiting Manager	$ 85,000	30%	55,407 – 83,279	BS or several tours of Recruiting Duty
Security Manager	$ 78,700	9%	4,297 – 16,918	BS or Military Law Enforcement
Traffic Manager	$ 78,800	13%	11,701 – 29,660	Service in Military Related Field
Warehouse Supervisor	$ 49,100	3%	19,735 -172-898	HS Grad + 4 years

Data for Chart Courtesy MONEY magazine.

Operations or Intelligence Analyst
(No corresponding O*Net SOC)

With the advent of the "war on terror" after September 11, U.S. security assistance and stabilization operations in Iraq and Afghanistan, the rise of Global Hawk and Predator UAV programs, a renewed emphasis on Signals Intelligence, and the growth of the C4ISR occupational field, the Operations or Intelligence Analyst has become a key player in providing time sensitive support in all of these areas. As evidenced by the ten-year job growth in this field as shown on the Best Jobs in America chart, it is the one occupation where there should be a wealth of opportunity for the retiring or separating servicemember.

Transitioning into a defense contractor position in support of any of these intelligence areas, or a civil service position at any of the intelligence agencies, should be a relatively painless process given the right credentials. Most officers and senior NCOs serving in Intelligence or Operations Analysts assignments have a Top Secret SCI or SBI security clearance and at least ten years or more in the field with several joint assignments in the United States and overseas. Given this experience and their military intelligence education, the crossover to a position in this field should be one of the easier ones given the 36 percent job growth and number of openings from 2009 to 2016.

Comparable civilian occupations in the defense industry: defense operations analyst (all levels); intelligence analyst (all levels); all-source collections analyst; signals intelligence (SIGINT) analyst; airborne intelligence analyst; and human intelligence (HUMINT) analyst.

Network Systems Manager (O*Net 11-3021/15-1071)

According to the description for Network Systems Analysts in the *Occupational Outlook Handbook 2008–09*, network systems and data communications analysts—also referred to as network architects—design, test, and evaluate systems such as local area networks (LANs), wide area networks (WANs), the Internet, intranets, and other data communications systems. Network systems and data communications analysts perform network modeling, analysis, and planning, often requiring both hardware and software solutions. For example, a network may involve the installation of several pieces of hardware, such as routers and hubs, wireless adaptors, and cables, while also requiring the installation and configuration of software, such as network drivers. Analysts also may research related products and make necessary hardware and software recommendations.

If you participated in the major technology advances in the C4 field during your service career, you could easily make a contribution in this heavy growth industry. Many of those who have served in the communications and computer operations fields have excellent experience as network administrators, communications centers supervisors, help desk supervisors, and customer service representatives.

The computer and communications industry will continue to grow quickly with job opportunities that will exceed those in the healthcare field. Customer service representatives, computer repair technicians, and sales positions, both on-site and in the field, are often advertised.

In the area of telecommunications, we have seen the split-up of AT&T and the accompanying growth of competition for all facets of the industry, especially in the cell phone industry with the rise of Verizon, Sprint, AllTel, T-Mobile, Vonage, and others. Advances in technology in areas such as satellite communications, wireless fidelity (WI-FI), and integrated services digital networking (ISDN) have continued to place this industry on the threshold of even greater growth. With the breakup of the former Soviet Union and its Eastern satellite neighbors, foreign sales and installations have created an exploding job market overseas for former military communications and computer personnel.

Civilian occupations: computer operator; systems analyst, information systems programmer; supervisor, computer operations; electronic data processor; supervisor, machine records unit; electronic equipment repairer; business programmer.

Education/Teachers (O*Net 25-2020/2021/2022/2023//2030/2032)
According to the *Occupational Outlook Handbook 2008–09*, the number of elementary teachers, secondary school teachers, and special education teachers needed is expected to grow by 12 percent from 2006 to 2016. Fast-growing states in the South and West (e.g., Nevada, Arizona, Texas, and Georgia) will experience the largest enrollment

increases and thereby the greatest need for new teachers at all levels. The Midwest will hold steady, and the Northeast will decline.

Shortages in the overall number of mathematics, science, and special education teachers point to these as areas of definite opportunity for exiting servicemembers who have a desire to teach at the elementary and secondary level. Also, the number of non-English speaking students will continue to grow, creating a demand for more bilingual teachers.

For those not interested in the corporate ladder or the lure of sales commissions, the teaching profession offers a challenging and personally rewarding career. In order to teach in the public and most private school systems, you must obtain a teacher certification. Since certification requirements vary from state to state, check with the department of education in the state where you plan to settle to find out what is required. This is something you will need to be thinking about well ahead of your service separation or retirement, since the state may require you to take additional undergraduate or graduate courses for certification.

Shortages in the overall number of mathematics, science, and special education teachers point to these as areas of definite opportunity for exiting servicemembers who have a desire to teach at the elementary and secondary levels.

As an incentive to those who are willing to go into the teaching field, Congress has continued to place millions of dollars into the annual defense authorization bills for the "Troops to Teachers" program. Although funding has been reduced significantly since the start of the program, there are sixteen states that actively participate in it as of December 2008. The Department of Education operating rules for this program (shown below) have been in effect since September 2005. There are now two types of financial assistance being offered with the following stipulations if you elect to accept one or the other:

Stipend: Participants accepting the $5,000 stipend are obligated to teach for three years in:

(a) any school within a school district that has at least 20 percent of its students coming from families living below the poverty level,

or,

(b) a school house where at least 50 percent of the students are eligible for the free or reduced cost lunch program, or where a "high percentage" (determined annually) of students have disabilities, as long as that school is in a school district that has between 10 and 20 percent of the students who come from poverty level families.

Bonus: Participants may accept a bonus of $10,000 in lieu of the stipend if they are employed as a teacher in a school district that has at least 10 percent or more of the students coming from families living below the poverty line and are:

(a) teaching in a school house where at least 50 percent of students are eligible for the free or reduced cost lunch program, or,

(b) teaching in a school house that has a "high percentage" (determined annually) of students with disabilities.

For a listing of the states' support offices, visit their website at *http://www.dantes.doded.mil/dantes_web/troopstoteachers/INDEX. asp.*

Civilian occupations: elementary or secondary school teacher; counselor; special education teacher; English as a Second Language teacher; and foreign language teachers.

Engineering (O*Net 17-2000/2051/2081)

Computer software engineers, civil engineers, and environmental engineers will be in the greatest demand in the twenty-first century. Computer software engineers are the key systems integrators for software that is part of all the new technology consistently multiplying in terms of the burgeoning hardware evolution. Civil engineers will come to the fore under the administration's plan for improving and repairing the infrastructure of America's roads, highways, and bridges. At the same time this infrastructure upgrade is happening, the need for environmental engineers to ensure compliance with environmental regulations for cleaning up existing hazards will make their field more in demand, too. Environmental engineers will be part of the fastest growing field with an increase of 25 percent within the projected 324,000 new jobs in the engineering field.

Civilian occupations: computer software engineer, civil engineer, environmental engineer, petroleum engineer, chemical engineer.

Environment (O*Net 11-9199/13-1061/17-2081/3025)

With the implementation of Executive Order 13423 and the pollution prevention (P2) programs at all of the DOD bases worldwide, environmental cleanup and environmental management services continue to be a big business. With the most recent Base Realignment and Closure (BRAC) Commission in 2005, it was determined that previous BRAC closures from 1988 to 2001 produced net savings of $17.7 billion, including the costs of environmental cleanup. BRAC 2005 consolidations, closures, and realignments are estimated to produce another $7 billion a year in savings to DOD, which again would include the associated environmental cleanup. It therefore makes sense that BRAC closures and consolidations would bode well for the individual services' environmental management system (EMS) programs, which provide ongoing short- and long-term employment opportunities to those separating or retiring as EMS specialists.

Currently, the services have a number of EMS positions that use both military and contractor personnel as hazardous material (HazMat) or hazardous waste (HazWaste) handlers, HazMat technicians, or environmental control specialists in the various HazMat/EMS Centers or HazMat Pharmacy organizations and units aboard bases and Navy ships. Most of these individuals have acquired formal training in their respective service to meet the requirements associated with their command EMS programs. Many of these individuals have left the service to transition to jobs opening up on a daily basis in companies that provide these services to various bases and naval units.

Civilian occupations: environmental consultant/engineer, environmental management systems (EMS) director, hazardous waste engineer, hazardous materials inventory control database management specialist, hazardous materials stock clerk.

Healthcare (O*Net 11-9111/31-9092/29-2012/51-9080/29-2071)

Healthcare professionals make up approximately 4 percent of the population in the Army, Navy, and Air Force and include doctors, nurses, dentists, physician assistants, pharmacists, hospital administrative personnel, medical technicians, dental technicians, and hospital and field corpsmen or medics. Projections provided in the *Occupational Outlook Handbook 2008–09* indicate that ten of the thirty occupations with the fastest projected growth rates during the period 2006 to 2016 are in the healthcare services field, which is expected to increase for some healthcare occupations by as much as 50 percent in the ten-year period. The demand, in some areas of the country, for medical professionals to fill jobs in the healthcare field even continues to outpace the demand for jobs in the computer field.

The health industry is centered on drug and pharmaceutical companies, healthcare service companies such as nursing homes and walk-in clinics, and medical supply companies. While drug and pharmaceutical company hiring will remain fairly specialized, the other two areas of the health industry—healthcare services and medical supply sales—will constantly be on the lookout for new talent. As hospitals fight the rising costs of inpatient care and are forced to close their doors, the healthcare service companies will fill more of the void left by failing hospitals. The outpatient burden will be taken up by the civilian equivalent of the military's Primus clinics (emergency or routine medical care clinics), which will start to show up more and more in suburban shopping centers.

With an aging population, a lower mortality rate, and a consistent trend to increase routine healthcare for the average citizen, the health industry will continue to offer excellent opportunities to qualified military medical professionals separating or retiring in the twenty-first century. The growing need for more healthcare services and Medicare and Medicaid programs, as well as the inception of the military's TRICARE For Life program, will require more agencies to process and administer the paper flow that accompanies all of these programs.

Civilian occupations: medical doctor, registered nurse, medical service technician, dental laboratory technician, physician assistant, orthopedic assistant, medical records administrator, radiologic technologist, hospital or clinic administrator, home care health aide, dental assistant.

Industries with the fastest-growing wage and salary employment, 2006–16

Industry description	2002 NAICS	Thousands of jobs		Change	Average annual rate of change
		2006	2016	2006–16	2006–16
Management, scientific, and technical consulting services	5416	920.9	1,638.7	717.8	5.9
Individual and family services	6241	973.6	1,687.0	713.4	5.7
Home health care services	6216	867.1	1,347.6	480.5	4.5
Securities, commodity contracts, and other financial investments and related activities	523	816.3	1,192.4	376.1	3.9
Facilities support services	5612	122.8	179.1	56.3	3.8
Residential care facilities	6232, 6233, 6239	1,316.7	1,829.2	512.5	3.3
Independent artists, writers, and performers	7115	46.8	64.8	18.0	3.3
Computer systems design and related services	5415	1,278.2	1,767.6	489.4	3.3
Museums, historical sites, and similar institutions	712	123.9	167.4	43.5	3.1
Child day care services	6244	806.7	1,078.4	271.7	2.9
Amusement, gambling, and recreation industries	713	1,404.4	1,876.8	472.4	2.9
Specialized design services	5414	135.8	179.3	43.5	2.8
Software publishers	5112	243.4	321.3	77.9	2.8
Funds, trusts, and other financial vehicles	525	93.1	122.4	29.3	2.8
Other educational services	6114–7	534.2	702.5	168.3	2.8
Promoters of events, and agents and managers	7113, 7114	100.0	131.3	31.3	2.8
Other support services	5619	305.4	399.0	93.6	2.7
Scenic and sightseeing transportation	487	27.0	34.7	7.7	2.5
Lessors of nonfinancial intangible assets (except copyrighted works)	533	28.9	36.6	7.7	2.4
Office administrative services	5611	363.4	456.4	93.0	2.3
Architectural, engineering, and related services	5413	1,385.6	1,731.0	345.4	2.3

Source: *Occupational Outlook Handbook 2008–09*

Human Resources (O*Net 11-3042/11-3049/13-1071)

While military members are not well versed in the principal areas that constitute the human resources field, i.e., personnel, compensation, benefits, and insurance, they are adept in training and counseling, both of which are increasing in importance as we advance in the twenty-first century. These are specialty areas where military members can compete, with some degree of success, with human resources professionals on an even plain. Those with previous military recruiting experience may find they have a reasonable chance of converting this experience into either an employment or temporary agency position, or a recruiting or sales marketing spot on a corporate headquarters staff.

If you plan on tackling a job in this field, it would be wise to pursue a certificate or master's program in organizational development. The area of human resources has become rather sophisticated over the past ten to fifteen years, and without the appropriate credentials, it is a difficult field to enter when searching for a job. If you have been serving in an Equal Employment Opportunity (EEO) or Affirmative Action (AA) assignment, you have some credibility, but without experience in compensation, benefits, health and life insurance programs, and in some cases, 401K programs, you don't have the qualifications that small- to large-size companies are looking for in a prospective HR professional. Don't confuse having worked in the personnel administration field as being all the background you need to successfully make the transition to this segment of the civilian workforce. You may be embarrassed when you find these credentials won't get you a visitor's spot in the company parking lot.

Civilian occupations: human resources records specialist, recruitment manager, training specialist, affirmative action specialist, temporary agency employee.

Internet and New Media (found under Desktop Publishing O*Net 43-9031)

Those with excellent computer skills and a knack for surfing the Internet may find that the lair of the World Wide Web appeals to their interest in marketing products online, managing and developing Internet computer technology, or becoming a webmaster for a small- or mid-sized company. This is a wide-open field, and because it appeared so suddenly and grew so fast at the end of the last century, it is not covered as a separate category as one of the 250 occupational fields in the *Occupational Outlook Handbook*, but rather can be found under the Publications–Desktop Publishing section.

Civilian occupations: webmaster, online content manager, director of networks, director of systems development, manager of Internet or intranet technology, desktop publishing specialist.

Law (O*Net 23-1011)

Members of the Judge Advocate General Corps of each of the services who separate or retire should find outside employment in the legal profession relatively lucrative depending upon the area they select. Government contract law and possibly trial law are two areas where the military lawyer may find the right fit as he or she leaves the military.

Computer Support (O*Net 15-1041/1071)

A quick check with the "Jobs Outlook" Section of the *Occupational Outlook Handbook* for 2008–09, shows that job opportunities for computer support specialists will increase by 13 percent by 2016. This is a decrease over previous predictions provided by the Bureau of Labor Statistics, which showed the computer support profession growing by 97 percent as it crossed into the year 2010. It would appear that the slowdown in the economy, the implosion in the tech stocks followed by large on-hand inventories in the tech industry from 2007 to 2008, the financial crisis of 2008, and the transfer of computer-related jobs to Third World countries have all contributed to this decrease in job opportunities for this field.

If you are exiting the military in the category of a network administrator, help desk supervisor, or computer security manager, you would do well to start your job search in this area. With the proper training, you will find the opportunities for advancement appear to be unlimited in this profession. You may even aspire to become a database administrator, and your work as a communications–computer support technician will give you an excellent background in this rapidly growing field.

Civilian occupations: network and computer systems administrators, network and data communications analysts, help desk supervisor, database administrators.

Management (O*Net 13-1111/11-1021)

The military is without a doubt one of the best prep schools for management in our society today. Command of an organization in the military and management of a large company in the civilian world have many similarities. The ones that immediately come to mind are the leadership of personnel or employees; managing large-scale budgets; transportation and movement by air, sea, or land of people and things; logistics and maintenance associated with supplies and equipment; and providing for the health, welfare, and morale of the organization. The majority of officers and senior staff NCOs have "been there, done that."

Military members have also served as project and program directors in the acquisition of new weapons systems or have overseen the installation of new command and control communications systems within their respective services. Heading up or being a member of a team involved in these stand-ups has provided another translatable skill to be used in the job search segment of the career transition process.

According to *U.S. News & World Report*, when Lt. Gen. Gus Pagonis, USA (Ret.), went to work for Sears, Roebuck & Co. after serving as chief of logistics during the Persian Gulf War, there was some doubt that his military logistics experience would translate into savings on a large scale for Sears. Within two years he had trimmed logistics costs by $45 million a year. This is one of the success stories that you hear about, but there are countless other logisticians who have left the military to successfully work in the civilian world.

Now that American business has taken on an international flavor, it will be looking for bilingual speakers and people familiar with other cultures to increase production and distribution goals around the world. Who is better qualified than a former military member who has served overseas and speaks the language and understands the culture?

Civilian occupations: senior management consultant, program manager, senior logistics management consultant.

Aerospace and Defense (O*Net 17-3021/23/24/25 and 17-2011)
This industry, which actually contains three major segments-aerospace companies, other defense contractors, and government support services contractors-is perhaps the top choice of many who are separating or retiring. This is true for several reasons. First, it provides the closest thing to your former job that you will find. If you have been working in a field such as research, development, testing, and evaluation (RDT&E), you may be able to find a similar position with a government contractor. Second, you may have an opportunity to apply your experience and expertise to areas that will make an impact on the services in the future, such as developing computer software for a government contractor or improving an existing UAV system in the field.

In response to the changing defense market, the aerospace industry is now in the process of shifting gears, moving from the military to NASA and the civilian sector. This is especially true in the lucrative airliner market, where there are already billions of dollars of backlog. While the workforce is being trimmed in some areas, job opportunities for exiting servicemembers with aviation-related skills should continue well into the next century.

Some economists thought that the easing of tensions in Eastern Europe would result in major cutbacks in defense spending, particularly in the shipbuilding and aerospace industry. But with a greater emphasis on peacekeeping and humanitarian assistance operations, military commitments around the world have actually taken on an increased operational tempo, causing a continuing review in the areas of roles, missions, and overall force structure. Recent multiyear increases in the Defense budget for this military "transformation" should result in an increase in defense contracting jobs with both hardware and software companies in the United States and overseas in such places as Afghanistan and Iraq.

Civilian occupations: airframe and power plant mechanic, shop mechanic, field service representative, airplane inspector, equipment tester, logistics planner, flight engineer, aerospace consultant, security officer.

Business Services and Supplies (O*Net 11-3011)

Paper, pens and pencils, office machines, temporary employees, janitorial services, and waste management are all part of the business services and supplies industry. Servicemembers who have spent a number of years in personnel administration and supply are usually knowledgeable about photocopiers, word processing equipment, and office supplies, without a doubt significant line items in every service's budget. The military is not alone in its constant need for office supplies and equipment. The average American worker would also be hard-pressed to accomplish any work without the convenience and availability of office machines, telephones, fax machines, paper and pens, and myriad other items. As a result, servicemembers experienced in procuring these items, or managing personnel involved in this field, should find themselves qualified for this growing segment of the job market.

The three major areas of this industry are business services (for example, secretarial and accounting temporaries, security guards, computer leasing firms); business supplies (for example, photocopiers, fax machines, postage machines, stationery); and industrial services (for example, waste management, janitorial services). Due to the constant and growing demands for their services, job opportunities in this industry should remain high well into the twenty-first century.

Civilian occupations: office manager, secretary, payroll clerk, purchasing agent, procurement manager.

Public Relations (O*Net 27-3031/11-2031) / Advertising (O*Net 11-2000/2011/2022) / Entertainment Industry (O*Net 27-4031)

Each service has a number of personnel dedicated to public relations (PR) and media affairs activities at installations, bases, stations, and aboard ships around the world. Public affairs professionals hit the pavement weekly in search of human interest stories, features, sports news, and articles on significant military events for installation newspapers and other publications.

To some extent, everyone who has served in the military has played some part in the public relations or media affairs efforts of her or his service. If you have served with local reserve units or recruiting stations, you have probably always been your own PR person, responsible for publicizing items of interest about the unit or service. You may have even appeared on a local TV talk or news show or been asked to speak at the local Lions, Rotary, or VFW on military-related events of interest to the general public.

With that in mind, consider what types of job opportunities exist in the entertainment and information industry. The best way to approach this is to break the industry down into its four major segments: broadcasting (radio and television), movies, publishing, and advertising. If you have worked in radio or TV in the military, you may focus your search on stations or companies in the area where you have decided to settle.

With continuing advances in the camcorder and digital camera industries, the video services industry has grown a niche of its own, providing training tapes, public service announcements, real estate promotions, tapes of weddings and reunions, and transfer from 8mm movies to videotape and from videotape to digital formats. Coming from a military public affairs background, you will be quite familiar with a number of the areas in which these video companies work.

The movie industry is more difficult to break into, especially since the first step may involve becoming a member of a union. Unions are firmly entrenched in everything that has to do with the writing, production, and distribution of films. Contacts and people already working in the industry will be your best source of job opportunities.

Jobs in publishing may be found on a continuing but limited basis in areas where there are publishing companies, trade magazines, trade or professional association newsletters, and local or major city newspapers. The publishing business, particularly the magazine and newspaper segments, suffered significant losses in their ranks over the past several years due to a severe drop in advertising capital as well as subscriber indifference. People today rely more and more on their Internet Service Provider (ISP) for the daily news, and they can retrieve the latest happenings using their cell phones and laptops en route to and from work. This has had a devastating effect on large city newspapers. For example, newspapers like the *New York Times* are in financial trouble and could go under in the coming year. Advertising has been pulled back due to the current recession and may not continue except on television where the appeal reaches a greater audience.

Jobs in the publishing field will be highly competitive, although salaries may be somewhat flat on the lower end of the pay scale. Don't let this discourage you. Related occupations include technical writing, ad copy writing, indexing, and educational writing.

If you have had public affairs experience at the base or joint service level, you may want to consider locating in an area where there are press services and other communications facilities. Again, consult the latest edition of the Gayle Directory of Publications and Broadcast Media since this is your best source for what's available in your area of choice. Your public affairs background also could qualify you as a candidate for a position in a trade or professional association on its communications or PR staff. Related fields include lobbying at the state or national level, fund-raising, and promotional management. You also may want to consider a position with a local chamber of commerce.

Advertising jobs are tough to land unless you have had some previous experience. If you worked in the visual communications field during your military service, you may want to consider graphics design as a good place to start your crossover training for gaining entry into the advertising industry.

Civilian occupations: public relations representative, reporter, lobbyist, translator, graphics designer, announcer, motion picture equipment supervisor, still photographer, program assistant (radio and broadcasting).

Logistics (O*Net 13-1081.00)

Every day, more than 500,000 military personnel are involved in logistics and transportation activities in the areas of scheduling, coordinating, contracting, and shipping military goods by air, land, rail, and sea. This movement of military supplies, equipment, and household goods represents millions of dollars in expenditures for all of the services annually. Yet this transshipment of supplies and household goods is not totally accomplished by military means, but rather is shared to a great extent by civilian air and land freight carriers and to a lesser extent by rail and sea carriers.

Within each respective service, there are logisticians of all ranks ordering, storing, and distributing all the parts and services that make their own service operate on a daily basis both in the United States and overseas. Supply chain distribution, warehousing, motor transport maintenance and overland hauling, petroleum storage and distribution, contracting, life cycle management, and integrated logistics support (ILS) all play a role in keeping our military on the cutting edge of warfare and humanitarian security assistance operations.

Projected growth in the field of logistics for the 2006 to 2016 timeframe is going to be faster than average and grow at a rate of 14 to 20 percent.

Civilian occupations: logistics management specialist, logistics engineer, ILS manager, logistics analyst.

EDUCATION, TRAINING, AND SKILLS

Based on the continued rapid advances in technology, technical knowledge and training will become more important for jobs in the twenty-first century, with the median educational level remaining at 13.5 years for over half of all the new jobs that are created.

Because the military has been at the forefront of emerging technology in the late twentieth and early twenty-first centuries, there should be no reason to doubt that it will continue to adopt new educational or training requirements in order to stay abreast of this technology well into the remainder of the twenty-first century. Not only will this training enable a person to be more productive while in the military, but service-acquired skills should provide a slight edge in competing with civilian counterparts for jobs in the more popular and growth-projected industries and professions.

KEY POINTS

- The occupational makeup of the workforce in American industry will not undergo any considerable change through the year 2016.

- Occupational training and job skills learned while in the military will make the exiting servicemember highly competitive as he or she applies for a position in the civilian workforce from 2009 through 2016 and beyond.
- Major trends developing in the workforce for the years 2009 to 2016 could have a favorable impact on those who will be exiting the service during this time.
- For servicemembers who elect to leave the military during the next five years, the ten areas that appear to offer the most opportunity for employment are banking and finance, computer support services, education, business professionals, engineering, environment, healthcare, human resources, leisure and hospitality, automotive repair and maintenance, Internet and wireless technology fields, law, and management.
- Other occupations that also may have job openings on a regular basis and opportunities for growth are aerospace and defense, business services and supplies, public relations, law enforcement and homeland security, and supply chain management.
- The required median educational level will remain stable at 13.5 years for the majority of occupations well into the twenty-first century.
- The current education level, training, and skills possessed by the average servicemember will be more than sufficient to allow her or him to transition to the civilian workforce upon completion of military service.

CHAPTER 3

JOB SOURCES

In order to gain successful entry into the civilian job market, you will need to research and investigate a number of job sources. When used properly, these sources will provide a valuable pipeline into the marketplace for identifying job opportunities in your area of interest. Job sources shown in this chapter represent a major sampling of those available to the average job seeker, as well as several that are available only to those leaving the military. They are discussed in descending order of importance.

MILITARY CAREER TRANSITION OFFICES

Currently, each service has a career transition office or center at each of its major bases around the world. As part of their services, they also conduct Department of Labor (DOL) Transition Assistance Program (TAP) workshops at almost eighty locations worldwide.

In October 2007, the Department of Defense issued the latest edition of its *Preseparation Guide* with instructions that the services execute a mandatory Individual Transition Plan checklist for all their separating or retiring servicemembers at the three- to six-month stage of their pending release from active duty. Because each service is unique in the way it handles its transition process, the name of the career transition office or center may vary from base to base. The current locations and terms for transition offices or centers by service are as follows:

- Army: Army Career and Alumni Program (ACAP) center. Currently located at fifty-three Army bases worldwide. If the Army base you are assigned to does not have an ACAP center, call (800) 445-2049 for the nearest ACAP center location.
- Air Force: Airman and Family Support Center. Currently located at eighty-six Air Force installations or locations worldwide.
- Navy: Fleet and Family Support Center. Currently located at fifty-two major naval bases and naval air stations worldwide.
- Marine Corps: Career Resource Management Center (CRMC), Marine and Family Services, Career Resources Center, or Career Resources Office. Located at eighteen Marine Corps camps, bases, and air stations worldwide.
- Coast Guard: Operates one-day seminars at thirty-three district, training center, or support center locations in the United States and overseas.

Army Career and Alumni Program (ACAP)

ACAP, the largest of the service-run career transition programs, serves separating or retiring Army personnel, their family members, retired Army personnel, other services' personnel in need of assistance (out less than ninety days, but on a space-available basis), and Army civil service personnel at fifty-three locations around the world. ACAP centers are normally found at every major division-size post in CONUS and overseas, and for the smaller posts and bases, a mobile ACAP team is provided. Each ACAP center offers a relatively struc-

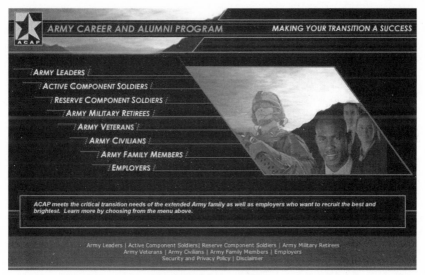

ACAP Home Page

tured program that starts at the six-month mark and includes all or most of the following services:

- *Mandatory Preseparation Counseling* (DD Form 2648)
- Individual Transition Plan—as shown in the DOD *Preseparation Guide*
- Review and counseling concerning information contained on DD Form 2586, *Verification of Military Experience and Training Document*
- Transition seminars and workshops:
  1. Three-day Department of Labor (DOL) Transition Assistance Program (TAP)
  2. Weekly ACAP workshops
  3. Interview workshops
  4. Small business seminar (depending on base)
- Computer support for:
  1. Preparation of a resume or cover letter
  2. Access to the Army "Hot Leads" Program database of available jobs
  3. Access to the Internet
  4. Review of jobs listed on the DOD Transition Bulletin Board (TBB)

5. Review of jobs listed on DOL's website (*www.careeronestop*
.org)

6. Review of information provided by state or local employment offices

7. "Troops to Teachers" program information by state and eligible school districts nationwide (*www.proudtoserveagain*
.com)

8. Review of jobs listed on the Office of Personnel Management
website (*www.usajobs.gov*)

- Reference library, state information, employer files, job hot line
directories
- One or more job fairs a year

You can get additional information on the ACAP program and a
base in your area by going online (*www.acap.army.mil*).

U.S. Air Force Transition Assistance Program

The U.S. Air Force has offered career transition assistance to its servicemembers and their families since 1992 and now operates eighty-
six career transition sites around the world. Each Military Personnel
Flight refers separating and retiring members to the transition office
as soon as they have made the decision to leave the Air Force. There
they receive information from a transition assistance specialist on all
the transition services and resources that are available; at the
ninety-day mark they are scheduled for TAP workshops. Each transition office offers a relatively structured program that includes all or
most of the following services:

- *Mandatory Preseparation Counseling* (DD Form 2648)
- Individual Transition Plan—as shown in the DOD *Preparation Guide*
- Review and counseling concerning information contained on
DD Form 2586, *Verification of Military Experience and Training*
- Transition seminars and workshops:
  1. Three-day Department of Labor (DOL) Transition Assistance Program (TAP)
  2. Interview class
  3. Resume class

- Computer support from the Employment Resource Center (ERC) for:
  1. Preparation of a resume or cover letter
  2 Access to the Internet, the World Wide Web employment office, and Adams Job Center
  3. DOD Job Search database registration for resume posting
  4. Review of information provided by state or local employment offices
  5. "Troops to Teachers" program information by state and eligible school districts nationwide (*www.proudtoserveagain.com*)
  6. Review of jobs listed on DOL's website (*www.careeronestop.org*)
- Reference library, state information, employer files, job hot line directories
- Fax machine and telephone numbers to contact potential employers in local areas
- One or more job fairs a year

Since the TAP workshop is usually located in the Family Support Center, transition assistance advisement, classes, and resource rooms are open to family members as well as the active-duty member or civilian employee. You can get additional information on the transition assistance program by going online to the to the Air Force Career Transition website at (www.afcommunity.af.mil/transition).

U.S. Navy Career Transition Assistance Program

The U.S. Navy has offered career transition assistance to its servicemembers and their families since 1993 and now operates fifty-two career transition sites at Fleet and Family Support Centers (formerly Family Service Centers) worldwide and through their career counselor force aboard Navy Atlantic and Pacific fleet ships wherever they might be deployed. Separating and retiring members report to their career counselor at their nearest Fleet and Family Support Center, or at sea online, to start their Individual Transition Plan checklists (DD Form 2648). They receive information on all the transition services and resources that are available; at the ninety-day mark they are scheduled for TAP workshops. Each Fleet and Family Support Center or shipboard career counselor offers a relatively structured program that includes all or most of the following services:

- *Mandatory Preseparation Counseling* (DD Form 2648)
- Individual Transition Plan—as shown in the DOD *Preseparation Guide*
- Review and counseling concerning information contained on DD Form 2586, *Verification of Military Experience and Training*
- Transition seminars and workshops:
  1. Three-day Department of Labor (DOL) Transition Assistance Program (TAP)
  2. Interview class
  3. Resume class
- Computer support for:
  1. Preparation of a resume or cover letter
  2. Access to the Internet and job search websites on the World Wide Web
  3. Review of jobs listed on the DOD Transition Bulletin Board (TBB)
  4. Review of jobs listed on DOL's website (*www.careeronestop .org*)
  5. Review of information provided by state or local employment offices
  6. "Troops to Teachers" program information by state and eligible school districts nationwide (*www.proudtoserveagain .com*)
  7. Review of jobs listed on the Office of Personnel Management website (*www.usajobs.gov*)
- Reference library, state information, employer files, job hot line directories
- Fax machine and telephone numbers to contact potential employers in local areas
- One or more job fairs a year

Since the TAP workshop is usually located in the Fleet and Family Support Center, transition assistance advisement, classes, and resource rooms are open to family members as well as the active-duty member. You can get additional information on the Navy's transition assistance program at the Navy Fleet and Family Support Center website (*www.nffsp.org*) under the FFSC Programs link.

U.S. Marine Corps Career Transition Assistance Program

The Marine Corps operates a Career Resource Management Center (CRMC), or a Career Resources Center (CRC) or Office (CRO), at all of its major bases in the United States and overseas. These centers provide career transition assistance programs for military members and local employment programs for their spouses. Each CRMC/CRC/CRO offers all or most of the following services:

- *Mandatory Preseparation Counseling* (DD Form 2648)
- Individual Transition Plan—as shown in the DOD *Preseparation Guide*
- Review and counseling concerning information contained on DD Form 2586, *Verification of Military Experience and Training*
- Transition seminars and workshops:
  1. Three-day Department of Labor (DOL) Transition Assistance Program (TAP)
  2. Interview class
  3. Resume class
  4. Disabled Transition Assistant Program
  5. The federal hiring process and OF 612 application procedures
- Career assessments to help define career options
- Biannual career fairs
- Computer electronic databases for jobs and education
- Career coaching
- Financial planning
- VA benefits counseling

At the major stateside bases, transition assistance services are offered to all Marines and other servicemembers within 180 days of separation. For information on the nearest career transition office, go to the Marine Corps Community Services website (*www.usmc-mccs.org/tamp*).

In addition, the Marine Corps now has fourteen Retired Activities Offices at every major base location around the world, and the Navy

Marine Corps Community Services Home Page

has Regional Retirement Activities Offices throughout the United States, providing seminars, workshops, and presentations on all subjects of interest to former and soon-to-be retirees from the services. In 2001, the Marine's started another new program, called the Marine for Life Program, at several major city sites throughout the United States. This program was designed to assist those former Marines who were having ongoing employment problems and were in need of additional job assistance after their separation or retirement from the Marine Corps. As of 2007, the Marine for Life Program was operational in eighty locations across the United States and manned by volunteers and active duty Marines willing to lend a hand to any or all of the 27,000 Marines separating each year in obtaining employment assistance in the community where they have elected to drop the hook. You can learn more about the types of assistance this program offers by going to the Marine for Life website at *www.m4l.usmc.mil* (requires TLS1.0 security).

U.S. Coast Guard Transition Assistance Program

Since the U.S. Coast Guard is not considered part of the Department of Defense for Operation Transition purposes, it operates a reduced-scale transition assistance program of its own. Working through Career Information Specialists assigned to the Work Life Staff at each major Coast Guard District, training center, or support center, it provides one-day seminars and workshops for both retirement and separation. These retirement and separation seminars are similar in scope to those offered by the other services at their bases and installations worldwide. Call the nearest Coast Guard District or Integrated Logistics Support Center to find a site near you.

MILITARY ASSOCIATIONS

Air Force Association (AFA)

The Air Force Association encourages its members to participate in the DOD's Operation Transition Program while offering them the added opportunity of having a professional resume prepared or one of their resumes reviewed and critiqued by AFA's Resume Preparation Assistance Service.

The resume preparation and review and critique services have been provided since May 1990, receiving highly favorable comments from AFA members over the years. A number of these resumes have been used as examples in appendix A of this book. A brochure describing AFA Benefit Programs to include the resume services is sent out to Airman and Family Support Centers and Consolidated Base

Personnel Offices at Air Force bases in the United States and overseas, as well as to any AFA member who requests one. AFA also advertises the resume services on its website (*www.afa.org*), under the Member Benefits section, and in *Air Force* magazine, the principal publication of the Air Force Association. Both services are reasonably priced, and with either service, AFA provides the member a copy of the latest edition of *Job Search: Marketing Your Military Experience*.

AFA has the added benefit of partnering with The Destiny Group, a recently added accession of RecruitMilitary.com, a web-based Internet site that provides a wide range of career transition services to separating, retiring, and currently retired or previously separated servicemembers. Chapter 6 has more information on the online services offered by The Destiny Group.

For further information, call the AFA Membership Services Office at (800) 727-3337 or (703) 247-5800, or go online at *www.afa.org*. Annual membership in AFA is $36.

The Military Officers Association of America (MOAA)

With 300,000 members, MOAA, formerly The Retired Officers Association (TROA), is without a doubt one of the largest of the military service-related organizations. Membership includes active-duty, former, and retired officers, warrant officers, and senior staff NCOs from each of the seven uniformed services. In addition to lobbying for veterans' benefits, publishing a monthly magazine, running a worldwide travel program, and providing supplemental TRICARE healthcare and life insurance plans, MOAA also has a career transition program called The Officer Placement Service (TOPS). The strength of the TOPS program lies in its overall education in the job search process, starting with a series of lectures given at bases around the world to officers and senior NCOs contemplating retirement or separation. The career transition services that MOAA has offered over the years have grown considerably and now include the following:

- Transition Assistance Lectures. Members of TOPS go on the road across the United States and overseas to military bases of all the services, providing 150 career transition lectures/ workshops a year. This has proven to be one of the most popular and well received of MOAA's transition assistance services, especially with all the servicemembers about to retire from the military each year.

- Publications. Members are given a free copy of MOAA's popular *Marketing Yourself for a Second Career*—a combination textbook and how-to guide for job searchers. A daily TOPS Job Bulletin Board on the MOAA website (*www.moaa.org*) contains a compilation of five hundred to one thousand job opportunities across the United States and is available to those members registered in TOPS (see below). MOAA also offers free online newsletters to veterans and retirees on areas of interest such as current legislation affecting medical and healthcare, pay and allowances, disability retirement, and more.

- Resume Critique. TOPS will critique a member's resume upon request. A standard checklist along with a marked-up resume is provided to the member for guidance in revising or writing other resumes. Before submitting a resume, the member should download a free copy of "Putting Yourself on Paper: Resume Guidelines and Samples" from the MOAA website and review it prior to getting his or her resume critiqued.
- Career Counseling. Members may schedule a visit with a TOPS representative in person, talk to one over the phone, or e-mail questions to *tops@moaa.org*.
- Career Research Center. Members have access to a library containing the latest reference material on career changing and job search, and a notebook updated weekly with current job opportunities from around the United States and overseas.
- Computerized Job Referral Service. In order to enter the TOPS database, a member must fill out a background data sheet. Registration is now done totally through e-mail at *tops@moaa.org*. Once the registration form has been completed and the resume has been posted on the website for retention on file, it can then be used for mailing to prospective employers as the need arises.
- The Military Officers Association of Networkers. TOPS has created an international network of MOAA members who are willing to be informational networking sources to fellow MOAA members in job transition. There are twenty-five hundred MOAA members in the network in the United States and in nine foreign countries. Members may obtain the phone numbers of mentors in their area by viewing the directory found on the TOPS website at *www.moaa.org/tops*.
- MOAA Web Page. This site offers eighty-five links to career transition services offered through TOPS and can be accessed online at *www.moaa.org/tops*.

For additional information call the Military Officers Association of America at (800) 234-6622, ext. 547, or (703) 838-0547 to speak to a TOPS representative. The annual membership fee is $26 for a current, former, or retired officer, warrant officer, or senior staff NCO.

The Non-Commissioned Officers Association (NCOA)

Operating out of its headquarters in San Antonio, Texas, NCOA offers a two-tiered, award-winning Veterans Employment Assistance Program that includes the following:

- Job Fairs. NCOA conducts two-day job fairs eight times a year at locations around the United States. These events are conducted on or near military bases and are designed to bring together companies and corporations seeking to hire separating military personnel. There are normally thirty to fifty prospective employers and hundreds of job seekers at each of the scheduled job fairs. A complete schedule of annual job fairs hosted by NCOA along with a Registration Form may be found on their job board at *www.militaryjobworld.com*.

- Job Board. The second tier of the NCOA Veteran's Employment Assistance Program is the Internet job board at *www.thejobleader.com*. This online job database is designed for you to post your resume with the hopes of reaching some of NCOA's Fortune 500 companies that may be searching for military retirees or separatees with specific qualifications for available job openings. Companies such as Lockheed Martin, Mantech, Northrup Grumman Technical Services, Sears, USAA, and Schneider International are just a few of the featured companies with whom NCOA has a contract. Human resources personnel from these companies are constantly accessing this job board in search of highly qualified former military personnel.

The annual membership fee is $20. The NCOA also welcomes spouses of veterans to participate in its programs. You can go online to *www.ncoausa.org* for more information on the NCOA Veterans Employment Assistance services.

Two other websites that strongly support transitioning service-members are Military Connection (*www.militaryconnection.com*) and Military Spot (*www.militaryspot.com*). The Military Connection provides information on primarily defense-related or federal jobs and has a virtual job fair running at all times offering positions available with member companies for twelve different occupational categories of employment. This website is referred to by several of the military service transition websites and the DOD website. Military Spot operates a Career Center with links to career transition assistance subjects that parallel the same services offered by the various military career transition offices. In this case, however, all of the transition subjects are through online sources. Both of these are excellent sites and should be consulted during the course of your job search research process.

Appendix C also provides a more detailed list of other military service–related organizations that have recognized the need to add outreach programs to assist former servicemembers in the areas of job search and employment assistance counseling.

NETWORKING

Networking is nothing more than getting the word out to the world that you are planning to leave the service soon and would like some assistance as you set out on your job search. What better place to start networking than with your immediate family, spouse's relatives, or close friends, some of whom may have only recently left the military themselves? Their contacts in the business world may be all it takes to get an interview that could start you on your way to that first position in your new career. Relatives (both sides of the family) can be very helpful in circulating your resume locally while keeping you informed of job opportunities in their particular area of the country. Make sure you let them know of your plans at the next family reunion. This will give them some time to gather their thoughts and get back to you with possible leads or contacts at a date that is closer to your separation or retirement.

If you are not interested in returning to your old hometown, or even your home state, you may find that friends will become your next best source of job assistance. They form the nucleus of a small but effective admiration society that will go to great lengths to aid your job search efforts. Friends who have left the service within the past year are veterans of the job-hunting process and will probably be more than willing to share their experiences with you, as well as assist you in your job search campaign.

Another major source of networking assistance will be professionals in your occupational field. Once you have located these people in the area where you are currently stationed or where you hope to settle, you will need to recruit their assistance in reviewing your resume and possibly identifying job leads.

Servicemember organizations such as the Military Officers Association of America (MOAA, formerly TROA) and the Non-Commissioned Officers Association (NCOA) are other good sources for networking opportunities. Constantly growing in strength, they currently offer selected transition and job search activities that include computerized resumes and job banks, job fairs, base visits, libraries, and written guides providing advice on the pursuit of a second career. See appendix C for addresses of military service-related organizations that offer job search assistance to former members of the military.

Building or expanding your network can also be facilitated by your own service, since all of the services now have Career Transition Offices or Family Support or Service Centers that provide basic information on job search and transition-related subjects to servicemembers and their dependents. The most thorough program is provided by the Army through its Army Career and Alumni Program (ACAP). In addition, most military bases periodically sponsor a retirement seminar program that features advice on career transition topics as well as service-connected benefits, financial planning, and other areas of interest to a veteran after separation.

How many people will you have to tell of your intentions to leave the military in order to show some return for your efforts in networking? As many as possible. Those who can successfully network with relatives, friends, and civilian professionals or through military service-related organizations shown in appendix C will no doubt be more successful than those who attempt to maintain a low profile as they prepare to exit the service.

Once you have formed all the various groups into a mutually supportive network, you will have taken a big step toward creating the ideal set of circumstances for leaving the service. In fact, someone in your newly established networking system could hold the key to the next step in your job search-an interview. It is important to remember early on that networking by itself will not guarantee you a job, but if handled in an organized fashion, it may prove rewarding in terms of job leads and interview opportunities.

Keep track of the list of names and contacts in your network the same way you would your telephone directory of relatives and friends. Why? Because networking is like having your own set of yellow pages with business contacts located in the various working professions.

Once your local area network is in place, you must remember to establish a responsive feedback system to track your networking progress and determine whether you are making any headway in the area of identifying job leads. A tracking chart similar to the one in chapter 4 may be useful. The old axiom "no news is good news" definitely does not apply to this phase of the job search, so don't let that phone sit on the desk and intimidate you when it's not ringing. Pick it up, dial your network, and energize things in the job search system!

As you draw closer to the end of your active service, the dynamics of networking will play a major role in helping you achieve one of your principal objectives in the job search process-obtaining an interview. How much effort you have invested in networking could determine your success in securing an interview or, better still, an interview that leads to a job.

THE HIDDEN JOB MARKET

A major source of potential jobs is what is commonly called the hidden job market. Since only 20 to 30 percent of available mid- and upper-level jobs are advertised in the media, that leaves almost 70 to 80 percent of the job opportunities unadvertised and known only to those companies or organizations with a need.

Is there a way to successfully penetrate the hidden job market? There is, but in many cases it will be more a matter of luck than design. The best way is to ensure that your network is growing steadily and that network members not only are spreading the word about your pending service exit but also are attempting to identify contacts for you. They may even be able to locate people in companies who may be willing to interview you for some of those hidden job openings.

Try to meet current employees in companies where you might like to work. They will always be your best source of information on the company, and their views on employment prospects may be quite useful. If you are unable to meet an employee from one of your companies of choice, then you may have to tap back into your network for some additional help in this area.

It is also wise to watch the business section in the local newspaper for companies receiving large contract awards. If the contract is in an area where you have some expertise, try to find out who will be in charge once it is awarded. Contact that person by phone to see if she or he will be hiring additional personnel. You may find that the company is just starting to work up the newspaper ad and is posting the new openings around the company. If your phone call produces the kind of information about your experience that may be needed for this contract, the person in charge may desire to see your resume.

Most companies publish a monthly listing of job openings by department or specialty and provide it to their employees. Friends who have preceded you into the marketplace should be aware of their own company's listing, which may contain job openings that may be ideal for you. The opportunity to interview for these job openings prior to separation will enable you to gain valuable insight into the hiring process while getting a good idea of how well your qualifications match those required for the position opening.

All companies are required by federal law to maintain a company bulletin board. In addition to the normal Equal Employment Opportunity (EEO) and Affirmative Action (AA) material that must be displayed, a number of companies post position openings. Ask your network to screen these bulletin boards on a regular basis.

JOB FAIRS

Job fairs have been around a long time but have increased in popularity in the past few years. They are designed to provide hiring companies a faster means of reaching a larger number of applicants in order to fill entry- to midlevel positions mainly in the high-tech and sales fields.

Job fairs are sponsored by an agency, an organization, or a military base transition office to fill a wide range of positions in occupations where there is constant demand at all levels. They are also sponsored by a number of companies in a given metropolitan area with similar hiring interests who agree to join together and set up booths at a central location, usually a hotel or convention center. Job fairs are also online at job-posting sites on the Internet (see chapter 6).

Job fair notices in the newspapers usually appear quite close to the actual date they are being held and often do not give you much time to prepare. Have your resume ready, and when possible, try to do a little research (see chapter 4) on some of the companies that will be represented. During the job fair, booths are staffed by company personnel, who informally interview applicants concerning position openings.

Those job fairs specifically designed for military participation are the regional job fairs put on by the Military Officers Association of America (MOAA), Non-Commissioned Officers Association (NCOA), RecruitMilitary.com, and local job fairs sponsored by base Family Service or Support Centers, a CRMC, or an ACAP office. The NCOA currently sponsors approximately eight job fairs a year around the United States and in Europe, usually at the same time of year in the same locations. They are almost always held in cities with multiple military installations or activities or areas with a large military presence.

NCOA job fairs have been relatively successful in attracting a number of major U.S. companies that are interested in hiring skilled technicians, engineers, computer systems analysts, retail sales and customer service representatives, healthcare professionals, and police and security personnel. Although job fairs sponsored by the NCOA were set up primarily for separating or retiring noncommissioned officers, they are now open to officers and interested civilians, since a number of the positions may require a college degree or advanced military specialty training.

When you attend a job fair, remember that most companies that participate in these recruiting ventures do not have large enough human resources departments to fully staff their booths with professional recruiters. Instead, they may send junior-level personnel from various departments to supplement the recruiting personnel and answer specific questions about their particular division. While well meaning in expounding the virtues of their individual companies, many are neither skilled in screening prospects nor adept in the preliminary interviewing process. If you find this to be the case, try to arrange to meet at a later time with another representative from that company who is better prepared to review your resume and assess your skills.

If you do attend a job fair, don't be discouraged if told you are too senior or overqualified for the position openings or underqualified for some of the more advanced high-tech positions these companies are trying to fill. Try to approach each job fair with an open mind. Realize that unless you become more knowledgeable about the types of job openings available in particular areas of the United States, the opportunity for you to find a position with a company having requirements matching your military experience could be very slim. If you do find a company that you might be interested in working for, try to stay in touch with the company in the event that it has a job opening in the future for which you might qualify.

FEDERAL AGENCIES
Both the Department of Labor (DOL) and the Office of Personnel Management (OPM) operate independent job search and career transition websites. DOL closed the previous America's Job Bank in July 2007 and opened a new job search and career transition website called CareerOneStop (*www.careeronestop.org*) shortly thereafter. Career-OneStop has a Military Transition link that will take you to other Quick Links and Hot Topics. Both of these links parallel the normal transition subjects found at the various military career transition offices, the only difference being that they can be accessed online from your own computer.

OPM has transitioned to a newer version of the former USAjobs website for finding federal jobs across the nation. This website offers a Veteran's Employment Resource Center, and the various links will take you through all the wickets necessary to finding and applying for a federal job in your occupational field of interest. You can get additional information by going online to *www.usajobs.gov*.

During 2007 and 2008, the Department of Defense Operation Transition website closed down, and the official DOD website for career transition assistance was shifted to TurboTap (*www.turbotap .org*). TurboTap inherited the bulk of the transition services found on the DOD transportal website and further extended these transition assistance services to members of the National Guard and the Reserves. At the same time, DOD opened another website called MilitaryOneSource (*www.militaryonesource.com*), which was a combined effort on the part of the DOD, DOL, and the Department of Veterans Affairs (DOVA). This was done to combine the financial benefits packages provided by the DOVA with transition assistance services from the DOD and DOL for both active duty and reserves. Links on this website go to TurboTap, CareerOneStop, and the individual military services.

Unlike the commercial sector, the federal government has its own form of resume—the Organizational Form 612 (OF 612). The government also has an added incentive for separating servicemembers called the veteran's preference. This provision is reserved for military veterans who are not retiring in the rank of O-5 or above (unless disabled). Depending on your length of service, whether you were wounded or are compensably disabled, or whether you served in a military action where you earned a campaign medal or award, you may qualify for an additional five or ten points on your application.

Although you may not be interested in transferring to a job with the federal government when you leave the military, it's still a good idea to complete an OF 612 and send it in to a government agency to obtain a civil service classification rating. Having a rating may come in handy, especially if you find there may be more opportunities for advancement in your particular career field in the government than in the civilian sector. Should you desire to pursue the civil service as an employment possibility, an example of a completed OF 612 can be found at the end of appendix A.

Department of Labor (DOL)

Under the DOL's agreement to provide employment assistance to the DOD during the military drawdown, the Transition Assistance Program (TAP) was started in the spring of 1990 and included six job fairs nationwide along with six three-day employment assistance workshops offered at select Army, Navy, and Air Force bases in the

United States. Today there are several hundred TAP workshop sites in the United States and overseas, with over half of them supporting the Army and the Air Force.

The TAP has two components: the Disabled Transition Assistance Program (DTAP) and the Veterans' Transition Assistance Program (VTAP). Both programs provide employment assistance to servicemembers by using automated information systems that incorporate a wide range of demographic job information data, an ability to convert military skills to civilian job titles, an automated multistate job bank, and a three-day workshop.

The TAP provides a three-day workshop that covers the basic career transition assistance services for any servicemember separating and retiring from the military up to ninety days before his or her expiration-of-service date. Currently both TAP programs are funded indefinitely by fiscal year.

Additional information on the DOL-sponsored TAP workshops, including the subjects covered during the three days, is available through your service career transition or Family Support and Services Center, or from your regional DOL Veterans Employment Office. Veterans and retired personnel who left the service but were unable to attend a TAP workshop before separation may apply for a TAP seat at the nearest military base or installation on a space-available basis.

The DOL is also tied in to O*NET, the Occupational Information Network. It replaced the *Dictionary of Occupational Titles* (DOT) and is a comprehensive database for collecting, organizing, describing, and disseminating data on job characteristics and worker attributes. O*Net currently includes 812 occupations with job descriptions, qualifications, and training information for those particular fields of interest. O*Net also provides a set of Career Exploration Tools for those who require additional insight into finding the right career path to pursue as they exit the military. O*Net can be accessed at *www.onetcenter.org*.

STATE AND MUNICIPAL EMPLOYMENT OFFICES

Every state, county, city, or township has an employment office or an office that handles the posting or advertising of job openings. Ads for these jobs appear in the weekly employment sections of the local Sunday newspapers and are posted on state employment websites. Position openings that seem to appear most often are for personnel with experience in administration, recreation, engineering, buildings and grounds maintenance, public safety, healthcare, vehicle or park maintenance, and social welfare.

If you are completing service in one of the many organizations responsible for the day-to-day operations of a large military installation, you may be attracted to some of these state and municipal positions. When applying, you will probably be required to submit a county or state application form along with either a resume or an OF 612.

U.S. EMPLOYMENT SERVICE

Operated in each state under various names such as the State Employment Security Commission, State Department of Labor Employment Service, or State Employment Service (Commission), U.S. employment service offices aid veterans in the areas of counseling, job market information, training programs, and referrals for jobs (when applicable to the veteran's background and experience).

Title 38 of the U.S. Code authorizes the secretary of labor to make available funds for each state to support a disabled veterans' outreach program (DVOP) to meet the employment needs of veterans, especially disabled veterans of the Vietnam era. As a result of this legislation, each state employment commission office may also have available one or more DVOP specialists (based on the number of Vietnam-era vets and disabled vets in the area) to administer this program.

In addition to the DVOP specialist, each office also has a local veterans' employment representative (LVER). Both specialists provide similar services to separating veterans, including access to a current microfiche file by occupational category of all jobs available locally, regionally, and nationally; a session with one of the veterans' employment representatives; access to the automated labor exchange search system (ALEX) that allows you to enter a computer database to search for job areas of interest to you; an opportunity to attend various workshops or seminars on resumes, interview strategies, and employment training; and, where available, access to a labor market information library.

The above services are normally reserved for veterans who have already left the military and who have not yet found that first job or are interested in seeking a better position than the one they currently hold. However, recently enacted legislation enables these offices to assist soon-to-be veterans (those who will separate within 180 days). For more information on whether you qualify for veterans' assistance, contact your nearest state employment commission job service office and ask to speak to the veterans' employment representative (either a DVOP or LVER specialist).

NEWSPAPER AND MAGAZINE EMPLOYMENT ADS

Once your decision to leave the service has been made, you will find yourself poring over the professional opportunities and employment section of the Sunday paper the same way you now read the daily message traffic in your current military position. At first, employment ads may be frustrating reading because you may not see anything that even remotely resembles anything you are now doing, or what you hope to be doing when you get out. Be patient. The ads will become easier to read as opportunities in your areas of interest appear from time to time.

Try not to put all of your job-hunting hopes in newspaper employment ads, though, because the ads you will be reading represent less than 30 percent of the available jobs that exist in your geographic area. In addition, for each employment ad you see that appears to be close to what you may have been doing in the military, there will be several hundred people just like you who will also be mailing in resumes for that position.

Should you decide to respond to a newspaper employment ad, do not be surprised if you never get a response. In fact, when you send a resume to a post office box in care of a major metropolitan newspaper, you can be assured you probably won't hear back. Ads for resumes sent to post office box numbers are usually placed by executive search firms hired by a company to find a specific person for an upper-level position. When their resume bank runs dry, they place an ad like this

---

SAFETY & SURVIVAL TECHNICIAN

Did you think that your experience with life rafts, life boats, oxygen, seat belts, blueprints, etc. wouldn't pay off after you left the military? Well, think again. Dayton T. Brown, Inc., needs military know-how in these areas to perform testing in our Safety & Survival Facility. If you have a working knowledge of pneumatics and mechanical equipment as a test technician on military airborne and shipboard survival equipment, we're looking for you!

Dayton T. Brown, Inc., is the largest independent Engineering & Test Lab on the East Coast. We're located on beautiful suburban Long Island. Our salary and benefits package is outstanding and includes medical, dental, profit sharing, tuition reimbursement, and much more. If you have recently been discharged, or expect to be discharged in the near future and would like to work in a challenging, diverse environment, call or write to us. You'll be glad you did!

Dayton T. Brown, Inc.
555 Church Street
Bohemia, NY 11716
(516) 589-6300

Equal Opportunity Employer   *M / F / V / H*

---

to see if any other candidates are available. Don't waste your time responding to these newspaper ads.

Army, Navy, and *Air Force Times* run weekly advertisements recruiting separating military personnel. Over the past several years positions for a variety of skill levels have been advertised, but the bulk of the higher-paying jobs appear to be in the technical fields. Take a moment to read the ad above for a safety and survival technician taken from a weekly edition of *Navy Times*. This ad is an excellent example of a company advertising a position that specifically relates to work currently being performed by a servicemember.

Weekly base or station newspapers also carry a number of employment opportunity ads that are targeted at a younger segment of the military population completing their initial enlistment. These ads are submitted by employers who are eager to hire separating servicemembers for entry-level positions whose enlistment guaranteed an occupational specialty such as aviation maintenance, communications, or computer programming and also included a highly specialized technical training school in one of these areas.

Job opportunities may also be found in selected association monthlies like that of the National Association of Contract Managers as well as trade magazines such as *Aviation Week, Maritime Reporter,* and *Marine Engineering*.

COLLEGE AND UNIVERSITY PLACEMENT SERVICES

Most colleges and universities have expanded their placement services to include alumni as well as upcoming graduates. These placement offices have extensive libraries on virtually every industry and major corporation that include specific position requirements. Some schools even publish job newsletters that are mailed out weekly or monthly and contain available positions. Periodic seminars on job opportunities, school recruiting visits by representatives from major companies around the United States, and resume development are also offered as part of overall career placement services.

Job bank phone lines are another area that a number of colleges and universities are using. Using recorded phone messages that are changed on a weekly basis, they publicize jobs that are currently available or projected for positions on their campuses. Jobs being advertised are normally in the facilities and services areas, although some faculty positions requiring immediate placement also may be included on the recording.

If you are currently attending one of the many university and military-sponsored continuing education college or masters-level degree programs, you may want to check the campus career resource center to see what types of jobs are listed.

CITY DIRECTORIES AND MAJOR CITY JOB BOOKS

Once you have decided on your new career location, you need to compile a directory of information that will provide you with a listing of the local businesses and organizations you are interested in. The local chamber of commerce is an excellent place to start. In Washington, D.C., the reference book *The Capital Source* contains a great deal of this information. Published each spring and fall by the National Journal Group, Inc. (see appendix E), this book covers the who, what, and where in the greater Washington metropolitan area, including principal government agencies, major corporations, notable think tanks, trade associations, interest groups, the media, and international organizations.

If you're settling in a major metropolitan area other than Washington, D.C., you may want to see if there is a directory similar to *The Capital Source*. A check with the chamber of commerce may provide a listing of major organizations, companies, and agencies with local offices. Directories like these can be especially helpful in mounting a targeted campaign.

In addition to the normal job search books at your local bookstore or library, there is now a series of *Jobs in . . .* books for every major city in the United States and a few for overseas jobs. If you are interested in working in a major metropolitan area in the United States, a book in this series could be helpful to your Individual Transition Plan.

EXECUTIVE SEARCH FIRMS

Executive search firms are hired on a retainer or contingency basis by companies with specific needs for hiring upper-level management executives. Salaries for these positions usually start at $100,000 or higher. Unlike employment agencies, executive search firms do not charge the job hunter a fee for their services. Firms hired on a retainer basis are usually paid with progressive payments by the hiring company over the life of a search or searches for prospective employees. On the other hand, contingency firms, or fee-paid recruiters, work on a commission basis, which is usually a set percentage (up to 30 percent) of the starting salary for each position they fill.

For the most part, executive search firms normally do not place people coming out of the military services. You may be matched with a position if your credentials fit a particular placement they happen to be working on, but don't count on it. They are more apt to be racing against the clock tracking down a short list of fast-rising executives in Fortune 500 firms-people who are willing to move quickly for the right price and a better position to an even more prestigious firm or company.

Although your education and professional background, especially in the high-tech areas, may equal or surpass that of your civilian counterparts, you may still not be accepted as a candidate for placement by an executive search firm because you are not already within the pool of executives employed by Fortune 500 firms. So, if you are politely rebuffed, try to understand that it probably has nothing to do with your ability or credentials to qualify for an executive position, but rather is due to the fact that a number of highly qualified civilian executives have already been identified as candidates for the job. Check the Internet for more information on how to find executive search firms in your area.

EMPLOYMENT AGENCIES

A small number of employment or placement agencies sprinkled around the United States recruit separating servicemembers for sales, manufacturing, distribution, finance, engineering, and consulting positions in industry. Agencies specializing in military placements advertise on a regular basis in *Army, Navy,* and *Air Force Times,* with an emphasis on recruiting separating junior officers or enlisted members with engineering experience.

Firms that specialize in the placement of junior military officers (JMOs) include the Lucas Group, Bradley-Morris, Alliance International, Orion/Career Network, and SOAR Consulting. A check with several of them revealed that their clients are generally junior officers with four to ten years of service who have been commissioned through either the service academies or ROTC programs at major colleges and universities.

According to Jim O'Neal of Lucas Group's Atlanta office, the majority of JMOs that they select for Fortune 500 matchups will have technical degrees positioning them for opportunities in engineering, production management, and sales in large companies. Prior to the downsizing, only one applicant in ten was usually selected for further matching with a client company (usually in the Fortune 500). With the completion of the downsizing and the growth of the economy, they are selecting one in five for further matching with client companies.

Candidates who are selected by the JMO recruiters (usually former JMOs themselves) are matched with six or more client companies at conference sites in the Dallas, Atlanta, Houston, Los Angeles, Chicago, Washington, D.C., San Francisco, and Philadelphia areas. The more established JMO recruiters are finding position matches in the traditional industries as opposed to defense.

Those selected for further interviewing by the client companies and eventually tendered job offers will generally be hired for entry-level sales, high-tech, engineering, and staff-related positions with 50 to 60 percent going into management. The fee (30 percent is not uncommon) for this service is normally paid by the employer once there is a successful match. The phone numbers for the major JMO recruiters can usually be found in the classified sections of the *Army, Navy,* or *Air Force Times.*

Be aware that many employment agencies offer both employer-paid and applicant-paid services. Generally the more qualified you are, especially if you possess a degree in a technical field, the more apt you are to be taken as a candidate for placement by an agency with an employer paying the fee. If you end up falling into the applicant-pays-the-fee category, you may want to be sure there are some guarantees of employment tied to the agency's services before you agree to this approach, and also that none of the fees are collected up front. Stick to the firms that advertise in the *Army, Navy,* and *Air Force Times,* and you should have a better shot at landing a satisfying and financially rewarding job.

OTHER MEDIA AND COMPUTERIZED SERVICES

Cable TV Networks
With cable television services available to the majority of residents in large cities and suburbs throughout the United States, prospective

employers have acquired another round-the-clock means of recruiting potential new hires. To assist the employers in their viewer areas, a number of cable TV services feature a weekly program format that advertises jobs in the office support, technical, services, sales, banking, computer, and healthcare fields. Alphabetized by subject areas, these ads include brief job descriptions and contact phone numbers.

Defense Outplacement Referral System (DORS)

DORS is a national resume registry and referral network designed by the Department of Defense to provide a ready source of exiting military members to more than 16,000 American industry employers. In keeping with the various governmental agencies' advances as they entered the new millenium, DORS moved to DOL's CareerOneStop website (*www.careeronestop.com*) when DOL shut down America's Job Bank. If you enter the former link, you will immediately be forwarded to the CareerOneStop website, where you will find a Military Transition link providing similar services to those of the old DORS.

The Internet

Due to the fact the Internet has taken on a much greater role in the job search process since the last edition of this book, it is covered in detail in chapter 6. Chapter 6 identifies a number of military-friendly websites for the job search campaign with links for identifying jobs, posting your resume, and seeking additional career transition assistance online.

KEY POINTS

- Use your service Career Transition Program office to develop and implement your Individual Transition Plan. If you are deployed and have the opportunity, prepare your plan online so that your career transition office can review it once you get back to the States.
- Use the career transition services provided by some of the more active military-related organizations (MOAA, AFA, MEA, NCOA, and AFCEA) as part of your networking efforts.
- Organize and put into operation a responsive network at least six months or more before you exit the service.

- Tap into potential job sources, including the hidden job market, as soon as you decide to leave the service.
- Seek counsel with former military friends who have preceded you into the civilian workplace.
- Establish a responsive tracking system to monitor networking.
- Attend job fairs as part of your job search.
- Complete an OF 612 in order to obtain a civil service rating, even if you're not particularly interested in further federal employment.
- Check with county and state employment offices or the U.S. employment office to learn about job openings in your area.
- Prepare broadcast letters to target a campaign in your field of interest. See chapter 4.
- Check with local college and university placement service offices for employment opportunities. Call in on job lines where available.
- Consider the use of an executive search firm if you are a highly technical specialist.
- If you are accepted as a candidate by an executive search firm, let it know if you have sent out any broadcast letters to preclude sending your resume to any of these companies.
- Use an employment agency only as a last resort. Be sure to read the fine print in the contract.
- Contact a JMO placement agency if you are separating prior to your tenth year of service to see if you qualify for their interviewing process with client companies.
- If you are an enlisted member with a technical occupational specialty that could be marketed with an employment or placement agency, check *Army, Navy,* or *Air Force Times* to find one that is advertising for positions in your field.
- Use your friends to check the monthly posting of job vacancies at their respective companies.
- Be aware of company bulletin boards in your travels.
- Take advantage of the jobs posted on the Transition Bulletin Board at your local Career Transition Office.
- Learn how to use the Internet and the recommended job search websites found in chapter 6.

   Naturally, you will locate other job sources to add to this list as you progress through your career transition to the civilian world. The key here is to remember that no job source by itself will be sufficient to guarantee a job. Instead, a number of the job sources mentioned in this chapter may open opportunities for you to pursue your dreams by allowing you to interview for positions that will meet your needs, both professionally and financially, once your life in the military is over.

CHAPTER 4

PREPARING FOR THE JOB SEARCH

THE COUNTDOWN

Ideally, you should start exploring the types of job opportunities available in the civilian sector about twelve to eighteen months prior to your intended date of separation or retirement from the service. Whatever you do, don't allow too little time (six months or less) to become familiar with the job market in the geographic area where you plan to settle, especially since it may be different from the area of your current assignment. Set up a countdown to employment schedule similar to the sample in this chapter, and try to divide your search efforts into three- to six-month increments down to the final ninety days.

Job Search Countdown Schedule

12–18 Months	9–12 Months	6–9 Months	2–6 Months	E-Day*
PERSONAL ASSESSMENT • Occupational Interests • Skills and abilities • Define goals • Career Assessment Inventories **IDENTIFY JOB SOURCES** • Relatives and friends • Professionals in field of interest • Military associations • Military related Web Sites (DoD links) • Civilian job-related Web Sites • Job Banks & Job Search Engines • Hidden job market **RESEARCH JOB MARKET** • Visit library • Start Internet job search • Demographics in second career area of interest • Contact recent retirees and separatees • Research company annual reports BEGIN TO BUILD CIVILIAN WARDORBE	**CONTINUE RESEARCH** • Research areas of interest to you by Google Search • Attend workshops/ seminars • Purchase several civilian Job Search guidebooks • Attend job-related courses or sign up for Certificate program in field of interest **OPEN NETWORK** • Relatives and friends • Professionals in field of interest • Find Mentor • Service Family Support Centers **INTERNET SEARCH** • Go online and check out various job search web sites/job banks/job bulletin boards/search engines • Sign up for Destiny Group and MOAA where applicable • Check out own service career transition web site and home page EXPAND CIVILIAN WARDROBE	**MILITARY ASSOCIATIONS** • Attend MOAA and NCOA Job Fairs • Get Resume review or critique from MOAA or Landmark Destiny Group **ATTEND WORKSHOPS** • DOL (TAP) • ACAP Workshops • Base career transition workshops or retirement seminars **CONTACT SERVICE TRANSITION ASSISTANCE OFFICE** • Start Individual Transition Plan • Request Verification of Training and Experience Forms • Review financial and medical plans • Sign up for TRICARE Prime and TRICARE Supplement EXPAND CIVILIAN WARDROBE	**GET RESUME OUT** • Via Network • Respond to newspaper ads • Post on selective Internet Job Search Web Sites **OBTAIN INTERVIEWS** • Local • Regional • Area of Interest • Broadcast Letters • Networking **ANSWER ADS** • Local papers • Internet • Company Bulletin Boards • MOAA TOPS Bulletin Board **START INTERVIEW PROCESS (2 months out)** • Terminal Leave starts 30–60 days out • Energize network EXPAND CIVILIAN WARDROBE	**FINAL INTERVIEW STAGE** • Offer Letter • Agreement to Hire CIVILIAN WARDROBE COMPLETE

When you reach the one-year mark prior to separation or retirement, think about where you want to locate, research the job market for this location, and attempt to determine what your prospects are for landing the type of job you feel would meet your expectations.

At the six-month mark, contact your base Career Transition Office or Family Services Support Center, and start putting together your Individual Transition Plan as shown in the DOD *Preseparation Guide* discussed in chapter 1.

If married, discuss your proposed job search efforts and countdown to employment schedule with your spouse so that he or she will have a better understanding of this challenging period in your life. Once your spouse has a better idea of what the job search process is all about, he or she will be more apt to provide moral support during the times you need it most.

RESEARCH

Demographics and Employment Profiles

As you start your countdown for exiting the military, understanding two factors about your region of choice will be necessary for achieving success in finding a job-demographics (the vital statistics of a given region) and the employment picture in the area where you choose to settle. With the advances in the Internet, you now have the capability to search out almost any demographic and employment statistic you need at any location in the United States and overseas. You also have access to all the latest data available in the variety of news and business-related magazines on areas of interest as well as occupations you may want to pursue. Simply enter the keyword in the browser on your computer screen, and stand back while the search begins.

Two magazines that continually track career growth in various fields are *Money* and *Business Week*. *Forbes'* January issue of each year will usually have career projections for that year. *Newsweek* and *U.S. News and World Report* are two other weeklies that will occasionally publish projected growth or cutbacks in the more popular careers of the day. As you saw in chapter 2, *Money* magazine's April 2007 issue had an excellent article for military servicemembers who are about to separate or retire on where the best jobs would be, the projected percent of increase in the occupational field, and the potential salary from entry to experienced.

While one cannot depend on *Money* magazine to publish this military-related job search article on an annual basis, the data published in the 2007 issue appears to be solid as this book goes to press and should hold up for several years. In the interim, there will be similar articles published in the magazines mentioned in the above paragraph, as well as in the biennial Jobs Outlook section of the current edition of the *Occupational Outlook Handbook*.

Library References, Trade Journals, and Annual Reports

In addition to maintaining a wealth of reference information on major corporations, occupational titles, and other job-related information, libraries are an excellent source of national newsmagazines, occupational outlook reference guides, and other industry and professional trade publications. Most libraries now have special sections of reference materials on career changing and job search information. Be sure to check your library and make this section the first stop in building your job search research file.

Business journals such as *Forbes, Fortune,* and *Business Week* are excellent sources of information on industry and commerce. They often run feature articles on specific trends or forecasts for various industries or professions. Other trade journals such as *Aviation Week, Maritime Reporter, Mechanical Engineering,* and numerous computer magazines provide current information on issues of major significance in their industries. Many of the trade journals also carry employment ads that will give you an idea of the types of jobs available in that particular industry.

The *Occupational Outlook Handbook*, published every two years by the Department of Labor, is a good reference book with which to start your research. This book describes what workers do on each job, the training and education required, working conditions, earnings, and expected job prospects for 250 occupations. Once you have identified a particular field or occupation of interest in the *Occupational Outlook Handbook*, go to O*Net online and look up each of the DOT numbers that were cross-referenced for that particular occupation.

Once you find an occupation that relates closely to your current position in the military (or another desired position), make yourself a Civilian/Military Occupational Profile chart similar to the one shown on page 81.

Once you have completed this chart, check the major directories or almanacs for more specifics on companies that employ personnel in this occupation or profession. References to assist you in this area are the *Dun & Bradstreet's Career Guide* (2008 or latest revision), *Career Information Center*, and *The Encyclopedia of Careers and Vocational Guidance*. A review of these references will give you insights on major U.S. companies (Fortune 500) and their principal areas of concentration (see appendix E). Now that you have a good idea of what occupation or career field you are interested in, you can continue your research with a better sense of direction.

Most metropolitan libraries carry Sunday newspapers that contain extensive employment ad sections from other major cities across the United States. A review of these newspapers will give you an idea of the types of jobs available in the occupational areas that interest you in other metropolitan areas. Regional libraries in some areas may also carry listings of state and county government job openings—other potential job sources.

Annual reports are another means to review companies that employ people in the occupations you have selected to pursue. The annual corporate reports contain a wealth of company information, including a profile that highlights major areas of concentration, corporate goals, acquisitions, marketing possibilities, financial reports to stockholders, and projections for future growth. These reports can be especially helpful in gaining an understanding of what these companies do, where their home and field offices are, and their prospects for the future.

Many of the larger companies print extra copies of their annual reports and offer them to the general public and prospective investors on a first-come, first-served basis. Check for notices of annual reports being offered by these companies in the June and July issues of *The Wall Street Journal*. The best way to obtain an annual report is to write directly to the company or request it online the year before you plan to leave the military.

CIVILIAN/MILITARY OCCUPATIONAL PROFILE
Electronic Equipment Repair
Occupational Field

OCCUPATIONAL PROFILE	Electrical and Electronics Installers & Repairers O*Net 49-2094.00	Fire Controlman USN NEC Advanced Electronics/Computer Field
WORK ENVIRONMENT	• Regular hours and shift work • Work in labs, offices, plants, electronic workshops, and on-site with customer. • May be exposed to shock hazards from equipment.	• Regular hours except for war or deployments. • Work aboard ship in Fire Control radar spaces, Combat Information Centers (CICs), gun directors, and tech shops. • May be exposed to shock hazards from equipment.
TRAINING/CERTIFICATION AND OTHER QUALIFICATIONS	• Certification programs for electronics repair and installation technicians are administered by one of two organizations: the International Society of Certified Electronics Technicians (ISCET), or the Electronics Technicians Association (ETA) • 2-year associate's degree program	• Basic electricity, electronics, computer systems, radar systems, and weapons fire control systems—28 weeks • Fire Controlman (A & C Schools)—U.S. Navy • AEGIS Weapons System School—U.S. Navy • TOMAHAWK Weapons System School • TRIDENT Weapons System School
SKILLS REQUIRED	• Select, install, calibrate, and check out sensing, telemetry, and recording instrumentation circuitry	• Ability to maintain, repair, operate, and troubleshoot complex/regular electronic and computer systems for weapons systems aboard ship.
EARNINGS	• Median Income: $47,100 based on 2002 DOL data extrapolated from the *Occupational Outlook Handbook*.	• Current income (rounded) as a single E-5 with 6 years at sea and special performance pay: $47,736 • Pension (rounded) as an E-7 at 20 years: $22,452 (earnings) based on 2008 pay and allowances

Internet Queries

The tool that will provide you with possibly the greatest wealth of information is the Internet. With a computer and a commercial online Internet service provider (ISP), you can connect in cyberspace with several of the most profitable and informational job-posting websites. Chapter 6 discusses computer requirements necessary to access the Internet and to find military-friendly job-posting websites.

MENTORS

A mentor is an invaluable player in your job search process. He or she is a person who is in a position to provide valuable and timely advice to you regarding your job search efforts and, in some cases, may be highly knowledgeable in your particular field of interest. Once committed, your mentor can provide a wide range of services that might typically include serving as a sounding board, cutting red tape in getting you an interview, and assisting you in refocusing the job search if necessary. A good mentor will give generously of his or her time and wisdom by showing your resume to interested parties, assisting you in determining a reasonable starting salary range, and seeing that you are properly prepared prior to any interviews.

Finding a good mentor is not an easy task, and it often happens more by accident than by design. In fact, you may not find a mentor until you are down to the final days of your military service. In some cases, mentors may be currently employed by your target company and can greatly influence the action on your behalf from the inside. Although a mentor may give freely of his or her time and advice, at some point in your job search it may become necessary to seek professional help in the area of resume writing or other aspects of the career transition process such as financial planning.

One example of former military personnel taking a more active role over the past few years in assisting their separating or retiring comrades is the West Point's Association of Graduates (AOG). Certain regional societies of the AOG have an active program of placing a volunteer mentor (usually a civilian executive) with a former academy graduate as he or she approaches the final months of military service. If you are a West Point graduate and a member of the USMA Association of Graduates, you may want to check with your local society to see if it offers this program. The Military Officers Association of America (formerly The Retired Officers Association, TROA) also has a volunteer mentoring program for its members that may be of assistance to you as you work through its officer placement program (see chapter 3).

FAMILY SERVICE SUPPORT CENTERS

Since early 1992, when a major drawdown of all the armed forces occurred, Family Support or Family Service Support Centers expanded their then limited services for their respective career transition assistance programs, in some cases growing to such a scale as to require a separate facility and program identification. For a long time, the Family Support Centers had been assisting military personnel in the areas of family assistance support activities, short-term financial aid, relocation assistance, and emergency help, but had done little in the way of career transition.

Both the Air Force and the Navy have used their respective Family Support or Fleet and Family Service Support Centers for the added responsibilities of providing career transition and job search workshops and seminars, resume preparation, interview technique classes, and job employment counseling and leads for both servicemembers and their dependents. In some cases, the centers are also able to assist soon-to-be-released servicemembers with personal assessments that may include the administering of one or more of the assessment instruments discussed in chapter 1. The Army and Marine Corps have set up separate transition assistance activities under the auspices of ACAP (Army) or the Career Resource Management Center (USMC). For those who are already out, the Marine Corps has recently established the Marine for Life Program, a job assistance program set up in several major cities throughout the United States to assist separating and retiring Marines in finding future civilian employment.

If you have been unable to attend one of the scheduled Transition Assistance Program (TAP) workshops put on by your base prior to separation, you may want to check out your Family Support Center, the ACAP office, or the CRMC to see what types of career transition or job search assistance is available to you and your spouse.

COVER LETTERS AND LETTERS OF INTRODUCTION

As you approach the six- to three-month mark on your job search milestone schedule, you should prepare a cover letter to accompany your resume. This is also a good time to draft a letter of introduction to send to companies that may be located in the area you are planning on settling in after leaving the service.

Broadcast letters are another form of introductory letter that will launch you into the job search marketplace. They serve to tell prospective employers you exist by highlighting noteworthy accomplishments contained in your resume as well as other background information. An example of a broadcast letter is provided to give you an idea of how to package your experience in a similar fashion, should you decide to use this approach in your job search campaign.

A broadcast letter is used when you mount a targeted campaign in a particular segment of the job market where you have a definite interest. Sending a broadcast letter to every company in this line of work in the geographic area where you are considering settling down after leaving the military could possibly net you an interview. There are no guarantees in the world of job searching, however, so try not to be too analytical in gauging your hopes should you decide on this approach.

The broadcast letter might also be sent as an e-mail attachment when time and necessity so dictate. While obviously a less formal manner in presenting one's credentials to a prospective employer, it definitely shows your flexibility and responsiveness given the nature of today's technologically advanced business marketplace. In a downsized market, every minute counts when you are up against a potential field of three hundred or more applicants for the same position.

There are many types and styles of cover letters and letters of introduction. The three letters shown in appendix B are representative examples that can be adapted to the types of situations in which you are most apt to find yourself.

The first of these is the cover letter, which is mailed out with your resume. Perhaps the most common, it serves as a brief means of introducing the resume you are providing in response to a newspaper employment ad. When responding to a newspaper ad, keep the cover letter brief unless the ad asks you to discuss some aspect of your

SAMPLE BROADCAST LETTER

Dennis A. Schoenski_____

5788 Ridge Valley Drive, Fayetteville, North Carolina 28394

March 8, 2009

Mr. Richard C. Boothe
President, Dunhaven Industries
410 Adams Federal Building
Louisville, Kentucky 40202

Dear Mr. Boothe,

I will be leaving the military within the next 60 days and am interested in applying for a position in your Human Resources department. I am a graduate of Western Kentucky University, Bowling Green, Kentucky, and have a masters degree (2002) in Business/Personnel Management from Central Michigan University.

I have over 16 years of experience involving personnel, recruiting, business administration, and budget control in the positions I have held in the Marine Corps. In addition, I am a hands-on manager with in-depth experience managing a variety of activities with an emphasis on problem-solving techniques, efficiency, and cost effectiveness. I thrive on challenges and would welcome the opportunity to apply previously acquired management experience to further increase the overall level of excellence at Dunhaven Industries.

Specific accomplishments include:

- Personnel director at headquarters. Handled the assignment, administration, career management of 800 midlevel managers in a variety of occupational skills. Developed and managed an operating budget of $1.4 million per year. Designed a cost control system for personnel assignments that saved the Marine Corps $50,000 a year.
- Regional personnel manager (Recruiting Station Director) of four-state area. Responsible for personnel recruitment of 1,200 new hires annually. Directed the activities of a 20-person sales force with an annual budget of $900,000. Introduced innovative sales training program, increased incentives for promotion, and employed participatory management techniques as part of ensuring achievement of all assigned goals on a monthly and yearly basis.
- While assigned to Marine Corps headquarters, designed and developed a management program for employees which classified and recommended assignments based on servicewide needs and employee availability. Wrote procedures for incorporation into administrative instructions and manuals governing employee benefits, wages, and salaries.

I will be in Louisville April 10–13, 2009, and will be glad to further discuss my qualifications and background during a personal interview. You may reach me at the office (919) 572-6735, or at home after 5 P.M. at (919) 876-9378.

Sincerely,

Dennis A. Schoenski

experience in detail. In the event only the company name appears in the ad, call the company and try to determine with whom you should correspond. If the company prefers not to provide a name for the ad, follow the recommended approach as shown in the cover letter in appendix B.

Cover letters are better received when they succinctly address the areas requested in the ad that are not covered in your resume. On occasion, you may have to expand on your applicable experience to let a potential employer know that your experience is directly related to the position that needs to be filled. As a minimum, assist the reader in correlating his or her position to your proven experience in easily understandable and relatable terms.

The second type of cover letter is to a specific person you may or may not know, who has asked you to submit a resume to his or her company. More personal than the employment ad cover letter, it should nonetheless not be used as an opportunity to paraphrase your life history. Respond in less than a page-preferably no more than three-quarters of a page. If asked for specifics on a particular area of your experience, provide these as briefly as possible and preferably in bullet format. Try to gain interest with key points that can be explained in more detail during an interview.

The third type is the "goin' fishin' letter," which is an introductory letter to prospective employers in your particular field. It is sent out in hopes of getting a "bite," even though a job opening has not been advertised and personal contact has not been made. This letter tests the water in a number of areas where a requirement might exist for someone with your experience and skills. This style of letter should be used when you have reason to believe that the company or individual you are addressing may be interested in employing people with your background and experience. If you feel you have identified an opportunity that falls under this category, try the example in appendix B.

Two additional suggestions are recommended when putting together a cover letter. First, don't make the cover letter an extension of your resume. Second, cite any additional experience examples in the cover letter only if they will strengthen the credentials presented in your resume.

Also send a thank-you letter to those firms who were gracious enough to interview you for a position. Although the interview may not have resulted in a hiring letter, sending a thank-you letter is a matter of courtesy and diplomacy. One never knows-it could cause your name to be retained in the active file for strong consideration for other position openings that might occur in the future. An example of a thank-you letter has been provided in appendix B.

RESUME DISTRIBUTION

Once you have field-tested your resume and are confident that it meets your job search needs, get it into the marketplace. The best time to do this would be with three months or less remaining before you exit the service. Keep at least fifty copies of your resume on hand at the start of your distribution and mail-out effort, and as you get closer to job acceptance, reduce the number to twenty or fewer. It is also wise to keep a copy of your resume on a flash drive or CD-ROM so that you can use a personal computer to update it or tailor it if the occasion calls for another approach.

Depending on your progress in finding a job, you may want to consider sending your resume to an executive search firm for possible use in its search and placement efforts. Before you make any decision in this regard, refer to the section on executive search firms in chapter 3.

You should also develop an electronic version from your final resume for possible inclusion on one of the many job search bulletin boards on the Internet. Whatever occurs in the future job market, having an electronic resume will prepare you to pursue the many employment opportunities offered by the different online bulletin boards or individual companies soliciting resumes in the form of e-mail attachments.

FOLLOW-UP

Once you are into the resume mailing or distribution phase, prepare a resume mail-out and tracking sheet (see example) to ensure that you have a good idea of where your resumes went and when you sent them. This way, if you want to query a company that has not responded to a resume you sent for its job opening, you can note specifically when, where, and to whom you sent it.

RESUME MAILOUT AND TRACKING SHEET

COMPANY MAILED TO	DATE	RESPONSE YES/NO	INTERVIEW

Not all companies that you mail your resume to may acknowledge receipt of resumes. Try not to take this as a rejection of your credentials; understand that most companies receive many resumes for their advertised positions. Some will send a postcard to acknowledge receipt and indicate that if you do not hear anything within two weeks, you are no longer being considered for the position. Other companies will send a form letter thanking you for your application but indicating that you didn't make the interview list.

A good rule of thumb is that if you have not had a response within a reasonable period of time (two weeks at most), you should make a telephone query to see if the company received your resume and whether it has filled the position. Most companies are receptive to queries of this type, and you may be pleasantly surprised to find out that you are still in the running.

This also applies in the case where you provided a resume to a mentor or associate who took it directly to a company representative for an unadvertised position opening. If the company hasn't gotten back to you within ten days, ask your contact to check on the status of the opening so you can either retain the lead or eliminate it from your follow-up list.

Follow-up on the part of an introductory or broadcast letter may be a bit more difficult to handle since you sent an unsolicited letter to the company. If you received an answer indicating that the company does not have an opening for someone with your particular experience, send a thank-you letter and check in a few months to see if there has been any change in the hiring outlook.

BUILDING A CIVILIAN WARDROBE

Building a civilian wardrobe should be an ongoing process from the time you make your decision to leave the military until the day you accept that first job. Before your first purchase, check some of the major department stores or clothing store chains and do a little comparative shopping. You may also want to review any annual reports you may be holding to see what the employees and managers are wearing in the working areas and offices of these various companies.

In spite of the shifting trends in women's and men's fashions over the years, a few basic guidelines for wardrobe building have remained constant. First, dark suits or dresses seem to be in style no matter what the season of the year or the location in the country. Second, the woman's basic pump and the man's wing tip have managed to outlast all the other footwear competitors as the shoes of choice in any basic wardrobe. But who knows-casualness creeping into the workplace soon may make the wardrobe information provided here obsolete.

Here are a few fashion suggestions to assist you as you put your wardrobe together.

For Men

When selecting a suit, grays (all shades) and navy blues in solids and pinstripes are your best bets, with wool as the fabric of choice. As of 2009, solids appear to be the style of choice over pinstripes. Belts and shoes should be the same color or as close to the same color as possible (usually brown, black, or cordovan should be worn for interviews). Ties should be distinctive and in popular patterns (for example, stripes, paisleys, tapestries, plaids) for the season of the year.

For Women

Unless you are already comfortable with the civilian wardrobe you have in the closet, you may want to check the current best-selling women's fashion guide at your local bookseller. Naturally you will need to keep abreast of any changes in styles in the workplace, but dress only as stylishly as your budget can afford. With the number of ongoing sales in regional or local clothing store chains, you should be able to comparison shop and eventually acquire the items necessary to build a practical and fashionable wardrobe for the civilian workplace.

KEY POINTS

- Start exploring job opportunities in the civilian sector twelve to eighteen months prior to leaving the service.
- Prepare a milestone schedule at the twelve- to eighteen-month mark and divide your job search efforts into three- to six-month increments.
- Research all available corporate, financial, and other information about companies or firms in which you have a strong interest.

- Use the Internet, library references, trade journals, and financial planning and business magazines to research industries and professions of interest.
- If you encounter difficulty in your job search, find a mentor to assist in your ongoing job search efforts.
- Stop by your Family Support or Service Center, ACAP office, or CRMC to see what types of career transition and job search assistance is available.
- Once you are at the three- to six-month mark, get your resume into the marketplace, prepare cover letters and a broadcast letter, and respond to employment ads and job opportunities as they arise.
- Follow up on resumes that you have mailed out or entrusted to friends for positions where you feel you have the requisite experience to qualify for an interview.
- Acquire a conservative yet stylish civilian wardrobe.

CHAPTER 5

RESUME PREPARATION

We are more easily led part by part to an understanding of the whole.   *—Seneca*

The preparation and production of a concise and clear resume is the cornerstone of the job search process. Your resume introduces you to a prospective employer and summarizes your skills and qualifications for the available position. It can also serve as a calling card, to be placed by friends, relatives, and other professionals with firms that may be in the market for new hires.

Before proceeding with what it takes to develop a resume that satisfies your job requirements and career goals, let's establish a few ground rules.

YE OLDE GROUND RULES

    1. Well-meaning friends are your most trusted allies in every facet of the job search except resume preparation. Accept

their comments and editing at your own risk. Unfortunately, they tend to edit out the "real you" and substitute a vague composite of somebody like you. (If you are really curious, give your resume to three or four close friends and ask them for their edits, and see what you get back!)

2. Determine for yourself which *resume format*—chronological, combination, or curriculum vitae—best portrays your career experiences.

3. Whereas an *objective* normally served as a lead-in to a resume in the past, it is more common to find it embedded at the end of the *profile* or *qualifications summary* in today's resume. If so, it should be short and to the point, identifying exactly what it is you want to do or be.

4. State an *objective* in your resume only when you are interested in a specific position or particular line of work. Be aware that if an employer thinks you are interested only in a position similar to the one you have spelled out in your objective, you may not be considered for other job openings for which you also may be suited.

5. A *qualifications summary* or *profile* is an excellent way of concisely highlighting your career experience for a prospective employer. If you desire, you can tie in an objective at the end of this section. This way you save space and reinforce your qualifications.

6. An *employment* or *career history* satisfies the requirement for those employers insistent upon a chronological summary of your career. This would normally be included at the end of a combination formatted resume.

7. The category *personal* or *activities* should never be placed on a resume. In many cases, providing this information can have an adverse effect on your chances for an interview, especially if the reader is not favorably inclined toward your particular sport, religious program support, community service activity, or the fact that you are married with or without dependents. Don't open yourself up to rejection based on providing irrelevant information about yourself.

8. Buzzwords and acronyms are acceptable when they identify recent or past assignments that relate to current programs, systems, military hardware, or recognized government agencies (e.g., SDI, IW, ADP, LCAC, NASA, CIA, or DOD) with which you may have been associated and the resume is going to be sent to companies or individuals who are familiar with these terms. These acronyms are both acceptable and expected in applying for positions at defense-related companies.

9. Try to keep your resume to one, one and a half, or two pages in length. The exception is the curriculum vitae, which may go over the page recommendations cited above.

10. You may want to include a Computer Skills section, or at least a mention of such skills, on your resume. Computer skills are not necessarily assumed in spite of the fact that most people coming out of the military have had a good deal of computer experience with a number of civilian and military software applications, operating systems, and the Internet.

11. Do not use multiple fonts and lots of bolding in your resume. Presentation does count, and the use of multiple fonts, a variety of font sizes, and a heavy emphasis on bold fonts could have an adverse and distractive effect on the reader.

12. Don't spend a lot of money on letterhead stationery or typesetting your resume. If you have access to word processing software, a personal computer, and a laser printer, you can produce a professional resume that is just as impressive as the typeset version and less expensive. When printing out your resume, use a heavy grade of copy or bond paper (24 lb.), available at office supply stores.

13. Under your memberships in associations or societies, do not include those that would allow a reader to discern that you are of a certain ethnic or religious background, as this could become an automatic disqualifier for certain employers.

14. Multiple addresses, phone numbers, fax numbers, and e-mail addresses are not necessary. Only use the evening phone number (which has an answering machine on it), one e-mail address, and a cell phone number if you travel a good deal of

the time. Try to use only your person e-mail address and not your military e-mail address in your resume.

15. When using multiple pages in your resume, always place your name and the page number at the top of each succeeding page. With the exception of a curriculum vitae, try and hold your resume to no more than two pages.

16. The statement "References Provided upon Request" at the bottom of the resume is not required. This is a given, and there is no need to waste space restating the obvious. The references themselves should be placed on a separate page and never embedded in the resume proper.

17. Never, but never, show your social security number (SSN) on a resume. While some government resume formats require this, no commercial or other type of civilian resume does. Be very wary about giving out your SSN under any circumstances. When in doubt, challenge the necessity of providing it. Most of the time, a potential employer will back off this requirement until after you have been hired; you will then need to provide it for your W-4.

18. Misspelled words, incorrect grammar, and invented words will ruin your chances every time. The reason being that with today's Microsoft Word, a red underline always tells you when you have a misspelled word. The green underline, which indicates a possible grammar disconnect, should be taken with a grain of salt; seven out of ten times, the grammar corrector on Word is wrong.

19. You run the risk of falling prey to age discrimination when you show dates over twenty-five to thirty years old on your resume. Stating that you served from 1979 to 1999, and then were employed for five to ten years as a civilian, puts you near or over fifty, and on your way to sixty in some cases. Once you do this, you make it easy for the reader to put your resume aside and move to a younger and possibly more computer literate applicant.

20. Never show graduation dates on your college degree unless it is five years old or less. Never, but never, show dates as far

back as the 1970s and even the early '80s unless you want to ruin your chances of being interviewed for a senior position given your qualifications.

21. Last, but certainly not of least importance, never use the pronoun "I" in a resume. Resumes are always prepared in the third person.

If you have been operating under the mistaken impression that military experience needs to be camouflaged because a prospective employer will somehow hold your military service against you, forget it. You could end up hiding not only your accomplishments, but also the skills and experience you gained during your service career. Be up front about your former military service when seeking a job. Stand tall and be recognized for who you are and what you have done! Civilian corporations and companies are frequently on the lookout for military professionals because of their management or technical experience, as well as the work ethic you have so amply demonstrated during your years of service.

Now that you understand the ground rules, let's proceed to the next step—determining the background information you will need to prepare your resume.

INFORMATION NEEDED

The length of time you spent in the military will determine the amount of personal data available for your resume. Gather this data and place it in a centralized file for easy access. Some of the information you will need includes the following:

- A chronology of your service, including any formal military schools (except basic training courses) attended.
- Job descriptions for positions held over the past three or four tours or previous ten years.
- Copies of whatever your service equivalent is for the fitness or performance report for the past ten years. (You may go back further if your service experience has been in one predominant field.)
- Any write-ups that were used to prepare noncombat award citations that you received over the past five to ten years.

- A list of specific accomplishments during the past ten years for which you were cited by your parent service, another agency, or another service within the Department of Defense.
- Any special qualifications you may have that could be useful to a prospective employer. These would include any foreign language comprehension you may have, certification as a Master Instructor, FAA certifications for power plant and commercial flying qualifications, and so on.

Once you have gathered this information, you need to determine what type of resume format will best convey your background, skills, and experience.

RESUME FORMAT SELECTION

The first decision to make in selecting a resume format is to determine which one will best portray your skills and career experience. These four formats are the ones most commonly used in the business and educational fields:

- *Chronological*—a listing of your career experience in reverse sequence, starting with the present position and going back ten years or more
- *Combination*—used when an individual has pursued multiple career tracks that include assignments in two or more occupational fields that do not easily lend themselves to the chronological format
- *Curriculum vitae*—a more detailed summary of one's professional experience and education
- *Electronic*—a scannable computerized version for companies looking for a specific type of background, with identifiable keyword and buzzword qualifications

Pilots seeking flying positions with airlines, air cargo carriers, or corporations often use a different format called a pilot resume, as shown in appendix A.

There is no magic formula for determining which resume format you should use. Your choice will depend on your service career pattern, education (both formal military and civilian), and accomplishments. Some guidelines may assist you in making the decision:

- *Use the chronological resume format when*:
  1. The bulk of your career experience has been in your primary occupational specialty or subspecialty, and you show a definite pattern of growth and strong capability in that specialty.
  2. Your job preference coincides with your previous record of military service.
  3. You are seeking employment in a high-technology field and want to show currency in a particular acquisition program, demonstrate your knowledge of computer systems, or show your background in research, development, testing, and evaluation (RDT&E) work.

Communications/Electronics and Aircraft Equipment Maintenance are excellent examples of occupational fields/specialties that lend themselves to the chronological resume format.

- *Use the combination resume format when*:
  1. Dates, job titles, and functional areas of experience over the last five to ten years of your career coincide with and support your overall job preference area.
  2. The chronological format does not lend itself to displaying or conveying related experience, achievements, or publications of interest to those in a specific career field (for instance, education, advertising, publishing, or journalism).

- *Use a curriculum vitae when*:
  1. Applying for a job with an institution of higher learning, and a more detailed description of your experience and education is required.
  2. The position is with a think tank or other type of research agency that requires significant educational credentials, professional society memberships, and a listing of previous publications or awards in the specific field.

- *Use an electronic resume when*:
  1. Applying for a technical job found on a job-posting site on the Internet.
  2. As an advance keyword and buzzword resume when a particular company has an urgent hiring need and requests that an electronic resume be submitted for the position opening.

Once you've decided on a format, you must decide which experience, skills, and accomplishments should be included. The following categories can help you organize your military experience so you can showcase your credentials to prospective employers:

- Qualifications Summary or Profile
- Education and Professional Military Training and Certifications
- Experience or Work History (paragraph or bullet (•) style)
- Special Qualifications, Related Experience, and Security Clearances
- Computer Skills (operating systems and software applications, commercial and military)
- Achievements, Awards, and Honors
- Papers and Publications
- Employment or Career History (in reverse chronological order, starting with current job)
- Associations and Affiliations (professional as opposed to service-related organizations)
- Community Service (if relevant, i.e., not-for-profit work is your objective)

Now review the resume examples for the format you have chosen (see appendix A), and select the headings from the list of categories that best characterize your background and skills. You are now ready to proceed in the organization and construction of your resume.

ORGANIZATION

Qualifications Summary or Profile

The Qualifications Summary or Profile is a concise recap of your military experience translated into comparable civilian skills in a shopping list fashion. It provides prospective employers with an overview of your qualifications and highlights key experience areas. This introductory section should serve as the building block for the rest of your resume, particularly the Experience and Special Qualifications sections.

The following are examples of typical qualifications summaries and profiles for personnel who are leaving the service after six to thirty years:

Example 1   **Air Force Colonel (Engineer)**

Qualifications Summary

Twenty years of progressive experience and documented success managing large-scale civil engineering and real property management programs for the U.S. military. Expert in all phases of constructing, operating, and maintaining multiuse industrial complexes and residential properties with special emphasis on aviation-associated facilities. Directed up to 800 employees servicing facilities worth over $2 billion. Highly knowledgeable in contracting, budgeting, energy conservation, environmental issues, and quality management. Current head of privatization program for military to civilian management of base facilities. Engineering professor at a major technical institute. Proven written, oral, and diplomatic skills honed under high-pressure operational conditions. Top people skills.

Example 2   **Marine Corps Lieutenant Colonel (C3)**

Profile

Seventeen years of specialized experience in the field of communications electronics, including all aspects of operational communications (ground and air), joint tactical communications (C3), telecommunications, human resources management, and fiscal accountability. Served in a management capacity with large-scale tactical electronic agencies in support of worldwide commitments.

Example 3   **Army Major (Logistics and**
                            Maintenance Management)

Qualifications Summary

Seasoned logistics management professional with eighteen years of technical, supervisory, and teaching experience in the areas of logistics, maintenance management and training, ordnance repair and overhaul, and materials analysis for petroleum-related equipment. Experienced in automotive instruction, end-item equipment repair, and foreign military sales (FMS).

Example 4   **Navy Lieutenant**
                         (Nuclear Submarines)

Profile

Six years of progressive experience and documented success in the areas of nuclear engineering, combat systems acquisition, submarine operations, training development, quality assurance programs, and human resources management. Seeking challenging nuclear engineering position with private industry or the state power commission.

Example 5   **Air Force Noncommissioned Officer**
                         (Aircraft Maintenance)

Qualifications Summary

Over nine years of technical experience as an integrated avionics systems technician/specialist and a missile systems analyst technician. Additional maintenance qualifications in fire control and flight control, and as an instrument specialist and a communication, navigation, and ECM specialist. Highly qualified supervisor with interpersonal skills to match.

The above are examples of suggested ways of translating your military career into marketable civilian qualifications. For each example, the total years of actual service experience for the individuals have been adjusted by two or three years to account for time spent in formal military schools or junior-level training. Time spent in junior- through top-level military schools or pursuing an advanced degree is actually time out of your career field and therefore should not be counted in your total years of experience.

To review resumes of individuals with military backgrounds that may be more similar to yours, check the resume samples in appendix A.

Education

The placement of education information on a resume may be critical to one's opportunities for employment. If you have a strong set of educational credentials, they should never be buried at the bottom of the final page of the resume. Prospective employers want to know early on whether or not you have a college degree and in what major. When they don't see this information, and they decide not to read any further than the first page of the resume, your prospects for employment have just gone south. So when in doubt, place your educational information as your second entry on the first page of the resume.

Conversely, if you do not have a college degree, it is best to place the education section of your resume after your experience section. This will allow prospective employers to focus their attention on your superior accomplishments and qualifications, so the lack of a college degree may have less of an impact on their decision to interview you.

Displaying one's educational background can sometimes be confusing. Should you put it in list form, run it all together in paragraph form, combine my civilian undergraduate education with military schools/courses, or what? Perhaps the cleanest way to display your educational credentials is as follows:

Education
Formal

College degree(s) with highest first (PhD, then Master, then Bachelor). Any other special advanced degree work or graduate level certificate programs also go here.

Professional / Technical / Certifications

All your service-related MOS/AFSC/Designator training in reverse chronological order. If this section goes beyond four or five entries, place the remainder on a supplemental page to your resume. Special certifications such as Certified Master Trainer, Certified Acquisition Professional, Level II in Program Management, and so on, would also be shown here.

Additional examples for displaying your education are provided below, starting with placement after the qualifications summary or profile (examples 1 and 2), and then after the experience section (examples 3 and 4). Example 3 could also show you as a bachelor of science (candidate) in civil engineering with an expected graduation date (for example, June 2010).

Example 1

Education

Master of Science, Systems Management, The George Washington University, Washington, D.C.

Bachelor of Science, Business Administration, Oregon State University, Corvallis, Oregon

Graduate, Industrial College of the Armed Forces (ICAF), Fort McNair, Washington, D.C.

Example 2

Education

Formal

Master of Science, Logistics Management, Air Force Institute of Technology, Ohio (Emphasis on Manufacturing Resource Planning, TQM, and Statistical Process Control)

Bachelor of Science, Political Science, East Carolina University

Professional/Technical

U.S. Air Force:

Maintenance and Munitions Officer Course (15 weeks)

Applied Maintenance Management Concepts

Certifications

Air Force Institute of Technology:

Certified Acquisition Professional Level 1, Program Management

Certified Acquisition Professional Level 1, Acquisition Logistics

Advanced Professional Designation in Logistics Management

Example 3

Education

Associate of Arts, Drafting, Northern Virginia Community College

Currently enrolled in undergraduate program leading to degree in Civil Engineering at George Mason University, Fairfax, Virginia, June 2007

Graduate, U.S. Army Rotary Wing Flight School—2004

Aircraft Maintenance Officer's Course—2005

Transportation Officer's Advanced Course—2006

Example 4

Education

Class A Basic Radioman School (24 weeks), U.S. Navy, San Diego, California

Class B Radio Technician School (36 weeks), U.S. Navy, San Diego, California

Technical Controller Course, Advanced Electronics/Troubleshooting (12 weeks)

Various communications and electronics courses on satellites, antennae, and HF equipment conducted under the auspices of the U.S. Navy or DISA, one week in duration

The above examples will provide you insight into how best to portray your own educational credentials. If you are concerned about how many military schools to list, the following suggestions apply: If you have an advanced degree and plan to pursue a civilian career in that field, then listing all your military schools is not necessary; if, on the other hand, your education does not coincide with your future job interests but one or more military schools you have attended may support your job goals, then cite those schools.

You will notice graduation dates for college and military schools have been left off most of the education examples. Using graduation dates could cause you to be dropped from consideration by employers who prefer hiring senior- or upper-level employees who have not yet reached their fiftieth birthday. So omit graduation dates unless you consider them absolutely essential or they fall within one to five years of your service exit date.

Experience

The experience section of your resume is without a doubt the most difficult to write. Prospective employers are interested in seeing your skills, capabilities, and past accomplishments portrayed in a complete, concise, and well-developed manner. The following suggestions should make this task easier:

- If you're writing a chronological resume, ensure that job titles and major commands are included wherever possible to highlight your career progression.

- Consider using bullets (•) or diamonds (♦) to highlight specific duties associated with the more significant (and attractive) jobs that you've held, especially those within the past five years.
- Avoid vague generalities when dealing with percentages. *Incorrect*: Reduced personnel turbulence by 20% the first year and a further 9% in the next 18 months. (Without the size of the unit, the significance of these percentages is meaningless.) *Correct*: Increased vehicle long-haul time by 10% to 500 hours per quarter while reducing annual maintenance costs by 15%, or $40,000.

Let's take a look at some examples that might be useful as models for your first efforts in the experience area. Examples shown were taken from chronological and combination resumes prepared by the author for officers and noncommissioned officers prior to their separation or retirement.

Example 1   Air Force Colonel

Experience

Government Contracting and Procurement—Responsible for DOD inventory control point (ICP) acquisition of weapons system spare parts and other hardware-related items. Monitored over 200,000 contract awards annually with an award value in excess of $600 million.

- ♦ Directed and implemented the Competition Advocacy Program for the Defense Industrial Supply Center, Philadelphia, Pennsylvania.
- ♦ As Director of Base Procurement at Scott Air Force Base, Illinois, supervised 40 personnel while managing annual expenditures in excess of $28 million requiring the interface of users, contractors, and industry management.
- ♦ Performed cost and price analysis for government use in contract airlift negotiations for worldwide transportation services.

Example 2   Marine Corps Colonel

Experience

Human Resources Management—Executive Assistant to the Director for Manpower responsible for all matters relating to planning, budgeting, research, information systems, employee relations (EEO/AA), personnel services, recruiting, finance, and office services for the Manpower Department with an annual budget of over $5.7 million.

- Directed and supervised the administrative functions of the office of the Deputy CEO for all Marine Corps matters.
- Initiated and coordinated Marine Corps-wide administrative review effort resulting in significant reduction of required reports.

Example 3   **Navy Commander**

Experience

July 2005–August 2008   Fleet Combat Training Center Pacific, San Diego, California

Director of Training and Division Head, Combat Systems

- Responsible for an annual budget of over $1.2 million.
- Directed all intermediate and advanced Combat Systems training for antisurface and antiair warfare. Designed curricula to support procedural doctrinal training for system operators.
- Employed a systems approach to training in developing curricula for 63 courses encompassing 1,000 hours in these areas: Conventional Combat Information Center, Electronic Warfare, Air Intercept Control, Battle Group Training, Tactical Action Officer, and Navy Tactical Data System.
- Initiated curriculum reviews and lesson revisions, and monitored the performance of 72 instructors and 11,000 students.

Example 4   **Army Lieutenant Colonel**

Experience

July 2006–June 2008   6th Infantry Division, Fort Richardson, Alaska

Comptroller and principal finance advisor for an Army installation consisting of three individual cost centers located in separate geographical areas. Total personnel supported included 18,000 military and civilians.

- Directed and supervised the development, programming, and execution of a $170 million annual budget and ensured compliance with all federal statutes. Reprogrammed funds when financial analysis dictated.

- Supervised the functions of all financial departments, including accounting, payroll, budgeting, and internal review and audit.
- Developed and automated an information network system that resulted in a 9% decrease (500 hours) in overtime and overall annual savings of $210,000.
- Represented the Army as the Banking and Credit Union Liaison Officer to four financial institutions serving the command.

Example 5   **Navy Chief Petty Officer**

Experience

September 2003–August 2006   USS JUNEAU (LPD-10), San Diego, California

Radio Chief-in-Charge of a communications department and 3M planned maintenance representative aboard a flag-configured amphibious ship assigned to duty on the West Coast and in the Far East.

- Planned and implemented a complex communications plan involving Naval combatants.
- Streamlined the training program for maintaining readiness that surpassed existing fleet standards for communications.
- Directed the effective use of the Navy's 3M system so that communications capabilities were fully operational for all exercises and readiness inspections.
- Planned and coordinated ship's force assets during an extended overhaul of the ship that resulted in major modifications and additions to the ship's communications capabilities.

While space does not permit experience examples from all occupational specialties, the above examples provide a variety of experience in fields related to all services. As you can see, they cite job descriptions and titles, budget amounts, high-visibility programs, and numbers of people supervised or directed. Experience summaries that identify major service programs and associated costs are a lot easier for a prospective employer to decipher than those with nebulous terms like *supply accounts, transactions,* and *weapon systems.* More importantly, these examples provide a thorough coverage of the types of activities associated with each of the categories or fields selected, while translating the various military experiences and job descriptions into relatable and identifiable civilian skills. Refer to appendix A for more resume examples.

Special Qualifications, Related Experience, and Certifications

The Special Qualifications section of your resume is well suited for information such as certifications, security clearances, pilot ratings or classifications, foreign languages spoken, special work-related hobbies, computer languages, skills, and any other educational or teaching credentials you feel are important. Examples of selected special qualifications summaries follow:

Example 1   **Pilot**

Special Qualifications / Certifications
> Command Pilot—6,150 flight hours
> FAA—Class I Medical
> Instructor, Air-to-Air Combat School
> Top Secret security clearance with current SBI

Example 2   **Officer (any service)**

Certifications / Related Experience
> Certified Professional Logistician
> Former Instructor, Defense Systems Management College
> Weapons System Acquisition Professional, Level II

Example 3   **Naval Officer (Nuclear Submarines)**

Special Qualifications / Certification
> Qualified Weapons Officer aboard nuclear submarines
> Top Secret security clearance with current SBI
> Certified by Director, Division of Naval Reactors, as Engineering
>   Officer

Example 4   **Senior Enlisted (Air Force)**

Special Qualifications / Related Experience
> Loadmaster on C-5A, C-17, and C-130 aircraft
> Certified Parachute Rigger, Parachute Club of America
> Secret security clearance

Example 5   **Officer or Senior Enlisted**
                                 (any service)
Special Qualifications/Related Experience
    Fluent in German
    Served as a NATO courier for classified material movement
        throughout Europe
    Secret security clearance

While the above examples are not all-inclusive, they do provide a sampling of information that demonstrates proficiency or cites qualifications that might be of special interest to a prospective employer. Do not fall into the trap of listing superfluous special qualifications just to fill a category. The information you include should specify additional skills as well as support your overall job search objectives. Remember that a secret or higher security clearance is good for only up to two years after you leave the service. If you want to continue to show it on your resume after the two years are up and you have not been working in a job that requires a security clearance, you should address this area on your resume as "previously held secret (or higher) security clearance" so as not to confuse your future employer or embarrass yourself.

Computer Skills
Since the last edition of this guide, computer skills have continued to grow in importance to the point where they require mentioning in their own section on the resume. Previously it was acceptable to use the term *computer literate* somewhere on your resume; today, however, that may not necessarily be the case. Employers are constantly looking for applicants who are familiar with three software applications that have become almost an industry standard of their own in the marketplace: Microsoft Word (current edition), Excel, and Power-Point. If you can master these three applications, your chances of obtaining long-term employment improve considerably. Microsoft Word and PowerPoint have undergone considerable user-friendly upgrades, and tutorials for each one of these programs is available on the Internet, at a relatively inexpensive price.

A few examples of the Computer Skills section follow.

Example 1   **Any Servicemember**
Computer Skills

- Proficient in the following operating systems and software applications: Windows 07, Microsoft Word, Excel, PowerPoint, Access, and Macintosh Desktop publishing.
- Military proficiency includes the following software applications (insert your service-specific applications that you use on a regular basis, e.g., SUDAPS, DEERS, FOMIS, CAMS, etc.).

Example 2   **Air Force Supply Officer**
Computer Skills

- Proficient in Windows 07/XP, Microsoft Word, Excel, Power-Point, and Microsoft Outlook.
- Military computer program proficiency includes: Environmental Management Information System (EMIS); MICAP Assets Sourcing System (MASS); Fuels Automated Management System (FAMS); and Systems Management Analysis Reporting Tool (SMART).

Achievements, Honors, and Awards

The achievement section of your resume should not be simply a laundry list of every medal, decoration, commendation, or unit citation you've earned in your career. Rather, you should cite honors that will highlight career achievements you've already mentioned in your resume.

There seems to be universal confusion over the placement and use of awards and achievements on resumes. Some individuals place their achievement and commendation medals in the Experience section for positions where they earned them, while others attempt to list them somewhere toward the end of their resumes. Since we have several types of achievement and commendation medals (own service, sister service, and joint service), it is probably easier to lump them under the category of Department of Defense commendations. One way to show them as a separate section within the resume is as follows:

Awards/Achievements

- Awarded three Department of Defense commendations for superior achievement and outstanding performance of duties in the areas of marine engineering aboard naval surface warfare ships.
- Honors Graduate at ITT Technical Institute.

Other examples of how to display awards/achievements follow.

Example 1   **Officer Any Service**
                       (Contracts Management)

Awards / Honors

- Recipient of 2001 Iowa State University Distinguished Alumni Award
- Awarded three Department of Defense Commendations for outstanding achievement and superior performance in the field of contracts management

Example 2   **Woman Officer in the Army/Navy/Air**
                       Force Medical Corps

Achievements / Honors

Listed in *A Directory of Women in the History of Science, Technology, and Medicine*, 2002; *The World Who's Who of Women*, 23rd edition, 2009; Biography included in *The Directory of American Scholars*, Volume VI, page 21

Example 3   **Senior Army Commander**
                       in the Pacific

Achievements, Honors, and Awards

- *Who's Who in America*, 2009
- Awarded Honorary Doctor of Law Degree, North Carolina State University, 2007
- Recipient of several Department of Defense Awards for Outstanding Achievement
- Awarded Republic of Korea Order of National Security Merit— Cheonsu Medal, 2008

Example 4   **Senior Marine Corps**
                                 Maintenance/Logistics Officer

Awards / Honors

- Commander of one of six units to receive Secretary of Defense Maintenance Award (2008).
- Recipient of Secretary of the Navy Unit Citation awarded to a Logistics Support Group for sustained superior performance with an unprecedented equipment readiness rate of 94%.
- One of seven distinguished alumni inducted into the first Hall of Fame for Brockton Senior High School in Brockton, Massachusetts, on the occasion of the school district's 100th anniversary.

Example 5   **Army Program Executive Officer**

Significant Achievements

- Served as deputy to Program Executive Officer (PEO) for Management Information Systems for programs representing $5 billion in life-cycle costs.
- Managed 11 major Army information system projects (e.g., ITMS, Supply 2000, Project 80-X, Supercomputer) with total budgets exceeding $2.4 billion.
- Designed an automated system to support selection boards involved in the promotion process for 95,000 Army officers.

How you handle personal decorations is more a matter of preference than necessity. While the inclusion of combat awards is not recommended for your resume, the citing of joint or meritorious service commendations received may be of some assistance when applying for a job in the defense contracting industry.

It also should be remembered that good conduct medals, campaign ribbons, and shooting medals are not considered in the same category as the respective Service Achievement and Commendation Medals and should not be included unless the latter have never been awarded.

According to one school of thought, citing large sums of money (that is, millions or billions) could cause a potential employer to think you are overqualified, especially if the budget figures you cite are larger than the company payroll or the combined worth of the company you would be joining. Nevertheless, if you work in systems acquisition, finance, or RDT&E; fly tactical, rotary-wing, or airlift aircraft; command over $50 million worth of M1A2 tanks at the battalion level; or command an aircraft carrier with over four thousand crew members and over eighty tactical aircraft, you are dealing with exceptionally high budgets. These are significant responsibilities. Your involvement in ensuring cost-effective financial management should be cited in your resume, especially if it is relevant to your target job.

If you are not comfortable with using these high dollar amounts, try to put a price tag on your particular part of the effort, providing you can break it out of the overall budget figure. Unless the person reading your resume is totally uninformed, he or she will be able to figure out that you didn't really hold the only checkbook for a $5 million or $5 billion program budget, and that you had plenty of help in spending the funds over that particular fiscal year or the lifetime of the program.

Papers and Publications

While not everyone is an accomplished writer or publisher, you may have literary efforts to your credit that would interest a prospective employer. If you decide to apply for a position in publishing or education, you may have to submit writing samples to prospective employers. Be sure to maintain a few samples of your literary or artistic endeavors on file in case you are asked to submit them with your resume or at the time of your interview. Below are recommended ways for handling your writing experience.

Example 1　　　　**Marine Corps Officer**

Publications

> Author: *The U.S. Marine Corps and Defense Unification: 1944–1947*, National Defense University Press, Washington, D.C., 2007

Example 2　　　　**Navy Officer in C4I Field**

Published Papers and Articles

> "Work Study Applications to C4I Design," C4I *Military Newsletter*, December 2008

"Combat Systems Integration in the U.S. Navy," *International Defense Review,* 2006

Example 3   Army Officer

Publications

Authored feature articles on defense preparedness in *Journal of Defense & Diplomacy, Armed Forces Journal International,* and *Defense Week*

Employment or Career History

Should you elect to use the combination resume format, you will need to develop an employment or career history section for insertion at the end of your resume. This is nothing more than a chronological listing of your service assignments in inverse order. The following are three representative samples of employment or career histories:

Employment History

2007–Present	Contracting Negotiator, MILSTAR Joint Program Office, Los Angeles AFB, CA
2003–2006	Special Assistant to the Deputy Chief of Staff, Contracting, Los Angeles AFB, CA
2000–2002	Flight Commander and Deputy Missile Crew Commander, Minuteman III ICBM, Los Angeles, CA
1998–2000	Contracting Officer, U.S. Air Force Systems Command Acquisition Center, Hanscom AFB, MA
1994–1997	Contract Manager, U.S. Air Force Communications Command, Computer Acquisition Center, Hanscom AFB, MA

Employment History

| 2008–Present | Flight Line Superintendent, Fighter Squadron, Moody AFB, Georgia |
| 2005–2007 | Product Improvement Manager, Logistics Group, Cannon AFB, New Mexico |

| 2001–2004 | Flightline Expeditor, Shift Supervisor, Maintenance Expeditor, and Crew Chief, Fighter Squadron and Aircraft Generation Squadron, Royal Air Force Bases, Upper Heyford and Lakenheath, United Kingdom |
| 2000–Prior | U.S. Air Force. Served in positions of increased responsibility in the aircraft maintenance field as a jet aircraft maintenance technician in Japan, the United Kingdom, and the United States |

Career History

| 2008–Prior | U.S. Navy Officer. Served in various flying and shipboard line and staff assignments in peacetime and during the Second Gulf War: as Chief, International Management Office for the Joint Tactical Command and Control Agency; on the NATO staff in Brussels, Belgium, as SACLANT representative for the NATO Airborne Early Warning Program; and as a Naval Flight Officer instructor in the Naval Air Training Command |

Associations and Affiliations

The associations and affiliations section should highlight professional or educational associations or affiliations you belong to currently, or plan to join prior to leaving the service. If you don't belong to any organizations that are associated with your desired career field, then it is all right to show memberships in military service-related organizations such as AUSA, MCA, AFA, or the Navy League. Provided below is a sample list of associations or affiliations selected as representative of the types that can be used in this section.

Associations

National Defense Transportation Association (NDTA)
Society of Logistics Engineers (SOLE)
Society of Naval Architects and Marine Engineers (SNAME)

American Society for Training and Development (ASTD)
Armed Forces Communications and Electronics Association (AFCEA)
Chamber of Commerce
College and University Alumni Associations

Affiliations
Adjunct Professor, DIA, Joint Military Intelligence College
Army/Navy/USAF/USMC Liaison to *Signal* magazine
Lecturer, Armed Forces Staff College

Organizations
The Company of Military Historians
Rotary, Kiwanis, or Lions Club
Professional Fraternities and Sororities

CURRICULUM VITAE
The curriculum vitae, or CV, is a more acceptable resume format for scientific organizations, colleges and universities, or think tanks in search of potential employees with graduate-level education, research internships, professional society memberships, papers or publications, community or public service, and specialized research. An Army Foreign Area Officer (FAO) or equivalent with advanced foreign language capability, foreign country residency, extensive overseas travel, and possibly a final tour at one of the senior intelligence agencies is a prime candidate for the CV. Examples of several types of CVs appear in appendix A.

THE ELECTRONIC RESUME
Electronic resumes posted on job search bulletin boards on the Internet in response to urgent hiring demands by employers nationwide and overseas are used as much if not more than the standard personal resume. Job opportunities by the thousands appear daily on job-posting websites on the Internet, and a number of employers prefer to screen applicants using the electronic resume or even a regular resume posted to their company website.

The decision on whether to post an electronic resume will probably coincide more closely with your expected expiration of service than the mailing of a normal resume, which takes place several months prior to your exit from the military. Once you have elected to use an electronic resume format, there are several guidelines to consider.

- Stick to the basic resume section headings as shown earlier in the chapter.
- State a specific objective.
- Use both keywords (aircraft maintenance, logistics, and so on) and buzzwords (for example, JAST, DOD, EWO, or IW).
- Use short synopsized experience statements with action verbs.
- Quantify experience into percentage of improvement, number of personnel supervised, budget savings, and specific accomplishments.
- List work experience only for the past five to ten years, or last three to five assignments.
- Avoid the use of personal information such as marital status, race, religion, political affiliation, and memberships in nonprofessional societies or associations.
- Don't use 10-point Times New Roman font, boldface type, italics, or special characters; don't tab over or use the space bar and return; and stick to the same size font throughout.
- Electronic resumes can exceed the traditional resume format in length but should not be more than three pages long.

An example of an electronic resume may be found at the end of appendix A.

THE OF 612

The standard government form for applying for a position with the federal government is called the OF 612. The OF 612 format is very similar to the resume formats discussed in this chapter. Since many readers will decide not to pursue this route for post-career employment, a discussion of OF 612 construction has been omitted. An example of a completed OF 612, however, has been included at the end of appendix A.

FIELD-TESTING YOUR RESUME

Once you have absorbed the information in this chapter, you will be ready to design your own resume. The resume examples provided in appendix A represent a cross section of the most common career patterns for members of all the armed forces. Refer to the index in the front of appendix A to determine which sample resumes contain experience examples that parallel your own career background, and then use them as handy references as you prepare your own resume.

After you have designed a resume, you will want to field-test it. Have a few of your friends who have successfully moved into second career jobs look it over to see what they think. Understand up front that any edits they may recommend are based solely on their own job search experience. If their backgrounds differ significantly from yours, seek other opinions before deleting any information that may be pertinent to your own search.

If you have less than six months before separation or retirement, you may also want to mail or even e-mail your resume to prospective employers whose advertisements appear in the Sunday employment section of your local newspaper. Although the probability of receiving a response may be slim, you might be surprised and may even end up with an invitation to interview.

The proof-positive for checking the marketability of your resume will be the number of interviews it yields. As soon as you have completed your resume based on valid comments and criticisms from those with experience in your particular field, then any mailing or direct passing to potential employers should result in some degree of interest (especially if it catches the eye of an employer who is looking for the qualifications that you possess).

KEY POINTS

- Review the ground rules for resume development to ensure that you have a good idea of how best to pursue this vital part of your job search.
- Gather personal military career data into a centralized file that can be converted to a reference library for use in preparing your first-draft resume.

- Service career pattern, education (both formal military and civilian), and accomplishments should dictate your selection of resume format.
- If an employer is seeking a more detailed resume with professional experience, educational credentials, publications, and professional memberships, then a curriculum vitae (CV) rather than a regular resume may be in order.
- Review appendix A to find a resume that most closely approximates your career experience. You may have to use a composite of several resumes to accomplish this task.
- Organize your resume by category, using the examples provided under the various headings in this chapter and in appendix A.
- Consider using the curriculum vitae format for your resume if your background and experience include an advanced degree, research internships, professional society memberships, publications or papers, community or public service, and specialized research.
- If you choose to post an electronic resume on the Internet, be aware that you are displaying it to the world. It contains your e-mail address and could open you up to unwanted e-mail spam and possible identity theft. If you are concerned with limited distribution, consider whether this is the best method of gaining entry into the civilian marketplace.
- Attaching your resume as part of an e-mail to a company that has specifically requested it should guarantee limited distribution.
- Once you are satisfied that you have prepared a representative resume, follow the suggestions recommended for field-testing it.

CHAPTER 6

CONVERGING TECHNOLOGIES

THE INTERNET AND ONLINE SERVICES

Next to networking, the Internet may well be your best resource for finding jobs currently being offered across the United States and overseas. Many of you use a personal computer (PC) as part of your regular military duties, and you have access to the Internet via the electronic-mail (e-mail) system provided by your individual service. In fact, nowadays most of you also own a desktop or laptop computer (PC or Macintosh) and have signed up with a commercial or local Internet service provider (ISP) for e-mail and other World Wide Web (www) searches. Some of the more popular ISPs include America Online

(AOL), Yahoo, MSN, Earthlink, AT&T Worldnet, Hotmail, Embarq, Cox, and COMCAST. In addition to the big-name ISPs, local towns and major metropolitan cities also have their own free nets or lower-fee Internet providers. Wireless access, or wireless fidelity (WI-FI), is another fast-moving technology that is rapidly becoming available in many organizations, businesses, and cities. Having an at-home computer offers you the opportunity to take a less stressful and non–time sensitive approach when viewing job-posting websites, job bulletin boards, and job search engines on the Internet.

USING THE INTERNET

Getting on the Internet has become easier over the years to the point of almost being automatic if you have access to a computer with the latest version of Microsoft Explorer, Safari (for Macs), Mozilla Firefox, or Opera. Many of you already have daily access right at your work site. If you are not one of these lucky people, then you will need three things in order to access the Internet:

1. Personal computer (either a Macintosh or a PC) with the latest operating system (e.g., Leopard or Windows 07/Vista/XP) and preferably the latest version of Microsoft Word (Mac or Windows) for e-mailing your resume via the Internet as an attachment to prospective employers, or posting it on one of the many job search bulletin boards
2. Modem with a processing speed of 56,000 bps (bauds per second)
3. An Internet service provider (ISP)

Using any word processing software other than MS Word may present problems in submitting your resume over the Internet. Since the majority of people operate desktop PCs with Windows operating systems, MS word is the preferred word processing software for transferring documents over the Internet. This usually guarantees the format will not fall apart en route. If you use other formats and word processing applications, you are doing so at your own risk.

Many people have elected to use broadband, cable hookup with high-speed access, or digital subscriber line (DSL) from their ISP for a monthly charge. The advantage of these high-speed hookups is that they provide continuous access to the Internet so that you are constantly logged on without the need to dial up each time you wish to connect to the Internet. The bad news is that your computer is continually susceptible to whatever viruses ("electronic AIDS") are flying around looking for a place to attach themselves. It would definitely be in your best interest to get a subscription to an antivirus service/firewall such as Norton or McAfee, both of which are renewable on an annual basis for a very reasonable price. McAfee now comes free with the latest AOL ISP software. There are also free antivirus services, one of which is AVG, as well as free firewalls, such as Comodo or Zone Alarm. Considering the damage that some viruses can do to your files and applications, you would be well served to investigate this antivirus protection if you don't currently have it on your computer.

Internet Terms

There are only a few terms you need to become familiar with in order to surf the Internet (check out different sites and links). Just like military buzzwords and acronyms, Internet terms also have unique meanings. Some of the more common terms are described as follows:

ISP. Your Internet service provider may be either a nationwide company or a local service. There is a monthly fee, usually $20 for the major providers and less for local providers. Most providers also offer McAfee or Symantec's Norton antivirus with the added advantage of backing you up in technical and administrative support when you need it.

Cable or DSL. These high-speed hookups give you twenty-four-hour access to the Internet. Cable works through your TV cable system and is independent of your phone line. DSL does not require a dedicated phone and can multiplex on your current phone line; you can use both simultaneously. Both are about the same price per month ($35 to $70) after the initial monthly phase-in offers (some as low as $19.95 for the first few months) expire.

URL. The ticket to get on the Internet, the uniform resource locator (URL), is the series of letters that distinguishes one website from another and provides a way for linking that site to the main resource locator through your ISP. A normal URL starts after the abbreviation http:// with the abbreviations www.something.something (and sometimes a few more somethings, such as numbers and symbols). For example, the website for the Army Career and Alumni Program is *http://www.acap.army.mil.* When using the ISP's online service, usually http://www. is already shown on the URL address line window.

Web Browser. Once you are on the Internet, you will need a web browser to find the various job search websites with their home pages and links to their resources and services. *Microsoft Internet Explorer (PC), Safari (Mac),* and *Mozilla Firefox* are probably the three most recognized web browsers. The web browsers take your URL commands and usually head off at breakneck speed to bring up the requested site on your screen. As you click the various underlined keywords (links) resident on your site, the web browsers provide hyperlink service by connecting you to the server to search for the next location you are seeking. If you use the Department of Defense website, DOD Transportal (*www.dodtransportal.org*), for your career transition needs, it provides a one-stop locator with these job search websites hyperlinked on their main information page. As of this writing, the DOD Transportal is in the process of switching over to *www.TurboTap.org*, which will take over the individual transition plan process and other features of the former site.

Hyperlinks. These connectors or category expanders are the individual subjects or categories that provide a further link with the click of the mouse to the subject matter you are interested in reviewing. Some are shown with underlines to indicate they are hyperlinks, and some you just click on to see if they will lead you to the next window on the subject.

Plog. A plog is a combination video and blog controlled by the author. A plog may be used to present a video resume of oneself or a video bio with monologue, depending on the situation and circumstances. For those with the computer savvy to put a plog together, this may be an excellent means of applying for a job long distance, especially if you are deployed and the timing of your return could work out with the position's hiring date. Some of the latest job search books have come out in favor of this method of presenting one's credentials, but it can also work against you if the plog presentation is not well-received by the prospective employer.

Search Engines. These are the dictionaries of the Internet. Access to the search engines is through the box with the window at the top of the Internet page. *Google, Yahoo,* and *Wikipedia* are examples of search engines. They will take the words you have placed in the search box at the top of the page and locate everything they can that relates to that particular subject. All definitions or categories located by the respective search engine have hyperlinks for further identification of the areas of interest.

World Wide Web. This series of networks residing on the Internet provides the world of sight, sound, colorful images, logos, videos, and useful information in textual and hyperlink formats, which can then be downloaded to your desktop, laptop, or even your iPhone, Blackberry, or other future devices with these capabilities. Unfortunately, over the years many websites have become more complex and sophisticated, and thus harder and harder (i.e., slower and slower) to use a dial-up modem for access. Even though your modem may be 56K for dial-up, the actual upload/download of data is almost always less (as low as 29,000 bpm) due to connections, older wiring, etc. Again, the use of DSL, cable, and WI-FI offer a better range of high-speed connectivity.

Web Home Page. An information page that describes all the features available to a particular website and provides keyword hyperlinks that allow you to move from one source of information to the next on the back of the search engine coupler. Web home pages are capable of being customized to your own online requirements. Check with your ISP to get more information on how to do this.

Webinar. A new term for *web conferencing*. Webinars are used to conduct live meetings or presentations via the Internet. Attendees normally go to a mutually supported URL, sign on, and then participate, but with limited interaction. This type of web conferencing can also include the use of a standard telephone line and speaker phone, which would allow for more interaction on the part of the participants.

WI-FI. The newest of the new-wave technology coming down the pike, Wireless Fidelity (WI-FI), or 802.11 as it has been categorized by some computer gurus, is making a significant splash in the workplace. Featuring a range of transmission from 150 to 300 feet at 11 megabits a second, it is ideal for the home and has also become a hit at your local Starbucks, Borders Books & Music, McDonald's, and other service retailers of the world willing to take a chance on a trial basis and hook you up with this technology. WI-FI requires a laptop with a WI-FI card and a service provider that can link your laptop to one of the 10,000 "hot spots" in over fifty cities across America and another 35,000 around the world. There are several WI-FI providers, but AT&T, Verizon, Sprint, and T-Mobile are the main providers at this time. You can also go to *www.wifinder.com* on the Internet for free WI-FI access locations; however, this free service is not secure so you could be setting yourself up for infection by the latest virus going around the world. In 2007, it was estimated that over 95 percent of laptop computers were WI-FI enabled. It would appear that WI-FI is definitely here to stay, at least in the case of the laptop.

CAREER TRANSITION AND JOB-POSTING SITES

The number of career transition online services and job-posting sites is growing exponentially, paralleling the rate of growth of websites on the Internet. By the time this book comes off the presses, the recommended websites for career transition assistance will probably have doubled again. Sifting through the amount of free advice, employment opportunities, online resume services, job search bulletin boards, and career resource centers is an endless task unless you narrow the search on the front end—just one more reason to opt for high-speed Internet access if you can afford it.

This chapter will provide you with some of the better websites for transitioning military servicemembers, as well as others offered by all online ISPs, such as America Online (AOL), Yahoo, and MSN, to name a few. Several of the better job-posting sites for separating military personnel are shown in the table on the next page, complete with website addresses.

The website home pages for The Destiny Group (now a Recruit-Military company) and CareerBuilder.com have been provided to give you an idea of the types of job search information and assistance that are available on a typical career transition assistance website. Each underlined word or phrase (for example, "Accounting" under the Search by Job Category on CareerBuilder.com), as well as the subjects shown in the various box arrangements in each website, serve

Key Career Transition Job Search Websites

Agency/Provider	Internet Website	Job Search Agents	Transition Support for
Department Of Defense	www.TurboTAP.org www.dodtransportal.org	No	All
Department of Labor	www.careeronestep.org	Yes	All
Destiny Group a RecruitMilitary Company	www.destinygrp.com	Yes	All
Military Officers Association of America	www.moaa.org	No	Officers & Sr. NCOs
Office of Personnel Management	www.usajobs.gov	Yes	All
CareerBuilder.com	www.careerbuilder.com	Yes	All
Military Advantage, Inc.	www.military.com	Yes	All
Alliance International	www.alliance-recruiting.com	No	Jr. Officers
Bradley-Morris, Inc.	www.bradley-morris.com	No	Jr. Officers
Lucas Group	www.lucasgroup.com	No	All
Orion International	www.orioninternational.com	No	Jr. Officers/ NCOs
MilitaryHire.com	www.MilitaryHire.com	Yes	All
VFW	www.vetjobs.com	No	All
American Military Retirees Association	www.amra1973.org	No	All

as hyperlinks that can be clicked on with your mouse, and the link then sends you to the subject or service selected.

The Destiny Group is unique in that it provides a number of services not readily available on other career transition websites. The Destiny home page has been provided to show you the types of job search information available on a military-oriented career transition website. In addition to the normal resume-posting service for those companies in search of separating and retiring military personnel, Destiny offers a recently established FasTrac program with two options for reviewing resumes. The basic program has a $29 fee, and for this the individual's resume is reviewed within seventy-two hours and placed in the FasTrac database for employer's participating in a fee-based program to view by occupational fields. The review process is sort of like a pass-fail exercise, and those whose resumes are in need of additional work are recommended for the full review and

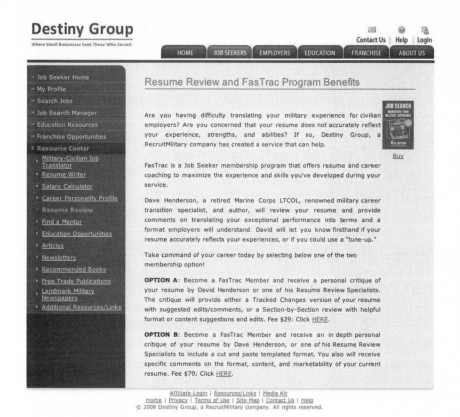

Destiny Group Home Page

critique option, which offers an in-depth analysis of their resume with either a marked-up version that they can repair or a redo in a sample format that can be pasted and further developed. The fee for the added review and critique service is $70. Persons using the Fas-Trac program may use their military e-mail address; however, once they separate from the service while in the database, they may want to consider switching to a personal e-mail address and deleting the military one.

The Destiny Group is much more than just a job board catering to the military experiences, skills, and values you have obtained. As a part of the RecruitMilitary group of career sites, it connects you with the nation's small businesses that provide unique and challenging career opportunities. By answering just a few questions, you can create a free, perfectly formatted resume on the site. Perhaps the best feature is a tool that assesses your personality and recommends what type of positions would best suit you. The Destiny Group's "smart" job board technology will then connect you to those opportunities presently posted, and all you have to do is click the "submit" button to pass your winning resume directly to the hiring manager. This new technology is free on a trial basis.

RecruitMilitary (*www.recruitmilitary.com*) focuses solely on matching up military veterans and their spouses with employers around the world. Whether you are enlisted or an officer, transitioning or have made the transition from the services several years ago, RecruitMilitary offers free, comprehensive job search and career transition services. It connects veterans and spouses with thousands of employers seeking quality candidates with the unique and well-rounded skill sets a military background provides. Through its direct placement division and its website, RecruitMilitary assists candidates with information about resumes, networking, and interviewing in its Career Center. It is also the largest provider of military job fairs in the country. You'll find regular and up-to-date search tips through their magazine, *Search & Employ*. All services are free to the veteran.

There are several other job-posting websites that should be considered during your job search campaign. The first is CareerOneStop (*www.careeronestop.org*), the Department of Labor's replacement for America's Job Bank, and the second is USAJobs (*www.usajobs.gov*), which is found on the Office of Personnel Management website. CareerOneStop is for all jobs in the commercial sector of the job market, and USAJobs is for federal job openings.

COMPUTER NETWORKING

Those of you with a certain amount of e-mail and Internet savvy are already tracking people in other DOD organizations at e-mail addresses around the world. In some respects you have already built a network of friends and working counterparts in your own service as well as the sister services. In fact, you know e-mail is clearly a "must" for anyone trying to stay current and accessible in his or her profession of arms. As soon as you start your job search and reach out into cyberspace for help, add these new URLs and e-mail addresses to a separate directory for easy reference and tracking.

Computer networking is just an electronic extension of the normal networking process you will already have in effect. Rather than maintaining a Rolodex of business cards and phone numbers for your contacts, you will be starting a useful directory of e-mail and URL addresses. Thus, computer networking becomes an easy, informal method of maintaining contacts before, during, and after your job search. Less demanding than a direct phone call and faster and more efficient than a letter, computer networking is the ideal way to nurture contacts in the geographic area where you want to pursue your second career.

THE ONLINE JOB SEARCH

There are a number of Internet job search books out there, but I believe one of the best is Alison Doyle's *Internet Your Way To a New Job*. This compact guide identifies all the key elements of putting together a solid online job search. If you place a lot of faith in your online experiences, then the helpful hints and procedures outlined in this book are for you. Some of the areas covered are as follows:

- Online networking and building an online presence
- Creating a profile on LinkedIn (*http://linkedin.com/home*) or FaceBook (*http://facebook.com*). LinkedIn is considered an advanced job search tool.
- Creating a professional presence, or "brand," so that potential employers can use Google to find your LinkedIn or FaceBook profile
- Online communications—e-mail, video resumes, profiles, blogging, and interviewing
- Privacy and safety issues and concerns
- Specialized job sites—6figurejobs.com (for executives) and DICE.com (tech jobs) are just two examples
- Online job search management tools such as JibberJobber (*http://jibberjobber.com*)
- Keeping track of jobs applied for online (tactics and techniques)
- Related sources section at the end of each chapter for further subject research

This book will go far in helping you develop a safe and strategic online presence for job searching and career transitioning. Keep it close to your desktop, or take it on the road with your laptop.

KEY POINTS

- Work with your Career Transition Office to learn the rudiments of surfing the Internet and the World Wide Web.
- Once you are comfortable using the various Internet websites, develop an organized approach to accessing applicable employment information on the recommended sites.
- Check out and use at least two or three of this chapter's recommended Internet websites and home pages for their job-posting data or their job search engines. Start with the DOD TurboTap website to see what is out there in the world of career transition websites, and then go to The Destiny Group, Careerbuilder.com, USAJobs, CareerOneStep, and the MOAA websites for more job search opportunities.
- Establish your own networking job search Rolodex of URLs, websites, and e-mail addresses to assist you in implementing your Individual Career Transition Plan.
- Remember that your ability to use a computer for research and communication has reached the point where basic computer skills are as indispensable as driving a car. You needn't be a full-fledged computer guru, but you can expect to be left behind if you are unable to readily, and with some degree of confidence, access the Internet and the various military-friendly job search websites.
- In keeping with the new technology, participate in webinars when and where you can to get familiar with the world of Internet teleconferencing.
- If you are into blogging, you may want to take your job search one step further and produce your own plog. Depending on the type of position you are seeking, it is important to remember that a plog can make or break your chances based on how well it is received by the prospective employer.

CHAPTER 7

THE INTERVIEW

All other job search efforts will seem rather ordinary when compared with the butterflies and white knuckles you will experience as you approach your first interview. For some it will be like an opportunity to audition for a lead role in a Spielberg movie; for others it will be like waiting for the command "Fire!" as they stand in front of a firing squad. The anxieties associated with interviewing are normal, so approach an interview as you would if you were preparing a briefing for a superior or a classroom presentation. This way you will maintain your composure and be more self-confident.

SOME DO'S AND DON'TS

As you enter this final phase of your job search, review the following do's and don'ts for handling typical situations you will encounter during the interview process. These are commonsense suggestions that will help to make your interview a success.

Do's:

- Be sure to research the company, firm, or industry for which you are interviewing. Not doing your homework can prove to be quite embarrassing, especially with all the Internet tools available to you today that can be used to complete an in-depth research file.
- Be enthusiastic—even if this is not the job you really want.
- Be on time for the interview.
- Shake hands firmly with the interviewer, whether male or female.
- Maintain good eye contact throughout the interview. It is important for you to look the interviewer in the eye and let him or her know you are prepared to answer any questions that might be posed during the course of the interview.
- Ask as many questions as you feel comfortable with on all aspects of the position for which you are being interviewed. By showing this sort of interest, you will impress the interviewer with your sincerity and eagerness to learn as much about the position as possible.
- Answer the questions posed by the interviewer in sufficient detail to give him or her a chance to make a quick analysis of your knowledge in this area. On the other hand, don't build a fort when a lean-to will do! Once the interviewer is assured that you have a good grasp of an area, he or she may choose to move on to other areas.
- Be candid but never critical, especially of former employers. If your military experiences were less than rewarding, don't spend your entire interview trying to drop napalm on those who may have made life difficult for you while you were on active duty. Stick to the positive things about your military career and you'll make a better impression.

- Listen and request clarification if you are not clear on the subject being discussed. Some interviewers assume too much and may throw out more information and buzzwords than you can digest in one session. Don't be afraid to speak up if you don't understand what is being said.
- Think and speak in civilian terms. Dropping military acronyms on an interviewer may prove counterproductive. Not every interviewer will have had military experience.
- Dress appropriately for the occasion (see the "Dressing for the Interview" section later in this chapter).
- Thank the interviewer(s) for his/her/their time.
- Mail a thank-you letter to each of the principal interviewers, regardless of the outcome of the interview or the manner in which you may have been treated while at their offices.

Don'ts:

- Don't smoke or chew gum during an interview.
- Don't provide more information than necessary.
- Don't wear your military dress shoes to an interview. This is a definite sign that your body is present but your mind is back on the parade field or ship's quarterdeck.
- Don't drink alcoholic beverages during an interview lunch. You don't have to make apologies or explain your feelings about why you prefer not to; just state politely that you don't care for anything alcoholic. By not drinking, your mind will be clear to answer questions.
- Don't discuss politics, religion, or activist group stands. These may be supersensitive issues with the interviewer, and the worst thing that can happen to you is to be on the wrong side of an issue that is special to the interviewer.
- Don't be glib, flip, sarcastic, or cynical in responding to questions you may feel are not worthy of any discussion on your part. This may give the impression of an air of superiority that is tantamount to employment suicide at an interview.
- Don't give the appearance of being too reserved, or you may come across as indecisive or difficult to relate to.

Check out the latest fashions in the areas where you plan to settle and observe what people are wearing to work. This way you will have a better idea of what to expect when you hit the interview trail.

For Men:

- A dark suit, preferably a solid blue or gray, should be in style no matter what the season of the year. For summer, a lightweight tan suit is an acceptable substitution.
- Leave the blue blazer and gray trousers in the closet until you get the job. This combination is a bit too casual for a formal interview.
- Hairstyles currently worn by men in the military (other than "white sidewalls") are acceptable for today's interview.
- Aftershave lotion or cologne may draw more negative reactions than positive ones—don't wear any.

For Women:

There are any number of books on this subject in the careers section of your nearest major bookseller. Most will recommend similar advice based on the current styles and fashions of the workplace today. Basic advice normally includes, but is not limited to, the following recommendations:

- Dress stylishly, but be conservative.
- Choose garments made from natural fibers when selecting your wardrobe. They look better, last longer, and are more comfortable than those made from synthetic materials.
- Keep accessories simple but large enough to be seen. (Accessories that are overdone become a major detractor to your overall appearance.) Some fashion consultants will recommend minimal accessories for the first interview.
- Stick to a medium-heel pump. Walk gracefully, wearing shoes and stockings that don't become focal points in themselves.
- Your hairstyle should project a professional image.
- Well-manicured nails and makeup with a natural look are important.
- Perfume or cologne should not be worn to the interview.

For the most up-to-date advice on what to wear to an interview, check out Martin Yate's *Knock 'em Dead 2009: The Ultimate Job Search Guide.*

WHAT TO TAKE TO THE INTERVIEW

There is nothing worse than getting to an interview and finding that you came ill-prepared for what lies ahead. There are certain items you will need, and there are others that should be left behind. On the take-to list, be sure to include the following:

- A folder with at least two or more resumes in it. While you might expect that you are going to interview with one person, you might be passed on to others. Human resources may also want a copy for their files as you leave the interview site.
- A sheet with your references on it. This is normally a supplemental page to your resume and should always be part of the resume folder you carry to the interview.
- Resumes carried to an interview should be on 24lb stock paper and not standard photocopy paper, which is usually 20lb. The major office supply stores carry a better grade of resume stock just for this purpose, so don't be afraid to invest in a box of this paper for resumes used at the formal interview process.
- Bring a pad of paper and at least two pens. If you bring just one pen, it will almost always fail to work, so bring two and check them out ahead of time.
- Depending on the company and what your research uncovered, bring a list of questions that might prove helpful during the interview and will also show that you did your homework on the company or firm.
- Leave behind at least one or two copies of your resume, and be prepared to leave your list of references if the interviewer requests them. If you have a military business card, it may be attached to your resume and also left with the interviewer.

THE SUCCESSFUL INTERVIEW

Not every interview will be successful, nor will a successful interview always lead to a job. Once the interview is over, however, you should try to review what has just transpired and apply what you learned to subsequent interviews. This will give you a better idea of whether you are coming across well. It can serve to identify and correct statements or mannerisms that may be sending the wrong message. But how should you gauge your progress, and what really constitutes a successful interview?

The successful interview is probably measured best in terms of positive reinforcements like the following:

- An interview that lasts forty-five minutes to an hour or longer would be considered an excellent interview.
- An interviewer who wants you to meet another person in the department, which in turn leads to a series of interviews.
- An interviewer who discusses salary during the first interview.
- An interviewer who explains how your position would fit in with the rest of the company.
- Receiving a compliment on the quality of your resume.
- Being asked back for subsequent interviews.

The tone, or tempo of the interview, is set within the first one to two minutes and goes either up or down from there. If the interviewer stays on the subject of the job opening at hand and pursues a line of questioning that appears comfortable to both parties, then you are correct in assuming that you are doing reasonably well. Should the interviewer decide that you ought to meet another person in that department, or another department that might make better use of your background, this is also a good sign. If your interview takes the form of a number of miniinterviews, this is an excellent sign that you have the skills and background that could nicely match the company's requirements.

THE PHONE INTERVIEW

When an interviewer has hundreds of applicants and an urgency to fill a position, he or she may resort to the phone interview. This type of interview may catch you off guard, but you should be ready with answers to possible questions just as you would for a face-to-face interview.

A phone interview usually lasts twenty minutes to half an hour and tends to be very structured, with the goal of weeding out the marginal or unqualified candidates. The surprise factor aside, it is very difficult to gauge just how well you did in a phone interview, since there was no eye-to-eye contact and no opportunity to see the facial expressions of the interviewer as you responded to the questions.

For more information on phone interviews, again refer to Martin Yate's *Knock 'em Dead 2009: The Ultimate Job Search Guide.* He includes an entire chapter dedicated to the phone interview and what to expect should you be called. You may also want to refer to Tony Beshara's *The Job Search Solution*, which has a chapter titled "Mastering the Dreaded Phone Interview." Both of these books cover standard and off-the-wall interview questions and how best to prepare for them.

REFERENCES

At some point in the interview process, the subject of personal references may come front and center. Generally, it is best to have at least three (preferably five) friends, associates, teachers/professors, or clergy (if applying for a nonprofit or charitable organization) in various lines of work who are willing to be contacted in order to attest to your character and abilities, both on and off the job. Depending upon the responsibilities involved in the position, it is likely that the hiring company will contact one, two, or all of your personal references to satisfy itself that you are the right person for this particular job.

In order to prepare yourself for this likelihood, keep a typed sheet with the names, work addresses, and office phone numbers of your personal references. When selecting these references, try to pick a fellow military coworker, a civilian professional (for example, a doctor, lawyer, or accountant), a clergy member, and someone who has already left the service and may be holding a comparable or higher position in another company similar to the one you hope to join.

Do not use relatives or any friends you have known for less than two or three years as personal references. People who are keenly aware of your previous positions and accomplishments over the past ten years are probably going to be the best choices as personal references. They will be especially helpful in providing a solid character reference to prospective employers interested in finding out about your work habits and temperament.

HOW LONG DOES IT TAKE TO GET A JOB?

How long it takes to get a job depends on how you respond to a position opening. If you are applying for a position based on a resume you passed on to a friend, you will probably get an answer in a reasonable period of time, usually within five to ten days. Provided you are qualified for the position, you may be called in for an interview. Other interviews may follow and are a positive sign. If you are accepted for the position, it will usually take a week or so before you receive an offer letter. In some circumstances, it is not uncommon to wait almost a month to receive an offer letter.

Conversely, when you elect to answer an ad in the newspaper, the time from submission to response may be much longer. For example, a friend of mine responded to an ad for an association position in Washington, D.C., on the first of July and heard nothing for almost a month. The first week in August he received a phone call from the association director indicating that three hundred resumes had been received for the position and that it had taken over a month just to go through them and cut the number down to ten, of which my friend's was one. The director then interviewed him by phone for almost thirty minutes. At the end of the phone interview, the director stated that he planned to cut the ten applicants down to five.

Two weeks later my friend received another call informing him that he was one of the five finalists and would be interviewed sometime in September. His interview was held toward the end of September, at which time he was told by the director that the list would be cut to three and the person selected from the remaining three would be hired by October 15. The interview lasted approximately an hour and a half, and he felt that he had done reasonably well. A week later he received another phone call to say that he had made the final three. He was then interviewed for the third time and was given an offer letter on November 10.

From start to finish, it took three and a half months to fill the position at that association. This is not unusual, especially when the number of applicants is in the hundreds. A former director of Job Placement Services for The Military Officers Association of America has stated that it takes at least six months to get hired from the time the search starts in earnest. Those who wait until they are out of the military could find themselves waiting even longer, unless they had strong leads prior to their exit date. During your job search you will need to continually expand your network in order to increase your opportunity for interviews, which in turn could lead to employment offers.

KEY POINTS

- Review the basic do's and don'ts prior to your first interview.
- Rehearse responses to standard questions usually asked at an interview.
- Research the firm or organization at the library, online, or with a current employee prior to the interview.
- Review any questions you may want to ask an interviewer.
- Prepare a manila folder to take to the interview with at least two or three copies of your resume and a sheet with your references on it.
- Locate the interview site before the actual interview date.
- Maintain a handy file of references who are willing to attest to your knowledge, abilities, and overall performance capabilities.
- Review the suggested wardrobe recommendations and dress accordingly.
- Send a thank-you letter within a week after the interview, whether you felt it was a positive experience or not.
- When responding to an employment ad in the newspaper, remember that the time frame of the employer could be three or more months from publication of the ad to hiring.
- Phone interviews are worse than attempting to cross a minefield blindfolded. Control rests solely with the interviewer, and the inability to view facial expressions based on your answers is not a great confidence builder. Do the best you can under the circumstances and try to maintain a positive outlook during the interview.
- Employers follow their own schedules for deciding when to hire after the completion of all interviews. In spite of your anticipation, be prepared to wait longer than you would if you were awaiting a major decision in the military.
- Call back a few weeks after you have sent your thank-you letter to the interviewer if you have received no word on whether the position has been filled. Sometimes this triggers speedier action, and sometimes it tells you that you are no longer being considered for the position.

CHAPTER 8

COMPENSATION AND BENEFITS PROGRAMS

Victory belongs to the most persevering.
—Napoleon Bonaparte

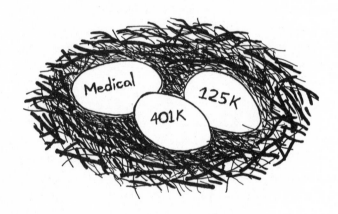

COMPENSATION

A civilian salary bears a strong resemblance to your present military pay and allowances in several ways. First, both have a taxable portion, usually based on a monthly or an annual dollar figure, and a nontaxable portion. How the taxable and nontaxable portions are determined, however, will vary according to employment levels (the military equivalent of pay grades) and possibly geographic location (United States or overseas). Second, although a civilian salary provides compensation for annual vacation and medical and insurance benefits, the level of compensation for paid vacation (usually two weeks as opposed to thirty days per year in the military) and the medical benefits package (free in the service; mutually shared in the private sector) may be much less than you now enjoy in the military. While there may be other similarities between civilian and military salaries, the nontaxable allowances (for housing and subsistence), overseas COLAs, sea pay, combat pay, and more to which you are now entitled are going to be hard to replace once you leave the service and accept civilian employment.

For the sake of comparison, let's review how a typical civilian salary might relate to your current pay and allowances. To start with, your salary would be paid at an hourly rate based on an annual industry norm of 2,080 hours per year. This figure is based on 1,880 work hours, 80 hours for federal holidays, 80 hours of vacation, and 40 hours of sick leave. Again, this is a norm; not all companies adhere to similar vacation, holiday, and sick leave figures, in some cases offering more vacation but less sick leave, or possibly making you take leave for sick days.

Out of your gross weekly wages are deducted federal and state income tax (if applicable), Social Security withholding (broken up into F.I.C.A. and Medicare), and possibly other deductions such as life insurance (for coverage over $50,000), your portion (if any) of medical and dental insurance premiums, 401(k) plan pretax contributions, a 125K deduction (should you choose to use this program), and any other deductions for company-sponsored programs. What is left is your net take-home pay.

Civilian salaries, or compensation packages, normally do not include any housing, subsistence, or cost-of-living (COLA) allowances unless you are accepting a position for an overseas assignment. Life insurance, for the most part, may not be as good as what you had in the military's Servicemen's Group Life Insurance (SGLI) program, as your civilian insurance is usually based on one or possibly up to two times your annual salary. Unlike your coverage under SGLI, the monthly premiums are usually covered by the company up to the first $50,000. The cost for insurance exceeding $50,000 is added as taxable income to the employee and varies by age. Smaller companies may not have life insurance programs, so it is wise to investigate this area thoroughly as you may have to take out additional life insurance to cover your family down the road. This would be especially true for long- and short-term health care insurance.

DETERMINING A STARTING SALARY

Now that you have a basic understanding of what makes up a civilian compensation package, your next step is to determine a marketable starting (or transition) salary figure for your new career. This should be determined before you find yourself in the interview chair.

Do a little homework. Your starting salary requirements will depend on several factors, the first of which is whether you are separating from the military with less than twenty years' service, or retiring after twenty-plus years. If you are separating after less than twenty years, your starting salary should be an amount that is equal to or close to your current pay and allowances and their equivalent value (the sum of the taxable income and nontaxable allowances) in dollars in the civilian sector. If you are retiring, you should pursue a starting salary that will bridge the difference between your retired pay and your active-duty pay plus your tax-free allowances in order to maintain your current standard of living. This does not necessarily mean accepting a starting salary that is less than your current military pay and allowances, but the bridging concept between retired pay and active-duty pay will give you a baseline for negotiations with the idea of getting as close to your current active-duty pay as possible. Should the trend of downsizing and streamlining in companies continue well into the twenty-first century as it has during the first few years, you may find that you will have to accept a salary that is lower than what you had determined was necessary to maintain your lifestyle. Do not take this as a failure on your part in salary negotiation.

In a downsizing job market, one may have to search for available jobs other than in the occupational field of choice. Whatever you do, never let pride or a superior attitude stand in the way of capturing a solid paying job with a bright future. Your performance alone will eventually gap the difference in pay, from what you had hoped for to what you are really worth, in that company or firm. It is not uncommon to receive early raises in the first year of employment for superior performance.

Another factor you may want to consider is trying to place a dollar value on your current healthcare (medical and dental benefits) and your Servicemen's Group Life Insurance (SGLI). To assist you in this task, check with *Army, Navy,* and *Air Force Times* for the most current version of their TRICARE Insurance Cost Comparison Supplement. This supplement lays out for comparison the various healthcare insurance plan costs for programs offered by various military associations and service-related organizations.

Conversion plans for your SGLI upon separation are also available, but they will be for less insurance at a higher cost per month than you are now paying. If you are retiring, take the retired equivalent of SGLI, or Veterans' Group Life Insurance (VGLI), for the five years it is offered, since it is relatively inexpensive and offers you and your family additional coverage at a reduced price compared with similar civilian life insurance coverage. If you are separating with less than twenty years of service, you may want to compare the SGLI conversion being offered with other available insurance programs before deciding.

If you feel that you are bargaining from a strong position, you may want to use your military benefits package for negotiating additional salary, particularly in cases where company-provided medical and insurance plans require you to share in the monthly costs. Point out that full medical coverage was part of your military compensation package, and the amount you are being asked to "share" with the company should be made up in salary.

Figuring out a starting salary is not as hard as it seems. Several examples in appendix D show how to calculate a starting salary for the purpose of salary negotiation.

NEGOTIATING A SALARY
There will always be a tendency to wonder whether you are worth more than the salary offered or, conversely, whether you should accept less than you had planned. It is imperative that you never go below your bottom-line starting salary figure unless you are willing to alter your lifestyle commensurately. When you have determined the bottom-line income required to support your current lifestyle, you have a ballpark figure on which to base all salary negotiations.

Some employers may try to catch you off guard early in an interview and ask you for a salary figure before you even have a chance to discuss the job. No matter when the subject of salary comes up, there is an easy and appropriate way to handle the issue. Simply ask what the salary range is for the position. If the employer provides one, and your previously determined starting salary is within that range, you will have a solid basis for citing an acceptable figure. Try not to cite any figure without first knowing the salary range for the position for which you are interviewing. This will preclude any embarrassment should you be way over, or under, the target salary figure for that position.

What if the company offers you a starting salary that is less than the amount you previously determined was your bottom-line figure for starting? If this is done during the final phase of the interview process, admit that the figure is a bit lower than you had expected for this position and that you would like a couple of days to think about it before accepting the offer. This prepares both sides for two things. One, the employer knows that you are not about to jump at any offer just to get a job. Two, it allows you an opportunity to call back in a few days and give a figure that is more in line with what you had considered your bottom-line salary to be. The new number becomes the negotiating chip for both parties. Be advised that this counter may jeopardize your chances of getting the job, but if the company is serious about wanting you for the position, you will hear from it shortly. In addition, this negotiating period gives you time to weigh any other job offers that may be more lucrative (both monetarily and professionally).

If the company refuses to budge on the initial offer, then depending on how badly you want this position, you will have to look at the long-term trade-offs in salary and benefits. Another approach might be to say that you would be receptive to the salary figure being offered provided you receive a salary review in six months. This gives you an opportunity to make up the difference in what you had set as a goal for your starting salary while allowing you to accept a job you feel will be professionally rewarding. If this also fails, then it will come down to how badly you want the position and whether you are willing to start at a lower salary.

Companies placing newspaper ads that ask for a salary figure with your resume want to eliminate you from consideration immediately if you cite a salary range that is either too high or too low. The best way to handle this is to indicate in your cover letter that you would be happy to discuss a salary figure during your initial interview with the company. If your resume meets the majority of requirements for the advertised position, you may be invited for an interview anyway. Additional advice and the types of questions you could encounter can be found in Martin Yate's *Knock 'em Dead 2009: The Ultimate Job Search Guide*, which has an entire chapter dedicated to the salary negotiation process. You can also refer back to the "Best Jobs in America" article from *Money* magazine mentioned in chapter 2 for additional salary information for fields in which you may be considering transitioning to and have an excellent opportunity in securing a solid position. The salaries cited in the accompanying chart are median salaries, so check the *Money* magazine article further for the high and low salaries within that field of interest.

COMPANY BENEFITS

Company benefits programs normally include medical and dental plans, life insurance, vacation, paid holidays, partial educational reimbursement for college tuition (not always), profit sharing, and a 401(k) retirement plan. Additional benefits may include bonuses (employee incentive programs), an annual salary review, and a flexible tax-free reimbursement program (cafeteria plan or 125K) to cover additional medical expenses.

Medical Plans

There are several types of medical plans that are offered by employers, but the most common ones are provided by either a health maintenance organization (HMO) or a preferred-provider organization (PPO). In addition, they may also provide short-term or long-term disability insurance coverage, or both, should you become hospitalized or unable to work. As part of your selected medical plan, you will normally be required to pay a portion of the cost on a monthly basis with a lump sum removed from each paycheck to cover your share of the plan. Your share of the pro-rated cost, and the annual deductible, could vary significantly depending on the company. Due to the rising costs in healthcare plans for all companies, trying to cite a baseline figure for your pro-rated costs and a reasonable annual deductible with which you could gauge your monthly costs is almost impossible.

It is important to remember that if you accept a company's health care plan, and pay into it on a monthly basis, your TRICARE plan then becomes secondary, and in some cases, you may still have out-of-pocket expenses after the claim has been paid by both parties. This is why it's a good idea to get a supplemental plan along with a company and/or TRICARE plan.

A quarterly TRICARE supplement (for inpatient care only), provided by one of the service organizations such as MOAA, the United Services Automobile Association (USAA), the Air Force Association, the Marine Corps Association, and several others, can help you control costs not covered by other insurance plans. As an example, for a family of three, the quarterly cost for inpatient care coverage is about $75 to $85 with a $200 deductible. Coverage lasts as long as TRICARE approves your hospital stay.

Dental Plans

Most companies now have dental plans for their employees. Typically, the employer pays for the employee, but you may find that dependents' coverage is available at your expense. Average dental coverage costs for employees range from $15 to $20 a month if you're single, $30 and up for a family of two, and $35 to $50 for a family of three or more. If you are responsible for any premium costs, there may be an offsetting tax-favored plan available.

There are three or four categories of dental benefit plans: preventive, basic, major, and orthodontic. The preventive plan usually covers 100 percent and includes cleaning, diagnostic services every six months, and x-rays every two years. The basic plans covers 80 percent (after the deductible) and usually includes restorative services (fillings). The major plan covers 50 percent for crowns, dentures, and other major work, such as root canals. Some plans will cover 60 to 80 percent of drugs, endodontic, periodontal, and oral surgery services. The orthodontic plan is usually 50 percent and will have a separate annual or lifetime maximum benefit. In most plans there will be an annual deductible (usually $50 per person). If your company does not have a dental program, the Department of Defense has approved a TRICARE Delta Dental program for uniformed services retirees and their dependents. Information on how to join this program is available through TRICARE or by e-mailing the Delta Select USA Tricare Retiree Dental Program, whose website is at *www.trdp.org*.

401(k) Retirement Plans

Almost every company with over twenty-five employees has a 401(k) plan. This is one area where one company can be significantly better than another in terms of when its plan starts and how much it is willing to match. Matching contributions by employers vary greatly. Some match dollar for dollar (rare); some match fifty cents on the dollar or some other percentage up to a limit; and some do not match at all. A general rule: You should contribute at least up to the matching limit; otherwise, you are leaving money on the table. Some plans allow the employer to make discretionary contributions on a profit-sharing basis, usually at the end of the business year. This would be on top of the matching contribution.

It is important to note that your 401(k) deferrals are excluded from your taxable income (that is, taken off the top of each paycheck), but not from the Social Security and Medicare tax. You will find differences in vesting in the employer's matching contributions, ranging from being fully vested immediately to a graduated vesting schedule over five years. Vesting means ownership. You are always vested 100 percent in your own salary deferrals, but you may not necessarily be fully vested in your employer's matching contributions should you decide to terminate your employment prior to reaching the set time for achieving 100 percent vesting in the company plan.

Participatory periods normally start in either January or July. An information packet usually arrives several weeks ahead, and a sign-up question-and-answer period is scheduled so that you are better prepared to make any decisions about the various instruments (money markets or mutual funds) that are available for you to invest in. Do a little homework ahead of the sign-up period to determine your comfort level in the risk of the instruments you select to invest in. Most 401(k) plans pick top-line mutual funds with solid performance records in both up and down periods of the stock market. For those whose threshold for financial pain is low, there is always the money market with a steady rate of interest that is usually slightly better than a bank savings account.

Some companies make you wait a year before letting you participate in a 401(k) plan, which costs you in the long run. If you want to join a company that does not allow participation in a 401(k) plan for the first year, try to get a financial offset in your salary negotiation phase that will compensate for this potential monetary loss.

OTHER BENEFITS

Some positions that you seek will have a well-defined bonus program as an added reward for your overall performance on the job. Bonuses may be structured or spontaneously offered, depending on how the company chooses to reward employees for their contributions. Do not be upset if certain positions you interview for do not have bonus programs as part of their employment benefits program. A number of other programs are available in the civilian job market in lieu of bonuses.

There are also a number of company benefits commonly referred to as "perks," which are provided to senior or upper management. These might include an expense account, a company car, extra paid vacation, fully paid medical coverage, deferred compensation plans (stock options), and business-class travel arrangements on business flights overseas.

A number of companies now offer a cafeteria plan, also known as a Section 125 plan (derived from the applicable section of the Internal Revenue Service code). This plan permits pretax deductions from your paycheck to cover certain expenses. The Section 125 plan is an important benefit because the amounts deducted from pay are pretax income, not subject to income, Social Security, or Medicare taxes.

Typically you will find two basic Section 125 plans. In a premium-only plan, you arrange an annual payroll deduction equal to any benefit premiums for which you are responsible. Corrections are triggered by family changes, premium changes, or plan changes made by the employer. In a flexible benefits plan, you specify a payroll deduction amount from which you can be reimbursed for allowed items such as healthcare deductibles, expenses for healthcare co-pay, day care, eye care, and others.

With the premium-only cafeteria plan, you can readily compute the pretax deduction. In contrast, the amount to deduct for the flexible benefits plan is subject to estimates of anticipated annual costs. This is a use or lose affair—you do not get reimbursed for unused deductions.

You may find that an employer will have a medical reimbursement plan rather than a typical group health insurance plan. These are administered by a third party (to be a qualified plan under IRS rules) and are essentially self-insured arrangements by the employer. Your medical costs, within certain limits, will be reimbursed by the company.

Items that might also fall into the other-benefits category include paid parking (very important in large metropolitan areas), day care for small children, and educational assistance programs featuring full or partial reimbursement for tuition, books, and fees based upon successful completion of a college-level course. Company-provided reimbursable educational assistance programs usually come with a payback requirement in terms of agreeing to remain with the company upon completion of your schooling for a specified number of years.

THE OFFER LETTER

An offer letter (see example) is a formal notification from the company that has expressed a desire to hire you. Such letters usually contain a brief summary of the terms of your agreement to become employed by the company. They may also include a set salary (expressed in pay per month or annual salary); a statement to the effect that your hire includes all standard company-paid benefits (vacation and sick leave) as well as life, medical, and in some cases dental insurance coverage; and any other stipulations or added benefits you were able to negotiate during your final interview.

Unlike a contract, an offer letter is not binding and does not contain any clauses that would stipulate the length of your hire. In many cases, you are expected to sign the letter as an agreement to join the company, although there is usually no set length of time you are required to remain after joining.

SAMPLE OFFER LETTER

January 31, 2009

Lt. Colonel Gordon W. Kennebrew, USMC
MOQ 2220
Camp Lejeune, NC 28542

Dear Colonel Kennebrew,

We are pleased to offer you a position as a Program Manager commencing on or about February 15, 2009, working in support of our contract to provide management services to the Department of Labor in the areas of industrial safety and workmen's compensation. You will report to Mr. Tom Jefferson, the Upper Brackets, Inc. (UBI), Project Director for this program. Your starting monthly salary will be five thousand two hundred dollars ($5,200).

UBI is pleased to offer you, as a full-time employee, a group medical, dental, and life insurance plan; short- and long-term disability coverage; an employee incentive plan; company-paid vacation (two weeks) and sick leave; participation in a matching 401(k) retirement program after six full months of employment; and voluntary participation in a Section 125 plan.

Please indicate your acceptance of this offer of employment by signing this letter and returning it to us no later than February 5, 2009. If you have any questions concerning this letter, feel free to contact either myself or the Director of Human Resources at your earliest convenience.

UBI looks forward to working with you in meeting all your professional and personal goals in the future.

Sincerely yours,

David G. Henderson
Director of Operations

Acceptance: **Upper Brackets, Inc.**

_____   _____
Signature/Date   Signature and Title

SAMPLE CONTINGENT HIRE LETTER

January 31, 2009

CMSgt. James F. Weston, USAF
1531 LeMay Circle
Langley AFB, VA 23605

Dear Chief Weston:

Upper Brackets, Inc. (UBI), is a management support services firm located in Burke, Virginia. UBI offers its full-time employees a group medical, dental, and life insurance plan; short- and long-term disability coverage; an employee incentive plan; company-paid vacation (two weeks) and one week of sick leave; participation in a matching 401(k) retirement program after six full months of employment; and voluntary participation in a Section 125 plan.

We are pleased to offer you a position as a (Job Title), contingent upon the award of a contract to UBI to provide (Description of Services) to the federal government under Solicitation DA 4423-66-C-09. The starting monthly salary for this position is three thousand six hundred dollars ($3,600).

In return for this contingent offer of hire, you agree to allow UBI to use your resume in solicited and unsolicited proposals to provide such services as outlined above, as may arise from time to time.

Please indicate your acceptance of this offer of employment by signing this letter and returning it to us no later than February 5, 2009. If you have any questions concerning this letter, feel free to contact either myself or the Director of Human Resources at your earliest convenience.

Sincerely yours,

David G. Henderson
Director of Operations

Acceptance: **Upper Brackets, Inc.**

_____   _____
            Signature/Date   Signature and Title

In the event that not all of the hiring information you agreed to is shown in the offer letter, or the salary quoted is not the same, call the company for clarification. If the salary is incorrect, make a line through the incorrect number and write in the salary you felt you had agreed to during the interviewing process, initialing both figures.

Another type of offer letter is the contingency hire offer letter. This letter (see example) is predicated on a possible hiring situation based on the award of an upcoming contract or possible follow-on business in an area for which you may be qualified.

Although an offer letter is not necessary in all hiring situations, it is the most common form of hiring agreement used in the market-place today. Other ways of becoming employed by a company might include a simple handshake agreeing to all terms of the hire, filling out company-provided personnel information forms and tax information forms after verbally accepting an offer for employment, or agreeing to be hired over the telephone. Depending on the job position, the size of the company, and the urgency of the situation, formalities involved in the traditional hiring process will vary.

PERFORMANCE REVIEWS AND RAISES

Performance reviews are the equivalent of fitness reports, or performance appraisals in the service, and are normally held at one of the following times during a company's financial year: on the anniversary of your employment hire date; at the end of a company's fiscal year; after the first six months of employment, and six months thereafter; or on your birthday, provided it is at least six months after your hire date.

Performance reviews are very important, and you should become as knowledgeable as possible in this area. Being able to negotiate a six-month performance review prior to joining a company, with the possibility of a salary increase as part of your agreement to become an employee, can prove beneficial in two ways. First, it gives you more incentive to show your new company just how good you really are. Second, it allows you another opportunity to excel and be recognized for your contributions when the annual pay raise time arrives. In a downsized hiring environment, however, the possibility of a six-month salary review may not be an option.

KEY POINTS

- Be familiar with what constitutes a civilian salary and compensation package.
- Understand what makes up a company's "standard" benefits program.
- Determine your desired starting salary prior to the interview in order to negotiate from a position of strength. Use the example for Computing Salary Requirements found in appendix D that most approximates your time in service and closest pay grade to assist you in this determination.
- Be aware that if downsizing and streamlining of companies continues well into the twenty-first century, you may have to accept a salary that is less than you desire in order to get the job that you want.
- If the need arises, use your military benefits (medical, dental, insurance) package as a tool for negotiating additional salary.
- Try to determine a reasonable value for your current military medical and dental benefits package. Don't forget to factor in a supplemental plan to cover any company and TRICARE shortfalls in payments of claims.
- Remember to ask for a salary range when the subject of salary is brought up—especially if asked up front how much you want to start. Never be trapped into blurting out a salary without getting the range first.
- Do not provide a salary figure when requested by an employment ad. Indicate in the cover letter that you will be glad to provide this information during the interview process.
- Be aware of any additional benefits other than standard company benefits.
- Be aware that many companies have bonus programs, so don't be afraid to bring up the subject of bonuses during an interview.
- Be sure the offer letter you receive includes all the important information that you negotiated with your new employer during the final interview.
- Review the sample offer letters to ensure that you understand the difference between a firm offer letter and a contingency hire offer letter.

- Become knowledgeable in the area of performance reviews. Try to arrange a six-month performance review as part of your hiring agreement, unless the economy and hiring environment at the time preclude this as a viable option.

APPENDIX A

RESUMES BY OCCUPATIONAL SPECIALTY AND FORMAT

Many of the sample resumes in this appendix are representative of occupational specialties common to all of the services; a few may be peculiar to only one service. The selected subject areas closely approximate civilian career fields, making them especially valuable to the servicemember whose current occupational specialty is in demand in the civilian marketplace.

Be sure that you understand clearly the differences in the various resume formats. If you are unsure, refer to chapter 5 to refresh your memory. Once you are satisfied with your understanding of the types of formats, try to select a format that will most aptly convey your military career experience. After you have done this, a prospective employer should have no trouble understanding just what it is you want to do, and whether you have the requisite skills, experience, and qualifications to fill a specific position in his/her organization.

Before you start to prepare your resume, refer to the "Resume Index" in this appendix and identify all the experience examples that relate to your career experience. Many of you will have served in multiple occupational fields over the course of your careers, so check out all the sample resume subject areas that may apply to your own particular service experience.

RESUME INDEX

CHRONOLOGICAL RESUME EXAMPLES
Specialty
> Aircraft Maintenance/Logistics/Missile Maintenance
> Electronic Maintenance Management
> Financial Management/Budget Analyst
> Fire Control and Electronic Repair Technician

COMBINATION RESUME EXAMPLES
Specialty
> Aviation Operations/Information Operations/Resources Management
> Communications/Electronic Warfare/Network and Space Operations
>   Systems
> Communications/Computer System Network Operations
> Computer Systems Maintenance/UAV Operations/Signals Intelligence
> Comptroller/Cost Analyst
> Disaster Response/Homeland Security
> Food Services/Fitness Center Management
> Hazardous Materials Management
> Human Resources Management
> Information Operations Management
> Intelligence/Acquisition/FAO
> Logistics/Supply Support/Maintenance
> Purchasing/Supply Chain Management
> Public Relations/Media Specialist
> Operations/Intelligence Analyst
> Security Force Operations/Homeland Security
> Telecommunications Maintenance
> Weapon Systems (RDT&E)
> Workforce Development/Organizational Training

CURRICULUM VITAE EXAMPLES
Specialty
> Architecture/Environmental Engineering
> Foreign Affairs Specialist
> Healthcare Management

ELECTRONIC RESUME EXAMPLE
Specialty
> Logistics

PILOT RESUME EXAMPLES
Specialty
> Airline/Air Cargo Pilot
> Corporate Helicopter Pilot

OF 612 RESUME EXAMPLE
Specialty
> Logistics/Supply Specialist

CHRONOLOGICAL RESUME
EXAMPLES

Richard L. Shelton Jr.

14507 Windy Creek • Helotes, Texas • 78023 • (210) 465-9425

rich30101@aol.com

PROFILE

Seasoned logistics and maintenance management professional with over 20 years of documented experience in the areas of logistics program management, aircraft maintenance, repair cycle management, and wing operations and plans. Additional expertise in nuclear assurance evaluations and combat crew training for strategic missiles (ICBM's) and tactical Ground Launched Cruise Missiles (GLCM). Detail-oriented, customer-focused professional with excellent verbal and written communications skills who has been consistently cited for logical and sensible approaches to problem solving in crisis response situations. Seeking challenging position in logistics program or project management, or nuclear assurance evaluation that will make maximum use of my proven leadership, logistics management, and strategic nuclear missile background. Current Top Secret SCI security clearance.

EDUCATION

Formal

Bachelor of Arts, Political Science, Texas Tech University

Professional/Technical

Advanced Logistics Officer Course
Jet Engine Mishap Investigation
Aircraft Maintenance Officer Course
Production Management Processes
Minuteman III ICBM and Ground Launched Cruise Missile (BG-09) Training
U.S. Air Force Senior Service Schools for Leadership & Management (Non-Residence/Seminar)
Computer literate in all Microsoft products and Air Force Maintenance Management Systems

SKILLS SETS

Aircraft Maintenance Management

Over eight years in the aircraft maintenance and quality assurance field, with responsibility for large body (C5A/C-17/C-141/KC-10) and mid-sized airlift(C-130H/J) aircraft maintenance meeting round the clock flying and periodic maintenance schedules.

Logistics Management

Managed and led a 50-person logistics support organization encompassing supply, transportation, and aircraft maintenance for a major airlift wing flying the C5 transport aircraft.

Wing Plans & Operations

Formulated, managed, and evaluated plans for maintaining a C5 airlift wing's combat readiness and crisis response capability. Served and deployed as an Airlift Control Element Operations Officer for Operation Desert Storm.

Nuclear Assurance Training & Evaluation

Responsible to the national command authorities for the crew proficiency, performance, and safe operation of the $170 million Minuteman III ICBM weapon system. Served as an instructor and evaluator for the positive control and execution of 16 Ground Launched Cruise Missiles (GLCM) at an overseas base.

EXPERIENCE

Commander, 433rd Maintenance Group, Lackland AFB TX (2006–Present)

Responsible for all organizational-level maintenance and logistics support for 16 assigned C5-A heavy transport aircraft assigned to meet Formal Training Unit (FTU) student flying hour requirements, non-FTU training requirements, and worldwide strategic airlift missions. Manage 800+ personnel in three different organizations, an O&M budget of $600,000, a personnel budget of $4 million, and an annual flying hour budget of $40 million.

Richard L. Shelton Jr., page 2

Accomplishments:

- Created process-driven approach to floundering maintenance practices
- Reversed negative aircraft fully capable mission status for first time in two years

Commander, Maintenance Group, Dobbins Air Reserve Base (ARB) GA (2004–2006)

Managed 300 personnel and directed and controlled aircraft maintenance and related activities of all assigned C-130H aircraft for peace time and aircrew training as well as crisis response operations.

Accomplishments:

- Streamlined flight line production—79% average mission capable rate exceeded AF standard
- Key player in Hurricane Katrina airlift support operations
- Time focused; forged facility review board for $10 million construction project milestones

Chief, Maintenance Engineering Branch, Dobbins ARB GA (2000–2004)

Managed and directed the activities of subordinate units comprised of 15 air wings and one support group, a total of almost 300 units with 25,000 reservists, 150 aircraft, and a budget of $200 million.

Accomplishments:

- Established viable Maintenance Standardization Evaluation Program (MSEP) for entire numbered Air Force (22nd Air Force)
- Initiatives led to reduction of isochronal Inspection fly-to-fly time by 43% and an improvement in aircraft mission capability from 65 to 71%.

Commander, Logistics Support Squadron, Dover AFB DE (1997 - 2000)

Commanded, managed, and led a Logistics Support Squadron responsible for supply, transportation, and aircraft maintenance for a major C-5A Logistics Support Group.

Accomplishments:

- Enviable organization safety record; zero reportable safety violations, over 23,000 mishap-free hours flown.
- Astute fiscal manager executed 99% of budget—met and exceeded all financial goals.

1996–Prior **U.S. Air Force/Air Force Reserve Technician.** Served in assignments of increased responsibility in wing plans and operations, as an instructor and evaluator for tactical missile (GHLCM) combat crews, and as a missile launch officer and flight commander for a strategic missile (ICBM) combat crew.

AWARDS/ACHIEVEMENTS

- Recipient of eight Department of Defense commendations for superior achievement and outstanding performance of duties in the areas of logistics and aviation maintenance management.
- Organizations commanded were selected twice for 21st Air Force Maintenance Effectiveness Award and as winners of the Air Mobility Command Maintenance Effectiveness Award in 1997.

ASSOCIATIONS/AFFILIATIONS

Logistics Officer Association

Albert W. King, Jr.

4230 Range View Court • Rapid City, South Dakota 57701 • (605) 343-8008

alking@rapidcity.com

ELECTRONICS MAINTENANCE MANAGEMENT

Objective: To obtain a challenging position in electronics maintenance management, quality control/assurance, or electronics training management.

QUALIFICATIONS SUMMARY

Over 20 years of specialized experience and documented success as an electronics maintenance manager for high-value U.S. national security resources, including radar bomb scoring sites and electronic combat training ranges. Expert at all maintenance management phases—planning, budgeting, contracting, acquisition, and operation. Operated and maintained facilities worth over $50 million; supervised up to 60 employees. As electronic training range manager, supervised over 20,000 simulated aerial bomb releases and 12,000 simulated aerial electronic combat attacks. An enthusiastic, take-charge leader.

EDUCATION

Bachelor of Arts (Candidate), Vocational Education, University of Southern Illinois

EXPERIENCE

2005–Present   **U.S. Air Force, Ellsworth Air Force Base, South Dakota**
Supervisor responsible for developing $300-million contract to convert 16 electronic training ranges from military to contractor-operated.
- On arrival, identified $130,000 in computer hardware for project office; placed immediate orders for proper equipment; prevented unnecessary project delays.
- Researched similar contracts, conducted fact-finding visits, obtained cost data and equipment inventories—detail-oriented approach ensured accuracy/avoided pitfalls.
- Ingenious approach to contracting—with minimal firm fixed-cost requirements—will produce maximum cost savings by allowing contractor to innovate.
- Provide incentives for contractor to meet easily measurable maintenance criteria thus ensuring maximum radar equipment uptime.

2000–2004   **U.S. Air Force, Electronic Combat Range, Wilder, Idaho**
Range manager responsible for operation and maintenance of facilities engaged in radar bomb scoring and electronic combat training of military aviators. Supervised 46 employees monitoring over 20,000 simulated bomb releases and 12,000 electronic combat attacks.
- Maintained radar uptime rates of over 90%—remarkable for aging electronic equipment.
- Experiencing 28% annual employee turnover, elected to train new employees in maintenance and operations simultaneously—made them effective in half the time.
- Operated radar while simultaneously moving five radar systems and seven portable buildings to a new site in only three weeks.
- Supervised the commissioning of $8.3 million in new radar systems and oversaw $4.5 million in new construction funds.
- Keen interest in employee welfare helped produce an error-free maintenance complex as noted by demanding inspectors of the Air Combat Command.

1996–1999   **U.S. Air Force, Scott Air Force Base, Illinois**
Senior technical expert on incentives to enhance employee productivity at radar maintenance locations worldwide.
- Detailed flow charts aided in evaluation of preventive maintenance schedules and saved thousands of man-hours evaluating future schedules.
- Efficient planning saved over $7,500 in travel costs for inspection of maintenance functions at 12 separate operating locations.

Albert W. King, Jr., page 2

1994–1999   **U.S. Air Force, Sembach Air Base, Germany**
Manager of U.S. military air traffic control and landing systems in Germany, Belgium, and the
Netherlands.
- Transported, installed, checked, and repaired dozens of precision radar systems in both
  urban and remote environments.
- Developed complete training program on newest state-of-the-art systems for students to
  apply their knowledge on advanced radar throughout Europe.
- Abilities as technician, trainer, and manager kept 30-year-old radar systems working until
  new radars could be procured.

1993–Prior   **U.S. Air Force**
Served as a radar instructor and instructor supervisor.

PROFESSIONAL DEVELOPMENT TRAINING

<u>U.S. Air Force Courses</u>

Basic Electronics (18 weeks)
Basic Radar (30 weeks)
Radar/Radar Simulator Maintenance (846 hours)
Computer Maintenance (160 hours)
Test and Measurement Writing (36 hours)
Technical Instructor (260 hours)
Instructional Systems Development (36 hours)
Academic Counseling (36 hours)
Military Management/Leadership Mid-Senior Level

<u>Certifications/Special Qualifications</u>

Master Instructor, Electronics Maintenance
Mobile Training Team Member for Security Assistance Program for Austrian Air Force
Air Traffic Control and Landing Systems Maintenance Management Specialist

AFFILIATIONS

Air Force Association

Ellen M. Gordon

7205 Boston Lane • Stafford, Virginia 22145 • (703) 424-7165

egordon@staffordrr.com

FINANCIAL MANAGEMENT

OBJECTIVE: Seeking challenging budget/financial analyst, program management analyst, or auditor position in state or city government, or the private sector.

PROFILE

Fourteen years of budgetary and financial experience as key budget and financial analyst for U.S. government information and weapons systems acquisition programs totaling 30% of the U.S. Army budget. Cited for meticulous accounting procedures, industriousness, and professional commitment to excellence. Closely monitored congressional actions affecting U.S. Army defense programs and reported to senior decision-makers within the Department of Defense (DOD). Proficient at cost estimation, accounting, and auditing military programs for fraud, waste, and abuse.

EDUCATION

Master of Business Administration, George Washington University, Washington, D.C.
Bachelor of Arts, Accounting, Niagara University, Niagara Falls, New York

EXPERIENCE

2007–Present   **U.S. Army, National Guard Bureau (NGB), Washington, D.C.**
Budget Officer responsible for developing, analyzing, defending, and executing the $1.6 billion information systems acquisition, operations, and maintenance budget for the Reserve Component Automation System (RCAS). Served as principal budget analyst to senior management on Department of the Army staff for input during program review cycle and congressional budget committee sessions.
• Managed all budgetary activities for this high-visibility program, ensuring that all budget actions were defendable.
• Consistently obtained congressional support for RCAS budget needs.
• Prepared timely reports on impending adverse DOD actions affecting technology, test, and acquisition programs.
• Timely financial management actions helped stretch remaining budget dollars, thereby reducing negative impact of budget cuts in program funding.
• Implemented budget automation system for RCAS program management office.

2003–2006   **Headquarters, Department of the Army, The Pentagon, Washington, D.C.**
Audit Analyst for Army Audit Agency evaluating management of programs worth $11.6 billion and activities of 52,000 employees at 11 separate installations. Developed procedures to ensure efficiency of operations and effectiveness of financial controls. Identified budgetary deficiencies and recommended immediate corrective action.
• Excellent grasp of Army accounting and finance systems enabled quick identification and correction of accounting irregularities in major acquisition program.
• Identified excess engineering equipment at base closure site worth $75,000. Turned over excess to Defense Reclamation Service after filling shortfalls for Army Reserve units.
• Close examination of temporary-duty travel accounting procedures identified areas with highest potential for errors and possible fraud.
• Identified wasteful practice of using contractor-supplied material when government-owned material of similar nature was available. Utilized Beneficial Suggestions and DOD Fraud, Waste, and Abuse Hotline programs to adopt better controls.

1999–2002   **U.S. Army Tank and Automotive Command, Warren, Michigan**
Budget Analyst responsible for computing tank-automotive operating hour costs and comparing them with funded costs per hour. Assigned ancillary responsibilities in contractor fraud and abuse investigations.
• Accurate analysis of $36.5 million operating hour costs ensured complex program was kept within budgeted funds at all times.
• Prepared tailored operations management system training program that was made available throughout the Army Materiel Command.
• Reviewed vehicle maintenance track and tire contracts. Recommended improvement in track and tire management that saved estimated $140,000 for major tank program and equipment transporter fleet.

Ellen M. Gordon, page 2

1998–Prior   **U.S. Army.**
Served in entry- and mid-level budgetary and financial positions in the United States and overseas.

Professional Development Training
U.S. Army Courses
Military Accounting Course
Budget Officers' Course
Comptroller Management Course
Finance Officers' Advanced Course
Finance Officers' Basic Course
Other
Lotus 1, 2, 3
Excel
PowerPoint

SPECIAL RECOGNITION AND AWARDS

- Outstanding Comptroller of the Year, 1993
- Recipient of several commendations from the Department of Defense for superior achievement and meritorious service in the financial management field.

Grady P. Parks
1534 Markson Road • Charleston, South Carolina 29414 • (803) 556-9845
Grady.parks@netzero.com

QUALIFICATIONS SUMMARY

Over six years of specialized training and experience in the operation of naval weapons fire control systems, including troubleshooting, repair, operation, and routine electronic maintenance. Previous experience in operating and maintaining electronic water cooling systems and induction melt furnaces (Inductotherm).

EXPERIENCE

2003–Present   United States Navy
Fire Control Technician assigned to a guided missile fast frigate operating with Atlantic Fleet units out of Mayport, Florida. Serve as work center supervisor within the Gunnery Department overseeing the training and daily work assignments of seven subordinate personnel assigned to the Fire Control Division.
- Responsible for the operations and repair of the Mk 92, Mod 2 (Sperry), Fire Control System (FCS) and the AN-UYK 7 computer.
- Troubleshoot, repair, and operate complex and regular electronic and electromechanical systems associated with radar and weapons systems.
- Repair analog and digital computers from circuit board down to component level. Operate various testing devices and equipment to locate malfunctions and failures in system equipment.
- Familiar with blueprints, drawings, and diagrams for all system components for the Mk 92, Mod 2, Fire Control System.
- Responsible for the operation, troubleshooting, and repair of command and control consoles for the Harpoon Weapons System.
- Assisted in preparation and installation of all Ordnance Alterations (Ord Alts) for affected FCS equipment or components.

2000–2003   American Foundry Group, Inc., Tulsa, Oklahoma
Melt Department Foreman responsible for directing furnace operations and procedures, maintenance of all melting department equipment, quality control, inventory of metal banks and related supplies, and the training and supervision of a 15-man crew.

SPECIAL QUALIFICATIONS

Qualified in the operations and maintenance of the following equipment:
- Mk 92, Mod 2, Fire Control System (Sperry)
- AN-UYK 7 Digital Data Processing Set (Sperry)
- Harpoon Weapons Control System (McDonnell Douglas)

PROFESSIONAL AND TECHNICAL TRAINING

Basic Electricity and Electronics (28 weeks), San Diego, California
Fire Control Technician "A" School, Great Lakes, Illinois—Analog and digital computer theory; servo systems; troubleshooting to component level on prototype computers and radars; repair of electromechanical systems.
Fire Control Technician "C" School, Dam Neck, Virginia—Troubleshooting and repair of Mk 92, Mod 2, Fire Control System (FCS), and associated equipment; FCS interfacing with Data Computer Processing set AN-UYK 7.
Harpoon Weapons System Technician School—Operation, troubleshooting, and repair of the command and control consoles for the Harpoon Weapons System.

COMBINATION RESUME
EXAMPLES

John A. Snider

14202 Madison Run Rd. • Gordonsville, VA 22942 • (540) 661-5154
jwsnider@aol.com

PROFILE

Highly qualified executive management professional with over 25 years of experience in aviation operations, international security assistance, strategic planning, resources and financial management, Information Operations, and operational flying experience in military jet aircraft. Managed and led organizations ranging in size from 300 to 7,000 involved in the implementation of high technology weapons systems in support of the National Command Authority worldwide. Seeking challenging position as a Sr. Business Developer for a defense aerospace company that can best use my knowledge and expertise of aviation operations, training, education, SECAF/CSAF level program management, and executive level management of large aviation organizations.

EDUCATION

Formal

Master of Aviation Science, Embry Riddle Aeronautical University, Florida
Bachelor of Arts (*cum laude*), Political Science, Duke University, North Carolina

Professional/Technical

National Defense Fellow, Atlantic Council of the United States, Washington, D.C.
U.S. Marine Corps School of Advanced Warfighting (Distinguished Graduate)
U.S. Marine Corps Command & Staff College, Quantico, Virginia (Distinguished Graduate)
USAF Weapons Instructor Course, Mountain Home AFB, Idaho (Outstanding Graduate)
Undergraduate and Advanced Flight Training/Instructor Training

EXPERIENCE

Resources and Financial Management

- Developed the policies and procedures and executed the personnel programs supporting 41,000 civilian and military personnel and 42,000 dependents stationed overseas throughout Europe and the Middle East. Provided personnel services to civilians in 26 countries and handled local national hiring and labor relations issues.
- Oversaw multidimensional programs to assist families across Europe and served as the principal liaison to the DOD Dependent School System supporting 16,000 students in six countries. Controlled a $25 million a year employee continuing education budget.
- Created programs for hundreds of volunteers, increased college enrollments by 11% among the workforce, delivered mentor programs, and improved family welfare, community support programs, and personal services across the European base structure.
- Infused discipline into civilian personnel program and energized dormant Civilian Resources Corporate Board to eliminate massive over-execution and cost overruns in $231 million program.
- Formerly responsible for the management of operations at RAF Lakenheath and RAF Feltwell in the UK, with assets valued at $8.9 billion including 720 facilities on 2,500 acres, 80 aircraft and associated support equipment, the second largest munitions stockpile in Europe, and the largest medical facility for U.S. Air Forces Europe.

Operational Flight Management/Training/Crisis Response

- Served as COO equivalent of the Air Force's largest, most dynamic and most heavily tasked Wing in Europe conducting U.S. and NATO air defense reconnaissance, air interdiction, and strike missions worldwide.
- Directly oversaw 82 F-15C/E aircraft flying 13,250 missions annually from two bases in the UK as the U.S. Air Forces in Europe lead Aerospace Expeditionary Force Wing. Started up the USAF's only Central Intermediate Repair Facility for F-15 avionics and F-100 engines contributing to a 66% increase in capacity and enabling over 908 missions and 3,262 flight hours in support of operations in Iraq and Afghanistan.
- As Commander of the 49th Operations Group, directed the flying and flight maintenance operations for a fighter Wing comprised of 80 aircraft valued at $3 billion.
- Managed all airfield operations, gunnery ranges, and coordinated/integrated the German Air Force Tornado Flying Training Center operations with annual budget of $30 million.
- Oversaw more than 40,000 accident-free flight hours in the F-117, F4F, and T-38 aircraft.

John A. Snider, page 2

Information Operations Management

- Authored, coordinated and implemented Information Operations (IO) policy and doctrine applying to the Unified Commands, Services, and national intelligence agencies while serving in the Directorate of Operations, J-3 of the Joint Chiefs of Staff.
- Served as lead Joint Staff Action Officer for the Quadrennial Defense Review IO Sub-Panel. Produced first-ever comprehensive assessment of Service capabilities to meet Commanders of Unified Commands IO requirements, which included critical intelligence and covert operations requirements.
- Led the development of the first automated analytic tool for deriving IO-related intelligence requirements.

AWARDS/ACHIEVEMENTS

- Recipient of 8 Department of Defense non-combat commendations and four combat-related medals for superior achievement and outstanding performance of duties in the areas of aviation operations, information operations, and resource management.
- Winner of the Commander-in-Chief's Direct Support Squadron of the Year for U.S. Air Forces in Europe.
- One of 22 Air Force Officers selected as National Defense Fellows—1994–95 academic year.

EMPLOYMENT HISTORY

2006–Present	Sr. Consultant, Aviation Operations, Gordonsville, VA
2004–2006	Director of Personnel, U.S. Air Forces Europe, Ramstein AB, GE
2003–2004	Inspector General, U.S. Air Forces Europe, Ramstein AB, GE
2001–2003	Vice Commander (COO), 48th Fighter Wing, RAF Lakenheath, UK
1997–2001	Commander (CEO), 49th Operations Group, Holloman AFB, NM
1995–1997	Special Technical Operations Officer, The Joint Staff, The Pentagon
1994–1995	National Defense Fellow, Atlantic Council of the United States, Washington, D.C.
1991–1994	Commander (CEO), 48th Operational Support Squadron, RAF Lakenheath
1990–Prior	**U.S. Air Force.** Served in assignments of increased responsibility as a tactical jet fighter pilot, instructor pilot, and flight examiner at multiple locations, and program element monitor at Headquarters U.S. Air Force. Completing service at the rank of Colonel.

Julie R. Fluhr

1029 Lambourne Lane • Virginia Beach, Virginia 23462 • (757) 961-6655
julie.fluhr@mac.com

PROFILE

Over 20 years of exceptional performance in the U.S. Naval Communications, Electronic Warfare, and Computer Network Operations fields. Led organizations where main mission was operational communications and computer network analysis and defense. Broad-based expertise in Signals Intelligence, Information Operations, All-Source Intelligence, Network and Space Operations. Seeking challenging program management position in the field of Computer Network Operations or business development where my previous Naval Security Group experience, Joint Computer Network Defense expertise, formal graduate education, language skills, and international background will best support the organization's objectives. Current Top Secret SCI Security Clearance.

EDUCATION

Formal

Master of Arts, National Security and Strategic Studies, U.S. Naval War College, Newport RI
Bachelor of Science, Political Science (Minor in German language), U.S. Naval Academy

Professional/Technical Training/Certifications

Naval Command and Staff College, U.S. Naval War College, Newport, RI
Joint and Combined Warfighting School, Joint Forces Staff College, Norfolk, VA
Russian Language Basic Course, Defense Language Institute, Monterey, CA
Cryptologic Division Officer Course

SELECTED ACCOMPLISHMENTS

Computer Network Defense Threat Analysis

- Recognized as command Subject Matter Expert on U.S. Strategic Command matters facilitating on-time accomplishment of over 500 staff taskings and preparation for three 3-Star level meetings and four Senior Warfighter Forums.
- Selected as Deputy Lead for the first-ever Operation Cyber Condition Zebra, a first-ever Navy-unique effort to eradicate malicious activity on its unclassified legacy network. Secured over 320 legacy networks, re-homed more than 100 bases/sites behind centrally managed security suites, and protected 225,000 users previously unprotected.

Joint Network Operations/Global Force Management

- Selected by the Commander, Naval Network Warfare Command to serve as the Primary Action Officer for the Joint Network Operations Concept of Operations. Prepared Navy Divergent View and built briefing materials for Joint Staff Operations Deputies' decision briefs.
- Coordinated Flag-level approval of the Base Plan and annexes for three major U.S. Strategic Command Contingency Plans.

EXPERIENCE

Computer Network Operations Intelligence

- Provided fused, all-source Computer Network Defense (CND)/Computer Network Attack (CNA) intelligence support, making significant changes to the Computer Network Attack/Computer Network Exploitation (CNA/CNE) Threat Warning Assessments for Russia and Cuba based on extensive research and revised rating criteria.
- Established a 16-person Computer Network Analysis Branch in less than six months to provide intelligence for CND missions with an operating budget of over $10 million. Built mission-essential intelligence relationships with the Department of State, CIA, NSA, and DIA as well as Canadian, Australian, and United Kingdom intelligence elements.
- Served as the Intelligence Representative to the Space Cell at the U.S. Strategic Command assisting in resolving issues associated with the merger of two unified commands.

Julie R. Fluhr, page 2

Communications/Electronic Warfare and Cryptologic Communications Support

- Led 80 technicians and communications specialists providing cryptologic communications support and JWICS network access to the commanders of the Fifth and Sixth Fleets, local commanders, Joint, NATO and bilateral forces operating throughout Southern Europe and the Indian Ocean.
- Ensured successful support of SCI Automated Digital Network System operational testing for the USS JOHN C. STENNIS Battle Group. Cited for excellent support in after-action report.
- Led activation of Joint Task Force NOBLE ANVIL Information Operations Cell. Coordinated essential communications equipment, network access, logistics, security, and administrative support. Achieved full tactical integration within 48 hours.

Corporate Executive Management Support

- Hand-picked to fix a dysfunctional front office. Mastered the key functions and implemented working groups to review, remediate, and reinvigorate every administrative function and collateral duty within the Joint Forces Headquarters-Information Operations at the U.S. Strategic Command.
- Selected by the Director of Global Operations based on broad operational knowledge of all command mission areas to be her Executive Assistant and the principal "go to" Action Officer for the Commander of the Naval Network Warfare Command. Managed and tracked over 250 staff packages from cradle to grave and assisted the Commander in the preparation of executive level meetings, conferences, speeches, and briefings.
- Shaped Navy position on Global Force Management issues and proposed changes to the Unified Command Plan. Heavily relied on by Navy Staff to prepare for the Joint Staff Operations Deputies' decision brief.

AWARDS/ACHIEVEMENTS

- Recipient of six Department of Defense commendations for superior achievement and outstanding performance of duties in the areas of communications and Information Operations management.
- Awarded the Navy Unit Commendation Medal for exceptional service while a part of Joint Task Force NOBLE ANVIL in operations against the Federal Republic of Yugoslavia and in support of humanitarian relief operations in Albania and the former Yugoslav Republic of Macedonia.

EMPLOYMENT HISTORY

2005–Present	Chief Joint/Fleet Plans Branch, Executive Assistant (06–07), Dep. Div. Director (05–06), Naval Network Warfare Command, Norfolk, VA
2002–2005	Executive Asst. (03–05), Chief Network Analysis-Computer Network Defense Branch (02–03), U.S. Strategic Command, Offutt AFB, NE
2002	Student, Joint Forces Staff College (3 Months), Dep. Chief, CNO Intelligence Branch, U.S. Space Command, Peterson AFB, CO
2001–2002	Student, U.S. Naval Command & Staff College, Naval War College, Newport, RI
1997–2000	Executive Officer, Naval Security Group Activity, Naples, Italy
1998–Prior	**U.S. Navy.** Served in assignments of increased responsibility in the Electronic Warfare, communications, Computer Network Operations, intelligence, and cryptologic specialist fields both in the United States and overseas.

ASSOCIATIONS/AFFILIATIONS

U.S. Naval Academy Alumni Association
Naval Cryptologic Veterans Association

Susan R. Alaniz

19 Neptune Drive • Mary Esther, Florida 32569 • (850) 581-3099

skinnynsue@aol.com

PROFILE

Over 20 years of exceptional performance in the U.S. Air Force communications, electronic warfare, information operations and political-military affairs fields. Led organizations where main mission was operational communications and information technology. Wide Information Technology background in voice/data networks and various radio systems. Led the creation of regional affairs education for Special Operations Forces (SOF) and international military and civilian students. Lived and worked in fourteen different countries. Seeking leadership position in the field of regional affairs policy, education, or program management where my previous White House Communications Agency experience, Air Combat Command, Pacific Air Command, and SOF operational experience, education, and international background will best support the organization's objectives. Current Top Secret SCI Security Clearance. Proficient in French and limited proficiency in Spanish.

EDUCATION

Formal

PhD (Candidate), International Development, University of Southern Mississippi
Master of Public Administration, University of Oklahoma
Bachelor of Science, Human Factors Engineering and minor in French, U.S. Air Force Academy

Professional/Technical Training/Certifications

Basic/Intermediate/ Advanced US Air Force Officer Professional Development, Air University, AL
Basic and Advanced Communications Officer Training, Keesler AFB, MS
Political Military Officer Orientation, U.S. State Department, Foreign Service Institute, Wash., D.C.
French Immersion, Accord School of Language, Paris, France
Methods of Instruction, Air Force Special Operations School, Hurlburt Field, FL
International Military Student Officer Certification, Defense Institute for Security Assistance Mgt.
Awarded Master Communications Officer Badge

SELECTED ACCOMPLISHMENTS

Information Systems Operations

- Recognized as command expert on the Mobile Microwave Landing System (MMLS); led entire Air Force in fielding essential capability for 759 Air Force aircraft for deployed precision approach services and flight safety.

White House Communications Agency

- Served as a Presidential Communications Officer at the White House Communications Agency responsible for delivering 24/7 operational voice, data, and video services to the U.S. Secret Service, National Security Council, and the White Executive Office of the President.
- Selected to lead teams of up to 72 personnel on Presidential official travel missions to the Asia Pacific Economic Summit in Shanghai, China, the G8 Summit in Calgary, Canada, and bilateral meetings in the host countries of the Presidents of Russia and Mexico.

Air Force Special Operations School

- Serve as Chief of the Regional Affairs Division responsible for 10 professors with advanced education and language qualifications and an annual budget of over $485k. Provide a real-time curriculum that keeps current with world events and meets the changing needs of more than 2,000 joint service students annually. Directed the revision/update of the Cross-Cultural Communications Course increasing the rigor and focus on operator requirements.

Susan R. Alaniz, page 2

EXPERIENCE

Communications/Electronic Warfare and Computer System Network Operations

- Led the modernization of the Multi-Service Electronic Warfare Data Distribution System, posturing the system for growth in the joint community in support of the Global War on Terror.
- Developed, staffed, and delivered successful plan to create a coalition electronic warfare coordination center at the Combined Air Operations Center in Qatar. Synergized similar organizations from DOD and two other countries to create more effective countermeasures for use against Improvised Explosive Devices (IEDs).
- Led 130 technicians/specialists in providing advanced program computer system networks to 300 worldwide locations valued at more than $5 million with annual operating budget of $1.2 million.
- Wrote the White House policy on the use of DOD non-telecommunications resources, a document consolidating DOD funding, human resources, and equipment to meet 200% surge in OPTEMPO.

Information Systems Operations Program Management

- Responsible for policy, modernization programs, and resources essential to the smooth operations and maintenance of command voice, visual information, video teleconferencing (VTC), meteorological and navigation, circuit management, and reprographics systems valued at nearly $50 million and operated by over 500 personnel command-wide.
- Directed an annual budget of $2.3 million and managed a $14 million POM.
- Orchestrated the Air Force Special Operations Command technical strategy for proliferation of SCI communications infrastructure.

AWARDS/ACHIEVEMENTS

- Recipient of the Defense Meritorious Service Medal, three Air Force Meritorious Service Medals, two Air Force Commendation Medals, and two Air Force Achievement Medals, along with numerous outstanding unit and other awards.
- Awarded the Presidential Service Medal, a controlled item that is numbered and authorized by the White House Military Office.

EMPLOYMENT HISTORY

2006–Present	Chief, Regional Affairs Division, Air Force Special Operations School, Hurlburt Field, FL
2003–2006	Director of Operations and Commander (CEO equivalent), 53rd Computer Systems Squadron, Eglin AFB, FL
2005	Staff Officer (Temporary duty), Information Operations Division, U.S. Central Command, MacDill AFB, Tampa, FL
1999–2003	Chief, Requirements & Operations Division/Presidential Communications Officer, White House Communications Agency, Anacostia NAS, Wash., D.C.
1998–Prior	**U.S. Air Force.** Served in assignments of increased responsibility in the communications, electronic warfare and computer systems fields. Completing service at the rank of Lieutenant Colonel.

ASSOCIATIONS/AFFILIATIONS

U.S. Air Force Academy Association of Graduates
Armed Forces Communications and Electronics Association
Air Force Association

C. Kevin Ammons

335 Ocean View Blvd. • Vandenberg AFB, California 93437 • (805) 734-1682

ckammons@gimail.af.mil

PROFILE

Seasoned information operations, technology and communications/computer systems manager with over 13 years of documented success in hands-on communications/information systems technology. Experienced with systems and equipment that include: Global Hawk, AN/GSQ-272 weapon system, U-2 Deployable Shelterized System, Predator and the National Deployable Transit–cased System. Previous experience in signals intelligence and in the avionics field as a technician working on high performance jet aircraft. Seeking challenging supervisory support position in the Information Technology Applications field that will make maximum use of my previous communications/IT experience, education and field technician training skills. Top Secret SBI Clearance.

EDUCATION

Formal

Master of Business Administration, California State University, Chico, CA
Bachelor of Science, Electronics Management, Southern Illinois University, Carbondale, IL
Associate of Applied Science, Instructor of Technology & Military Science, Community College of
    the Air Force
Associate of Applied Science, Avionics Systems Technology, Community College of the Air Force

Professional/Technical Training

Computer and Switching Systems (Honor Graduate)
Sun Solaris Operating System Training
F-111 Avionics Technical Systems Maintenance (Honor Graduate)
Mid-Senior Level Leadership & Management Training Schools/Courses throughout career

EXPERIENCE

Communications & Computer Systems Maintenance & Management

- Directed 24-hour operations and maintenance of Deployable Ground Intercept Facility-II, Common Imagery Exploitation System, Communications Operations Segment, and Ground Control Processors-VIII.
- Served as the Allied Information Flow System (AIFS) Manager and the primary system administrator for Joint Command South Center's AIFS, NATO's secure messaging system located in Larissa, Greece.
- Administered a computer network consisting of three Sun Ultra 10 and two Windows 2000 workstations. Trained personnel from nine countries in the use of the AIFS Integrated Message System message preparation software package.
- Discovered faulty Domain Name Server causing communications failures at 23 NATO sites; guided the Integrated System Support Center in Belgium to a fix restoring all AIFS units within 15 minutes.

Signals Intelligence

- Oversaw the installation of a new Global Hawk mission management cell and the upgrade of 54 imagery monitors. *Result*—Enabled analysts to cut processing time by 50% and ensured success of the 2005 Afghan and Iraqi elections.
- Supervised 40 military technicians and 43 field service contractors for Distributed Ground Station-2, the intelligence, surveillance, and reconnaissance (ISR) backbone for the U-2, Global Hawk, and Predator unmanned aerial vehicles (UAVs).
- Managed short-notice installation of Common Imagery Exploitation System upgrade during Global Hawk operational testing with zero loss.
- Coordinated support for the $28 million deployed Mobile Stretch (MOBSTR) data relay site. Performed equipment status reporting on 17 systems and 32 encrypted communication circuits.
- Led Signals Intelligence technology during 30 Operation Iraqi Freedom U-2 combat missions maintaining vital link with aircraft while ensuring seamless flow of real-time intelligence/battle damage assessments to the AOR commanders.

C. Kevin Ammons, page 2

Training Management/Quality Assurance Evaluation

- Currently serve as the head of a supervisory leadership/management school where the responsibilities include hiring and managing instructors as well as planning and executing the budget, including maintenance and improvements to the facilities.
- Instruct an intensive 192-hour curriculum that awards 10 semester hours of college credit to each graduate.
- Manage $250,000 worth of equipment/computers and an annual operating budget of $20,000.
- Convened the first Academic Review Board in 5 years; established the board process and upheld the highest academic standards.
- Cited for astute mentorship in garnering the first ever Airman Leadership School Instructor of the Year for Vandenberg AFB.
- Authored new Master Training Plan, which was recognized as Air Force Space Center Best Practice. Now available Air Force–wide.

AWARDS/ACHIEVEMENTS

- Recipient of seven Department of Defense commendations for superior achievement and outstanding performance of duties in intelligence, and computer and communications field.
- Communications & Informational Professional of the Year, Allied Command Europe
- Levitow Award (2) for Mid (5th of 253) and Senior Level (1st of 425) Leadership Schools
- Lance P. Sijan Award (Junior Level Winner), 480th Intelligence Wing
- Sr. Level Supervisor of the Year, NATO, Southern Region

EMPLOYMENT HISTORY

2006–Present	Flight Chief, Airman Leadership School, Mission Support Squadron, Vandenberg AFB, CA
2004–2006	Sr. Supervisor, Maintenance Operations Center and Computer Systems Maintenance, Intelligence Squadron, Beale AFB, CA
2003–2004	Sr. Inspector, Depot Maintenance, Distributed Ground Station, Beale AFB
2001–2003	AFIS Manager, Joint Command SOUTHCENT, Larissa, Greece
2000–2001	Communications Group Maintenance Training Manager & Quality Assurance Evaluator, Offutt AFB, NE
1996–2000	Strategic Automated Command Control System Technician ('98–'00), Computer Systems Training Manager ('96–'98), Offutt AFB, NE
1995–Prior	**U.S. Air Force.** Served in assignments of increased responsibility in the avionics technician field working on the F-111A/D, EF-111A, and F-15C/D aircraft, both in the United States and overseas. Completing service at the rank of Sr. Master Sergeant.

ASSOCIATIONS/AFFILIATIONS

Association for Educational Communications & Technology (AECT)
Air Force Association

Andrew J. Smith

9544 Sperm Whale Way • Bolder, CO 80908 • (719) 562-7742
financesmith@comcast.net

PROFILE

Skilled financial management specialist with over 20 years of demonstrated experience in the areas of cost estimating and life cycle costing for multimillion and multibillion dollar programs, forecasting, budgeting, trend analysis, economic analysis/cost/benefit analysis and as a comptroller at every level within the Air Force organizational structure. Seeking challenging position as a business manager/finance manager for a home builder or developer that will make maximum use of my previous cost estimating experience, educational background in real estate, and proven financial management skills.

EDUCATION

Formal

Master of Business Administration (*General MBA*), Rivier College, Nashua, New Hampshire
Bachelor of Science, Business Administration (*Finance & Real Estate*), University of South Carolina

Professional/Technical/Certifications (See *Supplemental Page* for additional courses)

Department of Defense Military Comptroller School
Air Force Professional Development Certificate, Financial Management Level III
Acquisition Professional Development Program Certified, Business and Economics Level II
Certified Defense Financial Manager

SIGNIFICANT ACCOMPLISHMENTS

- Recipient of Cost Analysis Officer of the Year from field of approximately 450 cost analysts in the Air Force.
- Cited for reinvigorating previously dormant position as financial management analyst and inspector for the Services Support Inspection Section while on the staff of the Inspector General, Headquarters, Air Force Space Command.
- As a senior cost analyst, analyzed contractor proposals for risk, reasonableness and completeness and provided cost basis for $185 million contract award.

EXPERIENCE

Financial Management

- Double-hatted as Senior Military Budget Analyst for two major commands at Peterson AFB in Colorado; charged with effects-based budgeting and execution of programs totaling $230 million.
- Former Chief Financial Officer for 38-employee accounting and disbursement office with control of $118 million in operations & maintenance funding, family housing, and health care funds for one of the Air Force's largest Intercontinental Ballistic Missile bases.
- Served as financial watchdog over $3.4 million in non-appropriated fund monies earmarked for welfare and recreational activities in support of 4,000 active-duty employees and their dependents.
- As Chief Financial Officer at Kirtland AFB, served as key financial advisor to the installation CEO. Supervised 122 personnel providing a full range of financial services to an entire base with funds exceeding $800 million.
- Cited for flawlessly managing the execution of $756,000 annual travel and inspection budget covering inspections at seven major commands and two numbered Air Forces.

Andrew J. Smith, page 2

Cost Analysis

- Served as Chief of the Cost Estimating Branch, Military Strategic and Tactical Relay (MIL-STAR) Terminal Systems Program Office responsible for building organic cost estimates for all acquisition, operations, support, and life cycle costs for the $6 billion portion of the Air Force Terminal Program.
- Supervised 14-person cost estimating team working for the Military Satellite Communications (MILSATCOM) Air Force Terminal Systems Program Office, which was responsible for MILSTAR and various other Air Force Communications systems.
- As Deputy Comptroller for Cost Analysis at Lajes Field, The Azores, Portugal, planned and directed all activities of the office. Developed, analyzed, validated and presented independent analytical cost estimate/analysis advisory services for the wing commander, his staff, and all tenant units at this overseas base.

COMPUTER SKILLS

Proficient in the use of Windows 2000/XP and Microsoft software applications, including MS Word, Outlook, Excel, PowerPoint, and Access.

AWARDS/ACHIEVEMENTS

- Recipient of eight Department of Defense commendations for superior achievement and overall excellence in performance of duties as a comptroller, cost analyst, and financial management specialist.
- Selected as the Military Airlift Command Cost Analysis Officer of the Year from a field of 30 cost analysts.

EMPLOYMENT HISTORY

2005–Present	Sr. Military Budget Analyst, Hqtrs. North American Aerospace Command & U.S. Northern Command, Peterson Air Force Base, CO
2003–2005	Comptroller, 90th Space Wing, and Commander, 90th Comptroller Squadron, Frances E. Warren AFB, WY
2000–2003	Chief, Plans & Programs Branch and Financial Management Inspector, Hqtrs. Air Force Space Command, Peterson AFB, CO
1997–2000	Assistant Professor of Aerospace Studies, University of New Mexico
1996–Prior	**U.S. Air Force.** Served in assignments of increased responsibility in the financial management and comptroller fields in the United States and overseas.

ASSOCIATIONS/AFFILIATIONS

American Society of Military Comptrollers
Delta Sigma Pi, International Business Fraternity
Air Force Association

Brice R. Huddleston

2016 N. Adams St. Apt. #206 • Arlington, VA 22201 • (703) 869-9335
briceh2@yahoo.com

PROFILE

Highly qualified executive management professional with over 25 years of experience in aviation operations, disaster preparedness, strategic planning, mobilization planning, and operational flying experience both as a pilot and a weapons system officer in military jet aircraft. Managed and lead organizations ranging in size from 20 to several hundred involved in the implementation of aviation weapons systems in support of the National Command Authority worldwide. Seeking challenging position as a Director or Sr. Analyst for a Homeland Security Defense contracting company that can best use my previous knowledge and expertise of disaster/crisis response operations at the federal, state, and local levels; aviation operations; National Guard Bureau (NGB)–level program management; and executive-level management of mid-size aviation organizations. Current Top Secret SCI clearance.

EDUCATION

Formal

Bachelor of Arts, Computer Science, University of Illinois, Springfield, IL
Associates of Applied Science, Engineering, Lincoln Community College, NE

Professional/Technical

Undergraduate Flight Training, Laughlin AFB, TX
Undergraduate Navigator/Weapon Systems Training, Mather/Homestead AFBs

SIGNIFICANT ACCOMPLISHMENTS

- Achieved Department of Homeland Security (DHS) policy that includes National Guard Bureau (NGB) Joint Operations Center (JOC) as one of 11 key operations centers of the National Command & Control Capability supporting domestic operations awareness of the President of the United States.
- Directed the Air National Guard (ANG) Crisis Action Team (CAT) in the first wave of Hurricane Katrina response to Louisiana in less than 8 hours. Provided 12,000 tons of emergency supplies and coordinated 3,400 missions moving 10,000 personnel into the New Orleans area, resulting in saving over 1,443 lives.
- Cited for implementing the NGB's Joint Enabling Team (JET)—Liaison Officers assisting the States during a crisis while providing accurate reporting and timely aid.

EXPERIENCE

Homeland Defense/Natural Disaster/and Terrorist Attack Training/Crisis Response

- Serve as the Chief of the Current Operations Division for the NGB Joint Staff, supervising a staff of 60 personnel charged with providing guidance and information on Domestic Operations involving the Non-Federal National Guard.
- Coordinate with federal, state, and local agencies to assist in the efficient movement of National Guard forces and equipment for homeland defense, enemy/terrorist threats, natural disasters, and terrorist attacks within the 54 United States and territories.
- Established policy for design and implementation of the NGB Joint Information Exchange Environment (JIEE), which has become the NGB operational collaborative toolset to share real-time operational information across the 54 states and territories for domestic National Guard (NG) missions.
- Evolved Joint Operation Center Situation Reports into world-class products lauded by the White House, Chief of the NGB, Department of Homeland Security (DHS), and USNORTHCOM, and at the Interagency level as the standard for operational reporting.
- Cited for skillfully leading the Current Operations Division during a period of extraordinarily high Operation Tempo that included over 500 domestic events involving the NGB to include wildfires, snowstorms, floods, hurricanes, and a state funeral for President Gerald Ford.

Brice R. Huddleston, page 2

Worldwide Aviation Operations

- Served as Commander (CEO) of an Operations Support Flight in the ANG responsible for aircrew flying and ground training, weapons and tactics analysis, flight and airspace scheduling, contingency planning, and various other support capabilities for an F-16 squadron and Operations Group personnel.
- Cited for crafting a concept for Joint Surveillance Target Attack Radar System Aviation Unit Type codes (UTCs) that linked employment from the continental United States to various UTC deployment package combinations to meet In-Theater Commander requirements.
- Previously served as the Deputy Chief, Deliberate Plans Branch at the NGB responsible for managing all ANG Air Defense fighter and bomber combat units. Expertly planned crisis response requirements for more than forty ANG fighter wings nationwide.

AWARDS/ACHIEVEMENTS

- Awarded several Department of Defense commendations for superior achievement and overall excellence in performance of duties in the areas of aviation operations management, national disaster response operations, and mobilization initiatives.
- Over 2,455 accident-free flying hours in jet aircraft to include the F-4, F-16, and T-37/38.

EMPLOYMENT HISTORY

July 2006–Present	Chief, Current Operations Division (J33), National Guard Bureau (NGB), Arlington, VA
Jan. 2006–July 2006	Deputy, Operational Plans & Deployment Division, Air National Guard Readiness Center, Arlington, VA
July 2004–Jan. 2006	Chief, ANG War & Mobilization Plans Branch, NGB, The Pentagon
Jan. 2003–July 2004	Air Force Mobilization Action Officer, NGB, The Pentagon
Feb. 2001–Jan. 2003	Commander, Operations Support Flight, IL ANG, Springfield, IL
June 1996–Feb. 2001	Chief, ANG Combat Plans, NGB, The Pentagon
May 1996–Prior	**U.S. Air Force /Air National Guard.** Served in flying assignments of increased responsibility as an F-16/F-4D pilot, instructor pilot, flight lead and weapon systems officer both in the United States and overseas. Completing service at the rank of Colonel.

Charles M. A. Dixon

PSC 37, Box 34 • APO AE 09459-0034 • 44-163 871 6283
Charles.Dixon@mildenhall.af.mil

PROFILE

Seasoned hospitality services specialist with over 18 years of food services, dining facility, lodging, storeroom, and fitness center management experience. Consistently cited as an astute, uncompromising, and cost-efficient manager in all fiscal dealings, and as a strong proponent of facility safety and sanitary cleanliness. Seeking challenging supervisory position in the hospitality management field or in the spectrum of hospitality services to the general public.

EDUCATION

Formal

Associates in Applied Science, Food Service and Hotel Management, Community College of the Air Force, Maxwell Air Force Base, Alabama

Professional/Technical Courses

Services Supervisor Course	EEO Awareness Course
Food Purchasing Training Seminar	Fitness Activity Management Course
Food Service Specialist	Biomechanics of Resistance Training
Supervisor Safety Training	Physical Fitness Specialist

EXPERIENCE

Food Services Management

- Supervised 40 local nationals and 12 military employees in the food handling, preparation, and serving of 120,000 meals annually, valued at $260,000, for the largest military-appropriated fund dining facility on the island of Okinawa, Japan.
- Responsible for the security and accountability of over $50,000 worth of grocery products and the safeguarding of cash receipts in excess of $10,000 monthly.
- Coordinated the $40,000 renovation project of the kitchen, serving lines, dining area, and bathrooms. Procured the new equipment and arranged the turn-in of over $250,000 in obsolete or unserviceable kitchen equipment.
- Managed "9-1" dining facility serving 60,000 hot meals and 2,000 box lunches monthly.
- Implemented Senior Cook Requisition for three meal periods that helped to reduce paper waste by 50% and saved up to 20 man-hours per week.
- Established first-ever Containerized Deployable Kitchen for use with overseas forces that was capable of providing 7,000 meals a month for flight line and flight crew personnel.

Supermarket Distribution Warehouse Management

- Implemented standards and inventory control procedures for a storeroom operation that processed $380,000 per month in supermarket commodity purchases/ issues with "0" errors.
- Managed the procurement and distribution of grocery products for 17 dining facilities and 53 U.S. Navy ships located on or in the vicinity of the island of Okinawa, Japan. Continuous oversight of warehouse operation resulted in recovery of $165,000 in missing and erroneous bills.

Fitness Center Management

- Manage the RAF Mildenhall fitness center, a $320, 000 sports complex in the U.K., used by 13,000 U.S. Forces personnel and their families monthly. Supervise 13 military and civilian personnel in the maintenance, safety, and use of 121 pieces of exercise equipment.
- Responsible for administering $55,000 in blanket purchase agreements and contracts for sports officials, aerobic instructors, and equipment maintenance, and $40,000 for awards, trophies, and athletic supplies and services (towels, laundry service, and resale).
- Cited for exceptional customer service to 125,000 annual users, the smooth operation of 28 instructed classes per week, and the 217% increase in the resale operation of the fitness center that was accomplished by reducing inventory and eliminating slow-moving stock.

Charles M. A. Dixon, page 2

COMPUTER SKILLS

- Proficient in the following PC software applications: Microsoft Office 2008, Access, and Per-Form Pro.
- Military software application proficiency includes Subsistence Total Order Receipt Electronic System and PC III.

AWARDS/ACHIEVEMENTS

- Recipient of four Department of Defense commendations for superior achievement and outstanding performance of duties in the food and hospitality services fields.
- Member of the customer service organization that received the 1999 General Curtis LeMay Award for Best Services Unit in the Air Force.
- Cited for Volunteer work in support of tax preparation for fellow service personnel, Special Olympics, and the U.S. Savings Bond drive.

EMPLOYMENT HISTORY

2007–Present	Fitness Center Manager and Services Specialist, Mildenhall Royal Air Force Base, U.K.
2003–2006	Chief Warehouse Operations, Dining Facility Manager, Kadena Air Base, Okinawa, Japan
2000–2003	Asst. Chef, Food Service Specialist, and Dining Facility Storeroom Manager, Misawa Air Base, Japan
1997–2000	Asst. Hotel Manager, Housekeeping Supervisor, Dining Facility Chef, Griffiss Air Force Base, New York
1999–Prior	**U.S. Air Force.** Served in assignments of increased responsibility in the hospitality services field as a line cook and storeroom clerk. Completing service in the rank of Master Sergeant.

Wayne I. Dailey

464 E. H Street Apt. 510 • Chula Vista, CA 91910 • (619) 476-9213

daileywaynei@hotmail.com

PROFILE

Seasoned occupational safety and health management specialist with special expertise in hazardous material (HM) handling and storage as it pertains to environmental services and pollution prevention. Key player in the stand-up and operation of the first Hazardous Material Consolidation and Control Center (HMC&CC) for a major U.S. Naval Air Facility in Japan. Former aviation fuels manager responsible for aircraft refueling under extremely hazardous conditions afloat and ashore. Excellent interpersonal and communication skills. Seeking challenging position in the environmental services industry dealing with Pollution Prevention and the storage, handling and issuance of hazardous materials. Computer literate.

EXPERIENCE

Occupation Safety and Health Management

- Served as primary Safety Inspector for major Naval Air Station conducting safety and health inspections to ensure installation was in compliance with local and Federal laws.
- Successfully conducted more than 60 safety and health inspections during tenure, resulting in enhanced safety for the installation and a major savings in maintenance dollars.

Environmental Services and Pollution Prevention (P2)

- Manage HICSWIN Program afloat for U.S. Navy in San Diego. Provide instruction and technical assistance for updating, restoring, inventorying, and maintaining HICSWIN aboard Navy ships.
- Screen material for offload; provide liaison for ships and HAZMIN Center San Diego to acquire HazMat; conduct informal training on HICSWIN for shipboard personnel; and coordinate underway and inport HazMat requirements.
- Served as the first Hazardous Material Consolidation & Control Center (HMC&CC) Supervisor for NAF Atsugi, Japan. Responsible for the storage, issue, and tracking of hazardous material (HM) for NAF Atsugi, NSF Kamiseya, Carrier Air Wing 5, and 24 other tenant commands.
- Supervised 13 U.S. and foreign national personnel issuing and/or delivering more than 500 line items of hazardous materials (HM).
- Implemented Shelf Life Program for reducing waste, saving the base $6,000. Installed the $10,000 PC-based Hazardous Inventory Control System (HICS) for inventory management.
- Key contributor to the consolidation of Hazardous Waste Sites into the Mobile Reuse Center and the elimination of 4 other HAZWASTE sites. Reduced onboard HM by 82%, from 2,200 line items to 500 line items.
- Managed HMC&CC budget of $225,000 annually, supervised 5,331 issues of HM with a value of $553,417. Saved Command $168,000 through utilization of cost avoidance initiatives with an emphasis on reuse materials.

Aviation Fuels Management

- Responsible for the safe refueling of all resident and transient aircraft aboard a major U.S. Navy aircraft carrier operating in the Western Pacific and Indian oceans. Supervised 60 refueling technicians manning 19 aircraft refueling stations and 5 deployable replenishment pontoons.
- Ensured the safe and efficient refueling and defueling evolution of more than 9,176 resident and transient aircraft, delivering in excess of 11,900,324 gallons of JP-5 jet fuel without incident.
- Supervised 15 refueler operators from the Mobile Refueler Department, delivering more than 30 million gallons of fuel to approximately 11,000 aircraft. Monitored and maintained all fuel records, planned work schedules, and conducted routine inspections of all operations procedures.

Wayne I. Dailey, page 2

EMPLOYMENT HISTORY

2006–Present	HazMat Technician, RCI, Inc., San Diego, California
2003–2005	Refueler Operator, Aircraft Service International, San Diego, California
1999–2002	Safety Inspector, Naval Air Station North Island, San Diego, California
1996–1998	Hazardous Material Supervisor, Naval Air Facility Atsugi, Japan
1992–1995	Flight Deck Division Supervisor, USS ABRAHAM LINCOLN (CVN 72), Western Pacific and San Diego, California
1991–Prior	**U.S. Navy.** Served in assignments of increased responsibility in the aviation fuels department ashore and afloat. Completed active service in the rank of Aviation Bulk Fuels Chief.

EDUCATION

Formal

BS (Candidate), General Studies, Southwestern University, San Diego, California
High school graduate

Certifications/ Technical Courses (U.S. Navy)

Certified First Responders Course for Hazardous Materials Incidents
Hazardous Material Control & Management Technician
Electrical Safety Standards
HICSWIN Training
Respiratory Protection and Prevention
General Industry Safety Standards
Hazard Communication Standard Training
Introduction to Navy Occupational Safety and Health Ashore

Lyman D. (Dave) Graham III

13109 Holly Leaf Ct. • **Woodbridge, Virginia 22192** • **(321)383-1210**

lyman.graham@gmail.com

PROFILE

Highly qualified Human Resources (HR) Management professional with over 10 years of experience in the areas of personnel policy, strategic planning, manpower management, recruiting, staffing, education and training, counseling and retention, awards and incentives, benefits, performance management, employee and labor relations, mediation, complaint resolution, safety, security, and disaster readiness and response. Additional 10 years experience in the Navy nuclear submarine field as a sonar technician/supervisor, a remote submersible pilot, logistics/supply, and a Navy Drill Instructor. Left the Navy to finish college. Excellent interpersonal and communication skills. Seeking a challenging HR management or training and development position that will make maximum use of my HR experience, education, and instructor (on-site and classroom) skills.

EDUCATION

Formal

Master of Education, Adult and Higher Education, University of Oklahoma, Norman, Oklahoma
Bachelor of Arts, Philosophy, University of Central Florida, Orlando, Florida

Professional/Technical

Manpower Staff Officer Course
Air Force Mid-Level Officer Leadership and Management Training, Top Third Graduate
Air Force Academic Instructor School and Navy Group PACE Instructor Course
Air Force Inspector General Investigator Course
Basic Submarine and Sonar Technician Training
Navy Basic Electricity and Electronics "A" School

Certifications/Special Qualifications

Senior Professional Human Resources (SPHR) (Candidate) Certification, 2009
Secret Security Clearance—Special Background Investigation (April 2007)

EXPERIENCE

Human Resources Management

- Currently serve as Deputy Chief of Strategic Plans on the Headquarters Air Force Manpower and Personnel Staff promoting the development and implementation of the Air Force's management strategy for a 750,000+ member Total Force and an Air Force HR investment of $36 billion a year.
- Managed Air Force Manpower, Personnel and Services community strategic planning. Initiated design/coordination of the 5-year Air Force Manpower, Personnel and Services Strategic Plan.
- Program Manager for Headquarters Air Force $500,000 Manpower, Personnel and Services community Strategic Research Budget, funding future years' HR innovation through full cycle of topic proposals, budget spending plans, contract competition, and contract award.
- Supervised staff of 16 HR professionals in managing all manpower actions for 10,400 positions located throughout the UK valued at $475 million to include force structure and organizational changes, advice to units on the most effective use of manpower resources, and the allocation and prioritization of civilian resources.
- Served as Director of the largest single HR Department in U.S. Air Forces Europe at RAF Mildenhall, responsible for implementing, administering, assessing, and improving the full spectrum of award-winning HR management functions and education and training services for 4, 000 assigned military and civilian personnel.
- Planned and executed annual $2 million budget for education and training programs.
- Led major aspects of an integrated recruiting and retention process improvement project that resulted in a critical 10% workforce increase in only six months.
- Responsible for program implementation and budgeting oversight of military retention incentives and civilian employee performance bonuses totaling $750,000 annually.

Lyman D. (Dave) Graham III, page 2

- Responsible for the Innovative Development through Employee Awareness (IDEA) program generating 162 suggestions, garnering $42,000 in awards, and savings of $597,000.
- Completed an Air Force–sanctioned Instructor Course and taught the Quality Facilitator Course at Luke Air Force Base, receiving excellent reviews from students and fellow faculty alike.

University Level Air Force ROTC Instructor

- Former Commandant of Cadets and Assistant Professor of Aerospace Studies at the largest AFROTC unit in the Southeast with 600 cadets. Instructed at the junior level of college on Leadership Studies, integrating both written and verbal communications skills into classroom instruction.
- Cited for developing an evaluation tool for cadet order-of-merit ranking and standing. Simple, yet fair and effective.
- Used manpower background to reorganize cadet wing to fit new Air Force Wing structure.

COMPUTER SKILLS/OTHER

- Proficient in the use of the following operating systems and software applications: Windows 2000/XP/VISTA; and MS Word, Excel, PowerPoint, Access, and Outlook.
- Qualified in Blackboard online instructional software.
- Editor of the A1 Review, Headquarters U.S. Air Force HR Professional Journal

AWARDS/ACHIEVEMENTS

- Recipient of four Department of Defense commendations for superior achievement and outstanding performance of duties in the human resources and manpower management fields.
- Guided Manpower and Organization Group to 2005 U.S. Air Forces in Europe Large Manpower Organization of Year Award, then Best in Air Force for 2006, and Best Air Force Military Personnel Support Team in Europe 2007.
- Best AFROTC Detachment in the Nation 2002.

EMPLOYMENT HISTORY   U.S. AIR FORCE (1998–PRESENT)

2007–Present	Human Resources Strategic Planner, Hqtrs. U.S. Air Force Manpower and Personnel, The Pentagon, Washington, D.C.
2005–2007	Human Resources Manager, 100th Mission Spt. Squadron, RAF Mildenhall, UK
2002–2005	Assistant Professor of Aerospace Studies, AFROTC Unit, Embry-Riddle Aeronautical University, Daytona Beach, FL
2000–2002	Organizational Design Manager, Hqtrs. U.S. Air Forces Europe, Ramstein, GE
1998–2000	Human Resources Requirements Consultant, 56th Fighter Wing, Luke AFB, AZ
1995–1997	Student, University of Central Florida, Orlando, FL
1995–Prior	**U.S. Navy.** Served in assignments of increased responsibility in the nuclear submarine field as sonar technician, remote submersible pilot, sonar division supervisor, and Navy Drill Instructor.

ASSOCIATIONS/AFFILIATIONS

Society of Human Resources Management (SHRM)
National Defense Industrial Association

William A. Ralston

941 Rancho Vista Court • Centerville, Virginia 22211 • (703) 876-9509
Will.ralston@ionfotech.com

PROFILE

Eighteen years of specialized experience and documented success in the areas of information systems management, operations analysis, acquisition management, budget formulation, and planning for the implementation of large complex systems. Current expertise in economic analysis, risk management, strategic planning, requirements analysis, and organizational integration. Proficient in use of FORTRAN and COBOL. Top Secret SCI Security Clearance.

EDUCATION

MBA, Information Systems (*cum laude*), Graduate School of Business, University of Georgia
Bachelor of Science, Engineering, U.S. Military Academy, West Point, New York
Graduate, Department of the Army, Information Systems Operation Officer Program
U.S. Army Command & General Staff College, Fort Leavenworth, Kansas

EXPERIENCE

Information Systems Management. Coordinated acquisition management activities between staff of 180 and Army/Defense/congressional authorities for $2.4 billion worth of information systems projects. Provided technical support, including program and database design, for information systems used by the American staff to track foreign military sales case data with the Republic of Korea. Managed the operation of four large computer systems and special-purpose database management systems using over 800 terminals integrated through a modern broadband LAN.

Operations Analysis. Conducted analyses of the Army Military Personnel Center's information systems requirements to support a worldwide operational strength figure of 780,000 personnel. Managed agency-wide study to integrate separate plans and staffs for office automation, telecommunications, and printing into the future Directorate of Information Management at the U.S. Military Academy, West Point.

Acquisition Management. Directed 40-person staff in the acquisition of hardware, software, telecommunications, and services for Army-wide support functions at four major data centers with a competitive contract valued at $283 million. Managed $1.5 million contract for integrated office automation resources totaling 100 systems for the Army's Military Personnel Center. Defined and proposed automation documentation that led to eight successful acquisitions for systems documentation, ADPE, software, WP equipment, and graphics with a value in excess of $675 thousand. Installed case-file documentation system to track approvals, estimated costs, and actual expenditures.

Budget Formulation. Prepared and coordinated the associated Headquarters Army Master Plan and local budget submissions while providing all documentation for the defense of a 10-year funding profile of investment and operating funds in the millions of dollars. Installed automated budgeting and tracking system at West Point resulting in more efficient contract management. As Deputy Director of Automation/AV systems, controlled annual automation budget of $3.5 million.

SIGNIFICANT ACHIEVEMENTS AND RELATED EXPERIENCE

- Served as deputy to the Program Executive Officer (PEO) for Management Information Systems for programs representing $5 billion in Life Cycle Costs.
- Managed 11 Defense-controlled Army information system projects (e.g., ITMS, DAIN, Project 80-X, Supercomputer) with total budgets exceeding $2.4 billion.
- Designed an automated system to support promotion and selection process for 95,000 Army officers.

William A. Ralston, page 2

EMPLOYMENT HISTORY

2004–Present	Executive Assistant to PEO for Management Information Systems, Fort Belvoir, Virginia
2000–2003	Deputy Project Manager, U.S. Army Military Personnel Center, Alexandria, Virginia
1997–2000	Deputy Director, Automation/AV Systems, U.S. Military Academy, West Point, New York
1996–1997	Information Systems Consultant, Joint U.S. Military Assistance Group, Seoul, Korea
1995–Prior	U.S. Army Officer. Served in junior/senior level assignments of increased responsibility in air defense artillery and the Adjutant General's Corps in the United States and Eastern Europe.

ASSOCIATIONS AND AFFILIATIONS

West Point Alumni Association
National Contract Administration Association

Thomas J. Mira

121 Abbott Lane • State College, PA 16801 • 703.402.1211
t.mira@att.net

PROFILE

Seasoned senior program intelligence analyst, systems engineer, and international security assistance professional; twenty years well-documented international security affairs, worldwide contingency air operations, joint personnel recovery, and specialized studies, plans, and programs experience. Former White House Aide, Reagan and Bush 41 Administrations, and Foreign Area Officer with Southeast Asia political-military regional experience. Seeking challenging senior intelligence analyst, systems engineer, program/project manager, or training/education position maximizing previous international political-military background, joint service and governmental Agency experience, and proven accomplishments. Current Top Secret SCI, Security Clearance.

EDUCATION

Master of Project Management, Penn State University, pending
Master of Management Defense Studies, (*with Distinction*) University of Canberra, Australia
Master of Business Administration, Florida Institute of Technology, Melbourne, Florida
Bachelor of Science, Edinboro University, Edinboro, Pennsylvania

Professional/Technical/Certifications

Six Sigma Specialist Qualification, May 2008
Raytheon Six Sigma Specialist Training, January 2008
PoSE (Principles of Systems Engineering) graduate, September 2007
Level II Acquisition Professional Certification
Contracting Officer's Representative (COR) and Federal Acquisition Regulations (FAR) Overview
Joint Personnel Recovery Agency Survival Training (Basic and Advanced)
DOD Hostage Survival Training
Analytical Graphics Satellite Tool Kit (STK) Training
Foreign Area Officer (FAO)

SIGNIFICANT ACHIEVEMENTS

- Directly contributed to Raytheon Intelligence and Information systems (IIS) Labor Secretary Opportunity Award win presented to one Federal contractor for instituting comprehensive workforce strategies ensuring equal employment opportunities.
- Served as Director, Joint Exercise Support, integrating space-based reconnaissance capabilities with Service-advanced Warfighting Experiments, Joint Doctrine development, Joint Force integration, and Advanced Concept Technology Demonstrations.
- Revised and enhanced Computer-based Training and NRO systems briefings, and spearheaded innovative use of voice-over capability for interactive NRO systems CD-ROM; a first of its kind 'leave behind' training tool. *Result*: Saved NRO thousands of travel dollars.

EXPERIENCE

Principal Systems Engineer, Raytheon, State College, PA

- Led four-man team working Phoenix-Silver Sword. Established Teaming Agreements with three industry partners and created a non-competitive procurement, sole-source contractual agreement. Raytheon share increased from 10% to 45%.
- Author and editor for the NGMARRC Operations and Maintenance ECP. Prepared comprehensive proposal and received ECP award.
- Assisted Air Force Special Communications (AF SC) in realizing actionable intelligence in the form of better geo-resolution for national tasking. Lead three-man team to data capture facility for briefings, and facilitated follow-on secure telephone conferences and coordinated previous test data delivery (a Raytheon first) for analysis.

Thomas J. Mira, page 2

Intelligence Analysis

- Served as Chief, Single Integrated Operational Plans (SIOP) and Exercises acting as Battle Staff Member for all real and exercise activity and higher headquarters inspections.
- Overhauled entire Wing SIOP Program following sweeping changes to USSTRATCOM OPLAN: Led team to produce three man-years of work in less than four months.
- Served as Subject Matter Expert (SME) responsible for all air operations while serving in Joint Reconnaissance Center (JRC) for Kosovo Forces (KFOR), Stabilization Forces (SFOR), and Operation NORTHERN WATCH (ONW).

Plans, Programs, and Specialized Studies

- Served as Operations Officer for Global Support, National Reconnaissance Office (NRO), delivering data exploitation solutions for Unified Commands, Services, Joint Task Forces (JTFs), and Combat Support Agencies; integrated multi-agency initiatives to ensure quick access to time-critical NRO intelligence data.
- As a GLOBAL GUARDIAN Exercise Analyst, cited for seeing shared situational awareness opportunity at all USSTRATCOM command nodes for NRO data applications.
- Saved the Marine Corps $2 million R&D funds. Tailored Topographic /Imagery Manipulation (T-TIMED), allowing deployed tactical operators to web-browse high data-rate asymmetric communications channels guaranteeing most accurate satellite-derived intelligence available.

International Security Assistance

- Dual-hatted as a U.S. Forces Advisor and Associate Professor, Australian Command and Staff College, Canberra; fostered understanding and appreciation of Aerospace Doctrine, Strategy, and Tactics while articulating Air Power tenets, creating networking vital to Joint and Integrated Southeast Asia operations.
- Earned Foreign Area Officer (FAO) designator, affirming ability to plan, formulate, coordinate, and implement Air Force aspects of international politico-military policies.

AWARDS/ACHIEVEMENTS/OTHER

- Recipient of eleven (11) Department of Defense commendations for superior achievement and outstanding performance of duties in the areas of intelligence, international security affairs, specialized studies and plans, and flying operations
- H. H. Arnold, Dean of Faculty Organizational Excellence Award, U.S. Air Force Academy

EMPLOYMENT HISTORY

2007–Present	Principal Systems Engineer, Raytheon, State College, PA
2004–2007	Sr. Intelligence Analyst, Joint Personnel Recovery Agency, Ft. Belvoir, VA
Jan.–Nov. 2004	Dep. Director, Specialized Studies, Plans and Programs, Air University, AL
2001–2004	U.S. Forces Advisor and Associate Professor, Australian Command and Staff College, Department of Defence, Canberra, Australia
1999–2001	Chief, Contingency Exercise Plans, 55th Wing, Offutt AFB, NE
1995–1999	Operations Officer, National Reconnaissance Office (NRO), Chantilly, VA
1994–Prior	**U.S. Air Force.** Assignments of increased responsibility; Air Force Academy Associate Professor, KC-135 Flight Commander, Supervisor of Flying, Chief, Plans and Readiness, Instructor Pilot, Flying Safety Officer.

ASSOCIATIONS/AFFILIATIONS

- Director-at-Large, Society of White House Military Aides
- Member, Armed Forces Inaugural Committee, American Bicentennial Presidential Inaugural
- Member, INCOSE (International Council on Systems Engineering)

David M. Bower

1207 Garston • San Antonio, Texas 78253 • (210) 679-5794

dbower1@satx.rr.com

PROFILE

Seasoned logistics management professional with over 19 years of demonstrated success in the areas of fuels distribution and storage management, maintenance management, supply chain management, and warehousing. Seeking challenging logistics management position that will make maximum use of my previous supply chain management and logistics experience and training. Currently hold Top Secret/SCI Security Clearance and valid US Passport.

EDUCATION

Formal

Master of Science (Candidate), Aeronautical Studies, Embry-Riddle Aeronautical University
Bachelor of Science, Liberal Arts, Bowling Green University, Bowling Green, Ohio

Professional/Technical

Advanced Logistics Officer Course
Supply Officers Course
Fuels Officer Course
Aircraft Maintenance Officers Course
Quality Assurance Evaluation Course

EXPERIENCE

Fuels Distribution/Equipment/Storage Facilities Management

- Supervised 496 fuels distribution personnel at 7 main, 3 stand-by, and 16 collocated operating bases managing more than 1,400 fuel equipment assets and facilities valued at over $500 million. Determined distribution of 692 pieces of fuels mobility support equipment stored at three locations.
- Wrote and submitted the fuels section of the U.S. Air Forces Europe (USAFE) Theater Air Space Engagement Plan, Annex D, within 24 hours.
- Cited as Air Force fuels visionary providing $7 million solution to Rhein Main Air Base Transition Program fuels systems cost overruns.
- Pioneered first-ever joint Air Force /U.S. Navy fuel equipment operations at Naval Air Station Sigonella, Sicily, quadrupling the output.
- Averted operational catastrophe at start of Operation Enduring Freedom in Afghanistan when 3 inbound tankers arrived in Theater with bad fuel. Worked nonstop with European Command, Defense Energy Supply Center, and the Turkish military. Reworked tanker schedule and brokered deal for 2 million gallons in Turkish Replacement-In-Kind fuel.
- As Deputy Chief of Supply for the 7th Air Force in Korea, managed three Mutual Logistics Support Agreements (MLSA) and the programming of fuel facilities within the Korean theater of operations while working with the Defense Fuels Office Korea, 8th U.S. Army, the Combined Forces Command in Seoul, Pacific Air Forces in Hawaii, and the Korean Air Force.
- Served as focal point for the thermal stability (JPTS) fuel conversion projects at Osan AB and Pohang Fuel Terminal in Korea, increasing peninsula JPTS fuel storage over 400% and saving $800,000 in annual transportation costs.
- Served as member of the U.S. negotiating team for petroleum pipeline support in Korea.

Maintenance Management

- Managed major parts supply program for six different tactical aircraft worth over $185 million and over $110 million in communications spares.
- Analyzed metrics and represented primary customer at logistics forums and briefings for corporate management in Europe.
- Set policies and procedures for the support of major aircraft organizations spread across Europe and developed mobility readiness spares packages (MRSP) valued at over $128 million.
- Served as Senior Maintenance Supervisor directing the efforts of 200 technicians providing support to three training squadrons utilizing $90 million worth of support equipment, 33 maintenance facilities valued at $20 million, and a $250 million munitions inventory.

David M. Bower, page 2

Supply Chain Management

- As Chief of the Supply and Transportation Division, developed and implemented Air Intelligence Agency (AIA) supply and transportation policies and provided surveillance over supplies, equipment, and vehicles valued at $200 million.
- Wrote Air Force Technical Applications Center supply chain management instruction, a first for AIA supply personnel.

COMPUTER SKILLS

- Proficient in the use of Microsoft software applications, including Windows 2000/XP, Microsoft Suite, MS Word, Excel, Access, PowerPoint, and Outlook.

AWARDS/ACHIEVEMENTS

- Recipient of ten Department of Defense non-combat commendations for superior achievement and outstanding performance of duties in the areas of fuels management, logistics, and supply chain management, and maintenance management operations.
- U.S. Air Forces in Europe Staff Fuels Officer of the Year 2001
- Logistics Company Grade Officer of the Year on two other occasions

EMPLOYMENT HISTORY

2006–Present	Chief, Materiel Management Division, Directorate of Logistics, Installations, and Mission Support, Air Intelligence Agency (AIA), Lackland AFB, TX
2003–2006	Chief, Supply and Transportation Division, Directorate of Logistics, AIA, Lackland AFB, TX
2001–2003	Chief, Command Fuels Management Branch, Supply Division, Directorate of Logistics, US Air Forces Europe (USAFE), Ramstein AB, Germany
2000–2001	Chief, Weapons Systems Support Branch, Supply Division, Directorate of Logistics, USAFE, Ramstein AB, Germany
1999–2000	Executive Officer to Wing Commander, 325th Fighter Wing, Tyndall AFB, FL
1997–1999	Maintenance Supervisor, 315th Maintenance Squadron, Tyndall AFB, FL
1996–1997	Deputy Chief of Supply/Staff Petroleum Officer, 7th Air Force, Osan AB, Korea
1995–Prior	**U.S. Air Force.** Served in assignments of increased responsibility within the logistics management field both in the United States and overseas.

ASSOCIATIONS/AFFILIATIONS

Logistics Officer Association
Air Force Association

Anita J. Fiedler

31 Jessica Drive • Nashua, New Hampshire 03060 • (603) 886-8068
ajfcm@beltway.com

PURCHASING/CONTRACTING/SUPPLY CHAIN MANAGEMENT

PROFILE

Twenty years of progressive experience serving in positions of increased responsibility as a contracts manager, resource management policy director, supply operations director, analyst, and technician. Solid track record managing large-scale, high dollar purchasing, contracting, and supply programs for the U.S. military. Hands-on, self-starting, people-oriented leader and manager. Computer literate in PC and Macintosh hardware and software. Seeking challenging supervisory position in purchasing, contracting, supply chain management, or facilities resources management.

EDUCATION

Formal

Master of Arts, Management and Supervision, Central Michigan University
Bachelor of Arts, Business Management, Park College, Missouri
Associate of Arts, Business Administration, University of Alaska
Associate of Arts, Materiel Management, Community College of the Air Force
Masters Level Courses, Principles of Government Contracting and Administration of Government Contracting, Western New England College

Professional Certifications

Certified Associate Contracts Manager, National Contracts Management Association
Designated Government Contract Management Professional by the U.S. Air Force

DEMONSTRATED EXPERIENCE

Contracts Management

- Director of Contracts for advanced research and development (R&D) projects. Planned, negotiated, and administered 27 contracts totaling over $70 million.
- Led negotiation teams of senior engineers, scientists, and price analysts. Determined contract types, drafted requests for proposals, and developed negotiation strategies for key acquisitions.
- Demonstrated superior leadership, relentless drive, and detailed know-how. *Result*: Awarded 18 new contract actions and exceeded program lead times by 10 to 20%.
- Resolved two-year stalemate with supplier for failure to deliver final technical reports in support of critical $2 million R&D program. Developed innovative $6 million bridge contract to sustain a vital test and evaluation program.

Supply and Purchasing Management

- Director for Materiel Management responsible for inventory control of 43,000 aviation-oriented supply and equipment items worth over $14.5 million. Supervised 29 supply and purchasing technicians in equipment management, retail sales, and stock control.
- Systematically identified and fixed all serious inventory control deficiencies. *Result*: Overall stock control effectiveness rate rose from 84.4% to 87.7%—an all-time high. Retail sales section rate rose to 95%. Supply management was soon rated "outstanding" by demanding inspection teams.
- Director for Resource Management for supply, fuels, and transportation at a remote airfield in Alaska. Supervised 38 technicians and maintained 79 general and special purpose vehicles. Handled $3.5 million fuel account and $6.6 million supply account.

Anita J. Fiedler, page 2

Supply Policy

- Director of Supply Policy for 25 Air Force bases with over $4 billion in assets. Supervised nine-person staff providing management oversight for all supply operations and took the lead in developing guidance and operating procedures for a warranty tool program. *Result*: Government Services Administration (GSA) adopted procedures as model for tool procurement policy throughout the federal government.
- Rewrote the Resource Guide for Materiel Managers—a key duties and responsibilities document; oversaw the successful installation of $3.5 million worth of mechanized materiel handling equipment; and validated 19 supply construction projects valued at $75 million.

SELECTED PROFESSIONAL DEVELOPMENT TRAINING
U.S. Department of Defense

Formal Schools

Supply Operations for Managers (Honor Graduate)
Inventory Management for Supervisors (Honor Graduate)
Central/Systems Level Contracting (Honor Graduate)

Courses

Acquisition Planning and Analysis   Government Contract Law
Introduction to Systems Acquisition   Contract Administration
Principles of Contract Pricing   Introduction to Labor Relations

Seminars

Defense Acquisition and Contracting Executive Seminar

HONORS, RELATED EXPERIENCE, AND SPECIAL QUALIFICATIONS

- Air Force Association Award for Logistics Acquisition
- Selected as participant in the Air Force's Education with Industry Program (Contract Management Option) with Boeing Defense & Space Group, Seattle, Washington
- Top Secret Security Clearance (SBI)

ASSOCIATIONS

National Association of Purchasing Managers
National Contracts Management Association (NCMA)

EMPLOYMENT HISTORY

1988–Present   **U.S. Air Force.** Completing highly successful career in the Logistics Acquisition, Contracts Management, and Materiel Management fields, having served in almost every position from technician and analyst up to manager and director.

C. Anthony Elder

5014 Snowy Creek Lane #104 • Millington, TN 38053 • (901) 216-7963
c.anthony.elder@gmail.com

PROFILE

Innovative and seasoned broadcast journalist with a 20-year track record in radio/TV broadcasting, media relations, community service events, strategic communications, photography, and live video taping for overseas closed circuit viewing. Proven troubleshooter who rapidly identifies potential media problems, formulates strategic plans, and implements new processes in challenging and diverse environments. Excellent interpersonal skills, former platform instructor, with extraordinary ability to execute media briefings on a moment's notice. Seeking a Director or Senior Level Management position in public relations or broadcast journalism that requires expertise in a variety of cross-functional areas of community affairs, media relations, and event and news coverage.

EDUCATION

Formal

Master of Arts, Communications Management, Webster University, August 2008
Bachelor of Arts, Communications Studies, University of Maryland

Professional/Technical

Defense Information School, Journalism and Broadcasting and Editor's Course
Department of Defense (DOD) Joint Short Course in Journalism, University of Oklahoma
Tactical Mobile Radio TV System Course (40 hrs)

EXPERIENCE

Public Affairs/Media Relations/Community Services Events

- Media Director at major Naval overseas base in Europe responsible for directly supervising a broadcasting staff of 20 military and civilian personnel hosting 3,000 live radio shows, 1,560 television and radio newscasts, and more than 8,000 community information spots to an audience of 3,000 base personnel and families and 25,000 local residents.
- Coordinated a three-day Radiothon raising over $9,000 for Sailors and families in need in Rota, Spain.
- Managed fast-paced, high visibility public affairs office at Naval Support Activity Bahrain supervising 8 journalists involved in developing public affairs plans, coordinating news coverage of special events and interviews between high-level military officials and local civilian media outlets.
- On assignment to Al Basrah and Khwar Al Amaya oil terminals in the North Arabian Gulf with the mission of generating news releases on enhanced security measures. Coverage served as a deterrent to terrorists and added a layer of security to Marines, Sailors, Coalition, and Iraqi forces operating in the general area.
- Served as the reviewing and approving authority for all written and broadcast products generated by Navy journalists serving in the Middle East resulting in consistent tone, quality, and message dissemination for all media products while fostering a clear understanding of Department of the Navy goals and objectives during Operation Iraqi Freedom and Operation Enduring Freedom.

Broadcasting/Journalism

- Assigned to cover the USS Milius, a Spruance Class Destroyer, supervising three journalists in shooting and transmitting via FTP, the first volley of Tomahawk missiles in the *Shock and Awe Campaign* on Iraq, providing U.S. media outlets with some of the first visual images of the operation as it was unfolding.
- Trained Guantanamo Bay's Naval Media Center Detachment personnel in scripting and producing spots, announcing skills, and newspaper writing resulting in the production of seven video stories, six radio spots, and two newspaper articles in the Base paper.
- Attended Tactical Mobile Radio and TV System (MRTVS) training, a 40-hour course designed to develop a proficiency in setting up and operating broadcasting and transmitting capability to forward deployed Forces in an expeditionary environment providing them with up-to-date security advisories in the North Arabian Gulf.

C. Anthony Elder, page 2

COMPUTER SKILLS

- Proficient in the use of Microsoft operating systems and Microsoft Suite software.

AWARDS/ACHIEVEMENTS/OTHER

- Recipient of seven Department of Defense commendations for superior achievement and outstanding performance of duties in the fields of journalism, radio/TV broadcasting, public affairs, and community event coverage.
- Current passport and Secret Security Clearance

PUBLICATIONS

- Published an article entitled "NPRST Forges the Future" in *The Tester*, designed to provide Navy District Washington readers with an insight into the mission and capabilities of the Navy Personnel Research, Studies, and Technology Lab in Millington TN.
- Published more than 40 news articles for release to *All Hands* magazine, the "Navy News Service" and "Navy Wire Service," while serving as Editor-in-Chief of the newspaper and Broadcast Operations Manager aboard the aircraft carrier USS John C. Stennis.

EMPLOYMENT HISTORY

2005–Present	Public Affairs Officer, U.S. Navy Personnel Command, Millington, TN
2004–2005	Media Operations Manager, U.S. Navy 5th Fleet, Manama, Bahrain
2000–2004	Media Operations Manager/Broadcast Journalist, Fleet Support Detachment, Naval Media Center, Norfolk, VA
1997–2000	Media Operations Director, U.S. Naval Station, Rota, Spain
1995–1997	Broadcast Operations Manager/Newspaper Editor, USS Stennis (CVN 74)
1994–Prior	**U.S. Navy.** Served in assignments of increased responsibility in the public relations, journalism and broadcasting fields both ashore and afloat. Completing service at the rank of Chief Petty Officer.

ASSOCIATIONS/AFFILIATIONS

Member, Public Relations Society of America

Glenn P. Jagger

3069 N. Kintrye Lane • Wasilla, Alaska 99687 • (907) 357-3069
glenn_jagger@mac.com

PROFILE

Highly skilled and trained intelligence analyst and antiterrorism/force protection advisor and specialist with over 18 years of documented experience in the areas of intelligence analysis, applications and systems, critical infrastructure protection (CIP) programs, and computer simulations. Seeking challenging supervisory position as an intelligence analyst or force protection specialist that will make maximum use of my previous experience, professional training, and proven skills. Currently possess Top Secret Security Clearance with SBI.

EDUCATION

Formal

Master of Science, Information Systems Management, Bowie State University, Maryland
Bachelor of Arts, Political Science, Swarthmore College, Pennsylvania

Professional/Career Related

Antiterrorism Force Protection Level II
Threat and Risk Assessment and Dynamics of International Terrorism Courses
Operations Security Program Manager Course #380 and 390, Washington, D.C.
Special Compartmental Information, Bolling AFB, Washington, D.C.
Intelligence Applications Officer Course, Lowry AFB, Colorado

EXPERIENCE

Intelligence Analysis/Management

- Served as Chief for COPE THUNDER (CT) intelligence operations ensuring that quality intelligence products, analysis, and support were provided to all users participating in CT exercises.
- Supervised the development, update, and intelligence support for CT's highly complex, state-of-the-art live fly and computer simulations designed to train intelligence personnel and aircrews.
- Served as unit budget analyst and coordinator for the $18 million massive combined exercise CT 99-4, hosting 16 nations and 18 separate aviation organizations involved in fighter, airlift, and rescue operations to a previously unattained degree.
- Cited for leadership excellence as Chief of Targets Branch for the Combined Air Operations Center Allied Forces, Vicenza, Italy directing 32 personnel from six NATO countries in managing the Joint Prioritized Targeting List and Master Target List.
- Provided direction and supervision for 30 intelligence personnel tasked with ensuring quality intelligence products, analysis and support to the 3rd Wing at Elmendorf AFB.
- Served as Chief, Intelligence Applications Branch at the Warrior Preparation Center (WPC) in Einsiedlerhof, Germany supervising a joint staff of nine intelligence specialists in the application of intelligence systems to support the WPC's highly complex, computer simulations, which trained 10 to 20 general officers and 1 to 3,000 members of their respective battle staffs annually.

Force Protection/Antiterrorism

- Served as principal point of contact for the development and improvement of the Alaskan Command's (ALCOM) Antiterrorism/Force Protection and Critical Infrastructure Protection (CIP) Programs.
- Designed a multi-purpose graphic for the Joint Task Force Alaska website to display critical information on force protection conditions for all DOD installations in the state of Alaska.
- Cited for providing AT/FP policy input into U.S. Pacific Command Instruction 3850.2, which combined two documents into one and helped define the ALCOM role in the AT mission.
- Initiated CIP analysis for all Alaska military installations, a first-time effort at a comprehensive look at vital installation facilities, which could become key to identifying and protecting joint rear areas.

Glenn P. Jagger, page 2

- Spearheaded the $123,000 Alaskan Command procurement of a headquarters building entry control system that proved invaluable as an added force protection measure during elevated threat conditions.
- Ensured compliance for operational security, operational reporting, physical security, disaster notification, and Open Skies Treaty obligations. Hand-picked to conduct staff assistance visits to assess component headquarters Command & Control functions.

COMPUTER SKILLS

- Proficient in the use of the following operating systems and software applications: Windows 2000/XP and MS Word, Excel, PowerPoint and Access.

AWARDS/ACHIEVEMENTS

- Recipient of eight Department of Defense commendations and one NATO Service Medal for superior achievement and outstanding performance of duties in the intelligence field.

EMPLOYMENT HISTORY

2003–Present	Asst. Professor of Military Science, University of Alaska
2000–2003	Senior Force Protection Officer, Alaska Command, Elmendorf AFB, AK
1999–2000	Chief Intelligence, Cope Thunder, Elmendorf AFB
1997–1999	Intelligence Unit Commander, Elmendorf AFB
1995–1997	Chief Intelligence, Warrior Prep, Einsiedlerhof, Germany
1993–1995	Staff Officer Intelligence Plans, Ramstein AB, Germany
1990–1993	Chief, Regional Air Analysis/Indications & Warnings, Boerfink, Germany
1989–Prior	**U.S. Air Force.** Served in assignments of increased responsibility within the aerospace intelligence field in the United States, Europe, and the Far East.

Joseph L. Rector

1060 Norfolk Dr. • LaPlata, Maryland 20646 • (410) 224-1841
josephrector@hotmail.com

PROFILE

Senior security force director with over 20 years of proven security leadership and management in the areas of air base security, antiterrorism operations, intercontinental ballistic missile security, overseas base installation security, security planning, programs, training, and law enforcement. Seeking challenging position as a Director of Security, Senior Security Specialist, or Security Program Manager where previous experience and training will make a maximum contribution to the safety and well-being of the organization or company.

EDUCATION

Formal

Applied Bachelors Degree in Peace, War, and Defense, University of North Carolina
Graduate studies in Public Administration, University of Oklahoma (30 hours)
Candidate, Master of Business Administration, California Coast University

Professional/Technical/Certifications (*See Supplemental Page for additional courses*)

Security Police Officers Course
Central Intelligence Agency Physical Security Seminar
Dynamics of Terrorism, Special Operations School
Homeland Security Planners Course, Joint Forces Staff College
Certified in Homeland Security Level III and IV
Certified Physical Security Professional
Certified Protection Officer Instructor

EXPERIENCE

Security Force Operations

- Directed 13-person multifunctional deployable Force Protection Integrated Support Team (FIST) consisting of security forces, communications, computer/electronics readiness, and transportation personnel.
- Lead 8 to10–person multidisciplined Vulnerability Assessment Team comprised of experts from security forces, emergency management, counterintelligence, information systems, medical, structural, and infrastructure engineering.
- Served as Security Force Director for 400-person organization providing the principal in-field response force, security forces command and control, and entry control security for 150 Minuteman II intercontinental ballistic missile (ICBM) launch facilities (LF) and 15 missile alert facilities spread over an 8,500 mile area.
- Principal Security Force Director for a 263-person organization providing security for special weapons movements and missile maintenance while augmenting launch facility security forces and the 15 missile alert facilities. Managed a $1.5 million budget in assets supporting 600 security force personnel in four separate organizations, 1,000 weapons, 133 vehicles, and all the equipment for five Air Base Defense Type Units.
- Provided security for daily maintenance activities and more than 100 weapons convoys. *Result*: Incident-free, airtight security for the 113 protection level one (PL-1) weapons movements.
- Directed 230-person Security Force responsible for critical law enforcement, weapons system security, and base defense for a multi-service overseas installation in northern Japan with 15,500 personnel while maintaining constant liaison with host government.
- Served as second in command of 220 personnel located in the Panama Canal Zone responsible for the law enforcement, investigations, liaison, contraband, military work dogs, mounted horse patrols, and security activities at Howard AFB, Panama.

Joseph L. Rector, page 2

Security Force Plans, Programs & Training

- As Chief of the Security Force Programs and Requirements Branch, responsible for five sections and 16 personnel providing command policy and guidance for the information security, personnel security, industrial security, antiterrorism, and force protection programs for the Air Combat Command (ACC). Manage $170 million operational budget in four program elements across 16 bases.
- Provided oversight of the ACC Security Forces Regional Training Center. Served as functional area manager (FAM) for 5,425 Security Force personnel at 16 bases, protecting 162,500 ACC personnel and $500 billion in ACC assets.
- Implemented Air Force programs and policies to secure aircraft, munitions, and other base resources for the only U.S. military–controlled C-5 jet capable runway in the Southern Hemisphere at Howard Air Force Base in Panama.
- Provided Security Forces to protect ground-based radar sites in South America and maintained trained mobility teams to support air base defense operations worldwide.
- Conducted two recapture scenarios for the PBS documentary *Avoiding Armageddon,* and selected to showcase nuclear Security Force operations for the History Channel series *Mail Call.*

COMPUTER SKILLS

- Proficient in the use of Microsoft software applications to include: Windows 2000/XP, Microsoft Suite, MS Word, Excel, Access, PowerPoint, and Outlook.

AWARDS/ACHIEVEMENTS/OTHER

- Recipient of twelve Department of Defense commendations for superior achievement and outstanding performance of duties in the areas of security force management, security plans & programs, anti-terrorism programs, and security force training and operations.
- Numerous Anti-terrorism awards/operational unit awards over career. (*See supplemental page*)
- Current Top Secret SCI Security Clearance.

EMPLOYMENT HISTORY

2007–Present	Chief, Security Forces Programs & Requirements Branch, HQ. Air Combat Command (ACC), Langley AFB, VA
2006–2007	Chief, Security Forces Training & Contingencies Branch, HQ. ACC
2006–2006	Chief, Integrated Base Defense Requirements Branch, HQ. ACC
2003–2006	Chief Aggressor Branch/Vulnerability Team Assessment Leader (05-06), Chief, Force Protection Integrated Support Branch (03-05) HQ. Air Force Security Forces Center, Lackland AFB, TX
2001–2003	Commander (CEO equivalent), Security Forces Squadrons (2), Minot AFB, ND
1999–2001	Commander, Security Forces Squadron, Misawa AB, Japan
1997–1999	Deputy Commander, Security Forces Squadron, Howard AB, Panama
1996–Prior	**U.S. Air Force.** Served in assignments of increased responsibility in the Security Field as the Chief of an Operations Division, Plans, Programs & Training Branch, Resource Management Branch, and an overseas Defense Force at Comiso, Italy. Competing service at the rank of Lieutenant Colonel.

ASSOCIATIONS/AFFILIATIONS

International Association of Counterterrorism and Security Professionals
American Society for Industrial Security International (ASIS)
American College of Forensic Examiners International (Member Emergency Management & Public Safety/Security National Emergency Response Team

Joseph L. Rector, page 3

SUPPLEMENTAL PAGE

RESUME OF JOSEPH L. RECTOR

Additional Course Work in the Fields of Security, Antiterrorism, and Law Enforcement

Air Base Ground Defense Flight Leaders Course
Advanced Security Police Officers Symposium
Sensitive Compartmented Information Management Course
Combating Terrorism on Military Installations
USAF Antiterrorism/Force Protection Level II Course
Crisis Response Senior Seminar
Commanders Responsibility Course Force Protection Level III
(*More than 100 additional law enforcement, security, investigations, and emergency management courses*)

Additional Certifications in the Fields of Security, Antiterrorism, and Law Enforcement

Certified Protection Professional
Professional Certified Investigator
Certified Protection Officer
Certified Security Supervisor

Additional Awards/Achievements

Aerospace Education Foundation, Jimmy Doolittle Fellow
Air Force Association National Medal of Merit
Aerospace Education Foundation, Ira Eaker Fellow
American Society for Industrial Security Professionals Organization Award (Air Force Security Forces Center)
Nominated for Spirit of Hope Award for the Air Force Security Forces Center
North Dakota Highway Patrol's Colonel's Award of Excellence for action during major motor vehicle accident

Brian D. Craft

183-G River Mews Drive • Newport News, Virginia 23602 • (804) 888-6575

Crafty1@msn.com

TELECOMMUNICATIONS MAINTENANCE

Objective: To obtain a career position in the telecommunications field in troubleshooting, maintenance, installation, and engineering of fiber optic and copper-core cable.

QUALIFICATIONS SUMMARY

Proven telecommunications maintenance specialist with demonstrated hands-on experience maintaining, troubleshooting, and repairing multimillion-dollar underground copper-core and fiber optic cables supporting worldwide U.S. Air Force command and control, communications, and computer systems. Highly expert at engineering telecommunications upgrades and emergency restoration of interrupted service, and improving voice/data transmission quality. Exceptionally customer-oriented and strongly committed to service excellence.

EXPERIENCE

2000–Present   **U.S. Air Force, Langley Air Force Base, Virginia**
Cable-splicing maintenance specialist, supervisor, and team chief, responsible for installation, maintenance, troubleshooting, and underground repair of copper-core and fiber optic cable; installation/maintenance/ repair of cable air-dryer and continuous-flow pressurization systems; maintaining communications and computer facility inspection records and technical orders.

- Working to provide essential programming enhancement for light-wave computer circuits; installed and spliced a 30-strand fiber optic link utilizing a fusion splicing tool and fiber-loc techniques. Successfully terminated and transferred the fiber with ST, SMA, and bionic connectors and field-tested the fiber for DB loss using an Optical Time Domain reflectometer and a Fiber Scout.
- Using a time-domain reflectometer and multimeter, located and repaired a water-saturated cable splice in a 900-pair cable carrying vital telephone and data circuits—restored service within three days.
- Investigated and fixed cause of cross-talk, noise, and service interruption in a 400-pair cable to a radar ground control approach facility—quick action kept vital voice communications clear.
- Worked overtime to install and splice 2,000 feet of 100-pair cable to replace old deteriorating cable. Service upgrade increased communication services to customers by 100 percent.
- Working in adverse weather, successfully trenched and back-filled 1,376 feet of 200-pair cable one week ahead of schedule—extra time enabled coworkers to exceed quality assurance standards for splicing, sealing, and terminating the cable.
- As team chief, planned, surveyed, and coordinated with other work centers the installation of 800 feet of 25-pair jelly-filled cable, providing telephone and security services for a new entry control gate. Completed job ahead of schedule, permitting gate operation much earlier than planned.

TECHNICAL TRAINING

U.S. Air Force

Cable Splicing Installation and Maintenance Course—510 hours
Fiber Optic Cable Installation, Splicing, and Maintenance Course—63 hours
Air Force Technical Order Systems Courses—23 hours total
Military Leadership Training

Jon R. Ball

36641 Tierra Subida Ave. • Palmdale, California 93551 • (909) 678-8914

JRBALL3491@aol.com

PROFILE

Consummate aviation and operations research professional with demonstrated experience in weapon systems development, resources management, customer service, and tactical flying under wartime and peacetime conditions. Also served as a military counsel to the Chairman of the Joint Chiefs of Staff for matters involving aviation force planning. Former City Manager equivalent for large military aircraft repair and rebuild depot with over 20,000 employees. Excellent interpersonal, communications and writing skills. Seeking challenging management position in operations research, program management, or in city or state government.

EDUCATION

Formal

Master of Science, Operations Research, Air Force Institute of Technology, Dayton, OH
Bachelor of Science, Economics & Management, Air Force Academy, Colorado Springs, CO

Professional/Technical

Graduate, Air War College
Air Force Command & Staff College
Undergraduate Pilot Training

EXPERIENCE

Weapon Systems Research, Development, Test & Evaluation (RDT&E)

- As head of the U.S. Air Force Unmanned Aerial Vehicle (UAV) Battlelab on the Florida Panhandle, direct a 25-member staff of aviators, engineers, analysts and support personnel with an annual budget of $4 million.
- Work with the military, industry, and the Air Force Material Command in investigating existing and emerging technologies to identify ways of enhancing UAV survivability, navigation, and mission capabilities under wartime and crisis response scenarios.
- Demonstrated UAV electronic warfare initiative that provided jamming support to fighter aircraft. Cited for "blazing trail through uncharted territory" from suppressing air defenses and directing close air support, to integrating UAVs with security and special operations forces.
- Served as Chief Analyst for the tactical air forces' (TAC) Air-to-Ground Weapons System Evaluation program (A/G WSEP), the Reconnaissance Evaluation program (REP), and the Precision Guided Munitions Analysis Program (PGMAP). Supervised five scientific analysts and two computer programmers in data collection, reduction, and analysis of weapon system effectiveness, reliability, maintainability and aircrew tactics.

Aviation Operations and Training

- Directed the daily flying operations of a 24-plane F-16C tactical jet squadron comprised of 44 pilots and 12 maintenance technicians. Supervised all scheduling, training, flight examinations, and wartime readiness capabilities for worldwide deployment.
- Served as chief flight examiner for overseas F-16 tactical fighter Wing. Supervised the Standardization/Evaluation Program for 130 pilots to include nuclear certification.

Jon R. Ball, page 2

Resources Management/Customer Services

- Served as City Manager equivalent for major Air Logistics Center directing the efforts of more than 1,200 military and civilian personnel, security forces, communications and computer, base and family support services, personnel, information management and education and training programs supporting 30,000 personnel and their dependents.
- Took stagnate program and revitalized it. Reduced crime, improved morale, welfare, and recreation activities. Focused on customer service mission with identifiable results evident within first six months.
- Created first-ever Community Action Information Board to focus human resources on most critical quality of life issues and needs. *Result*: Unique initiative enhanced services base-wide to more than 20,000 workers.
- Directed round-the-clock recovery and security efforts during devastating ($14 million) flood at Air Logistics Center.
- Identified $95,000 in capital expenditures to improve quality of life for base personnel. *Result*: Improvements contributed to overall increase in morale, welfare, and recreation (MWR) fund by $200,000.

AWARDS/ACHIEVEMENTS

- Recipient of five Department of Defense Commendations for superior achievement and outstanding performance of duties in the areas of operational flying, weapon systems research, development, test and evaluation, and city management.
- Expert oversight and management led to fourth consecutive Gold Key Award for temporary lodging facilities at the San Antonio Air Logistics Center.
- Two-year tenure as City Manager at San Antonio Air Logistics Center saw awards for the following: Best Child Development Center, Best Police Force, Best Youth Programs, Best Lodging, and Best Dining Facility in the command.

PUBLISHED PAPERS AND ARTICLES

- "Islamic Resurgence in the Middle East," *Essays on Strategy*, 1994

EMPLOYMENT HISTORY

1999– Present	*Director*, Unmanned Aerial Vehicle Battlelab, Aerospace Command, Control, Intelligence, Surveillance, and Reconnaissance Center, Eglin AFB, Florida
1997–1999	*Commander* (City Manager equivalent), 76th Support Group, Kelly AFB, Texas
1993–1997	*Deputy Assistant to the Chairman of the Joint Chiefs of Staff* ('94–'97), *Aviation Forces Planner*, J-8, the Joint Staff (93-94), The Pentagon, Washington, D.C.
1991–1993	*Student*, Air War College, Maxwell AFB, Alabama
1990–Prior	**U.S. Air Force.** Served in assignments of increased responsibility in the field of tactical aviation as a flight examiner, as chief analyst for several RDT&E weapon systems programs, and as a squadron pilot and aircraft commander flying the RF-4C, F-4D and the F-16 tactical jet aircraft. Gulf War Veteran. Completing service in the rank of Colonel.

Roger A. Cross

525 Sun Mountain Ave. • North Las Vegas, Nevada 89031 • (702) 370-2699

rogercross@yahoo.com

PROFILE

Skilled personnel management and human resources (HR) professional with over 20 years of administering, counseling, and instructing in all facets of workforce development, personnel management, foreign national and U.S. military training programs, and tactical air control party training, liaison, management, and combat operations. Excellent interpersonal communications and writing skills. Seeking challenging personnel management or HR position where previous senior level supervisory experience, resource management, HR, and personnel management experience match the needs of the company.

EDUCATION

Formal

Bachelor of Arts (Candidate), Management, American Military University, West Virginia
Associate of Arts, Liberal Arts, St. Leo College, Florida
Associate of Applied Science, Information Systems Management, Community College of the Air
    Force
Associate of Applied Science, Security Administration, Community College of the Air Force

Professional/Technical

Mid- through Senior-Level Leadership/Management Courses for Supervisory Personnel, U.S. Air
    Force
Middle East Orientation Course
Graduate, U.S. Army Airborne/Ranger/ Freefall and Air Assault Schools
Gettysburg Leadership Experience, Gettysburg, PA
Joint Aerospace Command and Control Joint Doctrine Air Campaign Courses

EXPERIENCE

Resource Manager and Principal Counselor/Mentor

- Advised and assisted the Air Support Operations Group Commander (CEO) on all HR, training, operations, and quality of life issues for 800-member organization at 17 geographically separated sites, providing base and deployed operations support to U.S. Army forces.
- Initiated weekly meetings with functional-level superintendents to identify and then resolve organizational level concerns/issues. Fostered an environment for open dialogue resulting in myriad improvements throughout the group.
- Pioneered efforts to fix manning issues for the Theater Air Control System in the war in Afghanistan, revamping and restructuring the Tactical Air Control Party Teams in country to better support Army and Special Operations forces requirements. Established and monitored metrics, visited Control Party Teams in both Afghanistan and Iraq, engaged with supervisors providing invaluable mentorship for hundreds in both areas of conflict.
- Cited as a visionary for establishing goals for professional development, training, housing and recreational facilities, quality of life programs, performance recognition, and stewardship to 415-member workforce located across Europe and deployed to Iraq.
- Counseled employees experiencing job, personal, financial, or relationship- challenges and, where necessary, referred them to expert agencies for further assistance.
- Served as principal supervisor for 89 highly trained specialists assigned to an Army Airborne Division providing joint airpower support for field exercises in the United States and ground operations in Afghanistan. Collateral duty of mentoring new supervisors on unit standards and readiness for deployment procedures.

Roger A. Cross, page 2

International Security Assistance/Training Management

- Served as the Senior U.S. Air Force Advisor to the Royal Saudi Air Force Air Ground Operations School (AGOS) as part of the U.S Security Assistance Training mission.
- Provided significant focus on establishing systems and standards of performance to the fledgling schoolhouse in order to bring credibility to the overall program.
- Coached and mentored 15 Royal Saudi Air Force Officers and enlisted cadre members on instructional issues to include planning, preparing, and executing both classroom and field training site instruction.
- Validated the development, revision, and implementation of all contractor-developed training products, ensuring statement of work requirements were accomplished to standard and on time.
- Spearheaded an aggressive train-the-trainer certification program without contractor assistance. A first for the AGOS.
- Driving force in the development of a digital electronic library of publications allowing one-stop shopping for doctrinal information. *Result:* Courseware for this library was developed three months faster than anticipated.

COMPUTER SKILLS

- Proficient in the use of the following operating systems and software applications: Windows 2000/XP/VISTA; and MS Word, Excel, PowerPoint and Outlook.

AWARDS/ACHIEVEMENTS

- Awarded 16 Department of Defense commendations for superior achievement and outstanding performance of duties in resource management and tactical air control party operations.
- Sr. Supervisor of the Year, 18th Air Support Operations Group
- Distinguished Graduate and Esprit de Corps Winner, Mid-Level Supervisors Course
- Distinguished Graduate/Commandant's Award, Tactical Air Command and Control Specialist School

EMPLOYMENT HISTORY

2007–Present	Group Superintendent (HR/Ops), 57th Operations Group, Nellis AFB, Nevada
2004–2007	Group Superintendent (HR/Ops), 4th Air Support Operations Squadron, Campbell Barracks, Germany
2002–2004	Chief Supervisory Manager (HR) and Operations Superintendent, 18th Air Support Operations Group, Pope AFB, North Carolina
2000–2002	Operations Superintendent, 14th Air Support Squadron, Pope AFB, North Carolina
1998–2000	Superintendent (HR), Royal Saudi Air Force Ground Operations School, King Khalid Air Base, Saudi Arabia
1997–Prior	**U.S. Air Force.** Served in assignments of increased responsibility in the Tactical Air Control Party field both in the United States and overseas. Completing service at the grade of Chief Master Sergeant.

ASSOCIATIONS/AFFILIATIONS

Golden Key International Honor Society
Air Force Association
Tactical Air Control Party Association
75th Ranger Regiment Association

CURRICULUM VITAE
EXAMPLES

Lemoyne F. Blackshear, AIA

807 Delaware Avenue, S.W. • Washington, D.C. 20024
(202) 484-4043 • *blackshearl@earthlink.net*

CAREER PROFILE

Registered Architect and environmental manager with over 20 years of documented success in the areas of large-scale management of high-dollar, environmental, engineering, and architectural projects both in the United States and overseas. Excellent oral communication and writing skills. Seeking challenging position as a senior research analyst or principal consultant for architecture design or environmental management program in the building and construction industry. Computer literate with current Top Secret Security Clearance.

EDUCATION

Formal

Master of Science, National Resource Strategy, Industrial College of the Armed Forces, 2000
Master of Architecture, University of New Mexico, 1991
Bachelor of Science, Architecture, University of Virginia, 1981

Professional/Technical

Imagine 21—Fast Track to Change Seminar, 2001
Hazardous Waste Operations & Emergency Response Course, 1999
Registered Environmental Manager Course, 1996
Princeton Groundwater and Hydrology Course

EMPLOYMENT HISTORY

Deputy Director, Critical Infrastructure Protection Integration Staff, Office of the Assistant Secretary of Defense for Command, Control, Communications & Intelligence, The Pentagon, Washington, D.C. (2001–Present)

- Lead efforts of representatives from 18 DOD agencies responsible for monitoring the identification of infrastructure assets critical to DOD and for overseeing that qualitative vulnerability and interdependency analyses are performed on these assets.
- Recently fielded work plan that describes a demonstration of the Critical Infrastructure Protection analysis/assessment process to include interdependencies of systems/functions.

Security Review Officer, Directorate for Freedom of Information and Security Review, The Pentagon, Washington, D.C. (2000–2001)

- Acted on behalf of the Secretary of Defense with full authority to review and clear defense information for release to the public and Congress. Handled over 300 security review cases clearing 240 cases for public release.
- Processed 46% of the division's completed FOIA cases—met all statutory response requirements with no appeals.

Student, Industrial College of the Armed Forces, Ft. McNair, Washington, D.C. (1999–2000)

- Completed highly demanding senior-level postgraduate program in National Resource Strategy as Award Recipient.
- Cited for insightful and innovative strategic-level analysis of information issues and policy options by instructors in the Executive Information Systems curriculum part of course.

Civil Engineer Inspector, Air Force Inspection Agency, Kirtland AFB, NM (1998–1999)

- Pioneered design and use of prototype data management computer program for adoption by Inspection Teams. Served as key member of Assessment Improvement Team.
- Developed and wrote solid recommendations for improving Air Force Hazardous Materials program. Wrote HAZMAT questionnaires, interviewed senior leaders at 20 installations, and set new standard for data collection.

Lemoyne F. Blackshear, AIA, page 2

Chief, Eastern Restoration Group, Air Force Center for Environmental Excellence, Brooks AFB, TX (1994–1998)

- Served as Project Director for environmental restoration projects at 11 closure bases valued at over $384 million. Drove 98 restoration projects totaling $43 million in FY96.
- Selected to serve as U.S. Project Officer to work with Russians and Norwegians to clean up nonradioactive contaminates at Arctic sites and later as environmental team member on United States delegation to Moscow.

Commander (CEO), Civil Engineer Squadron, Eareckson Air Station, Shemya Island, AK (1993–1994)

- Served as City Manager for small air station off the coast of Alaska. Managed all aspects of facilities/plant maintenance, fire protection, electrical power generation, housing, construction and service contract management for 125 major facilities and a population of 500-plus residents. Oversaw budget of $3.7 million and 69 vehicles valued at $6.1 million.

U.S. Air Force (1992–Prior)

Served in assignments of increased responsibility as a design architect, Associate Director for Engineering and Architecture, Programming Engineer, Chief Program Development and Requirements Division, and staff architect.

AWARDS/ACHIEVEMENTS/CERTIFICATIONS

Air Force Association Award for Excellence in Research and Writing, Research Fellows Program, Industrial College of the Armed Forces, 2000
Master of Ceremonies, U.S. Air Force Design Awards Ceremony, 1997
Women of the Year Award, Brooks Air Force Base, Texas, 1996
Air Force Center for Environmental Excellence, Superior Performer of the Year, 1996
Registered Architect, State of New Mexico
Registered Environmental Manager, State of Texas

ASSOCIATIONS/AFFILIATIONS

American Institute of Architects (AIA)
Society of American Military Engineers
Chairperson, Professional Development Committee, San Antonio Chapter, AIA
Air Force Association
National Registry of Environmental Professionals

Stanley R. Gray

7717 Shootingstar Drive • Springfield, Virginia 22152 • (703) 866-3124
stangray@chinagate.com

PROFILE

China Political-Military Affairs specialist fluent in the Mandarin Chinese dialect. Tenured faculty professor and former director of Chinese Studies at the United States Military Academy, West Point. Former military engineer with extensive mapping, charting, and geodetic background. Skilled communicator, proven writer, capable administrator, with demonstrated track record as a Principal China Analyst for the Defense Intelligence Agency. Chief editor for Congressional, National Security Council, DOD, and other high-level briefings on sensitive Asia-Pacific Rim issues affecting U.S. foreign policy decision making. Computer literate. Seeking challenging position as a Chinese political affairs analyst for a Washington "think tank," or as an instructor of Chinese studies and Mandarin Chinese with the National Foreign Affairs Institute, or at a college or university.

EDUCATION

Formal

Master of Arts, Summa Cum Laude, Asian Studies (China), Seton Hall University, NJ
Bachelor of Science, Engineering Studies, U.S. Military Academy, West Point, NY

Professional Technical Training

- Chinese Language School, British Ministry of Defense, Hong Kong
- Summer Language Program, Beijing University
- Defense Language Institute, Mandarin Chinese Language Refresher Course
- Institute for Military Assistance, Foreign Area Officer Course, Fort Bragg, NC
- Engineer Officer Basic and Advanced Courses
- Mapping, Charting, and Geodesy Officer Course
  - distinguished graduate

PROFESSIONAL EXPERIENCE

Foreign Area Officer and Engineer, U.S. Army, 1972–Present

Chronology of Career:

Completing distinguished Army career as the Chief of the Asia-Pacific Counterintelligence Branch, Defense Intelligence Agency (DIA) in Washington, D.C. Previous assignments include Chief, China-Political-Military Section, Asia Division, DIA; Assistant Professor of Chinese and Program Director (Chinese) at the U.S. Military Academy; engineer instructor and chief of administration, operations, and training for the Commandant of Cadets at the Virginia Military Institute; several tours as an Engineering, Cartographic, or Terrain Intelligence Officer with U.S. Forces in Germany and at Fort Bragg, NC; and as a Foreign Area Officer with DIA. Extensive travel in the People's Republic of China, Southeast Asia, and Western Europe.

Significant Accomplishments:

- Consistently cited for clear thinking, innovativeness, strategic planning, superb management, quality control, and outstanding leadership throughout career.
- Recipient of nine Army and DOD medals for meritorious service and superior achievement in the engineering, Chinese language instructor, and Foreign Area Officer fields.
- Responsible for increasing cadet enrollment in Chinese Studies at USMA by 400%.
- Recipient of Distinguished Writing Award from the Institute of Military Affairs.
- Selected as member of Phi Kappa Phi Society for academics while at USMA.

Stanley R. Gray, page 2

China Political-Military Affairs Specialist, 1985–Present

Chronology of Service:

— Chief, Asia-Pacific Counterintelligence Branch, Counterintelligence Research and Analysis Division, Defense Intelligence Agency, Washington, D.C. (1993–Present). Supervise 14 analysts, intelligence technicians, and clerical personnel in the preparation of high-level analyses of foreign intelligence threats to United States interests by Asian nations. Ensured smooth transition of branch to new organizational structure within DIA with shift in emphasis to nontraditional threat assessment issues, i.e., proliferation, technology espionage, and DOD acquisition.

— Chief, China Political-Military Section, Asia Division, Defense Intelligence Agency, Washington, D.C. (1990–1993). Devised well-conceived ambitious research production plan at critical juncture in changing U.S. policy in East Asia that became basis for DIA analysis of sensitive Chinese political-military foreign policy issues. Created new sense of teamwork while playing key role in the development of four major National Intelligence estimates on China's leadership succession, preassessment of the 14th Party Congress; military modernization plans and programs; and Taiwan's increasingly independent course in the region. Instrumental in energizing interaction with Department of State analysts that provided greater opportunity for input to U.S. policy initiatives toward China, Taiwan, and Mongolia. Supervised 10 political-military intelligence analysts in the preparation of over 70 biographical reports on key military leaders in China and other Asian countries for use by high-level government officials.

— Assistant Professor of Chinese and Program Director (Chinese), Department of Foreign Languages, United States Military Academy (USMA), West Point (1986–1990). Served as primary instructor for all Chinese language instruction at USMA, including core and elective courses. Introduced more dynamic textual material and modifications to the teaching of Chinese, thereby improving cadet comprehension and performance. Set up, coordinated, and conducted the USMA Academic Exchange Programs visiting the People's Republic of China, Taiwan, and Hong Kong. Principal point of contact for the East Asian Field of Study and academic counselor for 34 cadets concentrating in Chinese studies.

— Student, Foreign Area Officer Advanced Training Program, British Ministry of Defense Chinese Language School, Hong Kong (1985–1986). Schooled in the Mandarin Chinese dialect while conducting in-depth one-year study of natural resources conservation programs in China. Traveled extensively, conducting interviews and field research using source materials written in Chinese. Interviews were conducted with key Chinese officials in the Ministry of Forestry, the National Environmental Protection Agency, and nature preserves, and with academicians. Worked closely with the World Wildlife Fund Office in Hong Kong. Published major research paper on wildlife conservation in China.

PUBLICATIONS AND PAPERS

Authored following works:
— Thesis titled "An Analysis of the Ch'ing Central Military Organizations: The Eight Banners and the Army of the Green Standard"
— Research paper on "The Dynamics of China's Military Modernization"
— Research paper on "Wildlife Conservation in China"

ASSOCIATIONS AND AFFILIATIONS

Chinese Language Teachers Association
The World Wildlife Fund

Thomas J. Tegeler, RN, MPH, CNAA, BC

6241 West Post Rd • Chandler, AZ 85226 • (623) 256-9931
TTegeler@cox.net

PROFILE

Seasoned healthcare professional with over 25 years of documented success in the areas of nursing and medical administration, medical services (medical, dental, and aeromedical) support, TRICARE management, and medical operations management in large medical centers, stand-alone clinics, and a for-profit surgical hospital. Former Chief Nurse Executive and Vice President of Clinical operations at three facilities. Seeking challenging healthcare industry position in an acute care facility (hospital) or management company that works closely with the acute care industry.

EDUCATION

Formal

Masters in Public Health (MPH), University of Alabama at Birmingham
Bachelor of Science in Nursing (BSN), Northern Illinois University

Professional/Technical Training/Certifications

APIC: The Fundamentals of Infection Surveillance, Prevention and Control
TRICARE Management Activity Conference, Washington, D.C.
Interagency Institute for Federal Health Care Executives, Washington, D.C.
Department of Defense Patient Safety Course, San Antonio, TX
JCAHO Conference on Sustained Performance Success, Albuquerque, NM
Physicians in Management Courses I, II, and III, Sheppard AFB, TX
Several Air Force Executive Leadership Courses & Symposiums
Board Certified in Nursing Administration Advanced by the ANCC
Registered Nurse

SIGNIFICANT ACCOMPLISHMENTS

- Directed the efforts of a Medical Services Support organization's preparation for four Joint Commission on Accreditation of Healthcare Organizations Surveys and Health Services Inspections. *Results:* All four scored in the high nineties with one awarded "Accreditation with Commendation."
- Led the largest division in the U.S. Air Force's second largest medical center with six Departments (in- and outpatient), and three graduate medical education residencies.

CAREER EXPERIENCE

Health Care Administration/Management

- Recently served as Chief Nursing Officer for a major orthopedic surgical hospital with responsibility for interpreting, directing, and evaluating nursing practices to promote safe, efficient, and therapeutically efficient nursing care throughout the hospital.
- Developed policies, procedures, and staffing essential to the achievement of the philosophy and objectives of the hospital. Reviewed and revised same with the Administrator, nursing staff, and professional staff, maintaining currency in nursing practices and patient care.
- Served as Director of Medical Operations at Air Force's second largest medical center, the David Grant Medical Center. Supervised 520 medical personnel at two geographically separated locations and a budget of $33 million, which annually supported 2,972 admissions, 228,232 outpatient visits, 116 research protocols, and Clinical Phase II training programs.
- Cited for fiscal initiative with the VA developing an $800,000 sharing agreement for in-house dialysis services that expanded the care by 60%.
- Validated the benefit of an $86,000 drug dispensing machine for emergency services, ensuring 24-hour medication access and saving $300,000 per year in excess drug costs.
- Served as Chief Clinical Consultant for the $600,000 redesign of the U.S. Air Force Academy hospital ICU.
- Achieved position on Tucson Nursing Foundation Board of Directors linking Air Force nurses to the community.

Thomas J. Tegeler, RN, MPH, CNAA, BC, page 2

Medical Services Support/Medical Resource Management

- Cited for leadership while serving as Chief Nurse and Medical Operations Unit Director at the David Grant Medical Center in the organization's winning the 2001–2002 Picker Institute Award for the most patient-centered hospital in the United States.
- Led two different medical services organizations to a 97 and a 98 out of 100 points, respectively, on the Joint Commission on Accreditation of Healthcare Organizations Survey and Health Services Inspections, which reflected the organization's mastery in providing the highest standard of health care possible.
- Served as Administrator for case management activities for 88,600 TRICARE beneficiaries; responsible for providing health-care beneficiaries with medical administrative and ancillary services while executing a $4.2 million annual budget.
- Directed all nursing assets during four disaster preparedness exercises, which tested the National Disaster Medical System while training staff and maintaining patient access.
- Implemented automated ambulatory data system, thereby increasing data accuracy by 30% and saving three full-time equivalents.

AWARDS/ACHIEVEMENTS

- Recipient of five Department of Defense commendations for superior achievement and outstanding service in the health care and nursing management fields.
- Director of numerous organizations during Air Force career that were recipients of Health Services Organization Inspection and Quality Air Force Assessment Awards.

EMPLOYMENT HISTORY

2006–2007	Chief Nursing Officer, Arizona Orthopedic Surgical Hospital, Chandler, AZ
2001–2005	Commander (CEO equivalent 03-05) Medical Operations, Chief Nurse Executive (01–04), David Grant Medical Center, Travis AFB, CA
1999–2001	Medical Group Deputy/Nurse Executive (00–01), Director Medical Operations/Nurse Executive (99), Medical Group, Davis-Monthan AFB, AZ
1995–1999	Commander Medical Operations/Chief Nurse, Medical Group, Grand Forks AFB, ND
1994–Prior	**U.S. Air Force.** Served in assignments of increased responsibility in the health care/medical nursing fields as a charge nurse for the following: an ICU/CCU, Multi-Service Unit, Family Practice, and Outpatient Services. Completed service in rank of Colonel.

ASSOCIATIONS/AFFILIATIONS

Fellow, American College of Healthcare Executives
American Nurses Association and the Arizona Nurses Association
Sigma Theta Tau International, Honor Society of Nursing
Association of Military Surgeons of the United States
Association for Professionals in Infection Control and Epidemiology

PILOT RESUME
EXAMPLES

Robert. B. Manchester

14 LeMay Drive • Offutt AFB, Nebraska 68113 • (402) 596-7832
rmanchester@earthlink.net

Permanent Address
4217 Bayou Drive • Lake Worth, Florida 33463 • (954) 698-7245

Objective: Position as a Commercial Airline or Air Cargo Flight Officer

AIRCRAFT CERTIFICATES AND RATINGS

Airline Transport Pilot, Airplane MEL (Boeing 707/720)
Flight Engineer, Turbojet Written Exam (03/2004)
FAA Class I Medical (03/14/2006)
[COMP:See table in 4th Edition for formatting]

FLIGHT TIME   Total 4,332

Position	Hours	Other	Hours	T/M/S	Hours
Pilot-in-Command	2,536	Instruments	529	B-52G/H	1,750
Co-Pilot	492	Simulated Instruments	172	T-38A	1,198
Instructor/Evaluator	1,304	Night	443	T-37B	354
		Multi-Engine	3,304	RC-135V/W	136

PROFESSIONAL EXPERIENCE

May 2008–Present   **Vice Wing Commander (City Manager), 55th Wing, Offutt AFB, NE**
Deputy CEO for largest wing in the Air Combat Command with over 30 aircraft flying 19,000 hours and 3,300 missions annually. City Manager for base population of 12,000 and tenant facilities with an annual budget of $432 million and assets of more than $4 billion.

Oct 2006–May 2007   **Commander (CEO equivalent), 5th Support Group Minot AFB, ND**
Responsible for the infrastructure and associated support for B-52H bomber operations worldwide, as well as 150 Minuteman III Intercontinental Ballistic Missiles.

Oct 2003–Oct 2006   **Chief, Military Education Div., Joint Staff The Pentagon, Washington, D.C.**
Led accreditation team that assessed all Department of Defense intermediate and senior service schools for JCS.

Jun 2003–Oct 2003   **Commander, 559th Flying Training Squadron Randolph AFB, TX**
Commanded the Air Force's primary flight instructor school for training pilots in instrument, formation, and navigation flying in the T-37B.

EDUCATION AND SPECIAL FLYING TRAINING

- RC-135/V/W, Initial Training, Offutt AFB, NE, 1999
- T-37B, Pilot Instructor Training Upgrade, Randolph AFB, TX, 1998
- Student, Air War College, Maxwell AFB, AL, 1998–1999
- Student, Air Command & Staff College, Maxwell AFB, AL, 1990–1991
- MBA, Management, Troy University, Troy, AL, 1989
- T-38A, Initial Pilot Instructor Training, Sheppard AFB, TX, 1988
- B-52G, Aircraft Commander Upgrade, Castle AFB, CA, 1989
- USAF Undergraduate Pilot Training, Craig AFB, AL, 1986
- BS, Marketing (cum laude), Auburn University, AL, 1985

Personal Data: Available: August 2009

Mark H. Rohrback

3208 Sydenflicker Court • Santa Ana, California 90051 • (213) 275-4617
markrohr@rotorhead.com

QUALIFICATIONS SUMMARY

Nine years of progressive experience as an operational rotary-wing pilot, including time as Pilot in Command, flight instructor, ground safety and maintenance officer. Qualified in all-weather flying conditions with operations in high-density air traffic areas, both domestic and international.

EDUCATION AND FLIGHT CERTIFICATION

Bachelor of Science, Engineering, U.S. Naval Academy, 1988
Graduate, U.S. Naval Flight Training, Pensacola, Florida, 1989
    Commercial: Helicopter and single-engine land
    Instrument: Helicopter and fixed-wing
    ATP: Helicopter VFR and IFR written tests completed
    FAA: Class 1 Medical

Flight Time		Rotary- and Fixed-Wing		Type Aircraft
Total Time	2,800	Helicopter (Twin Turbine)	2,546	BH-212
Pilot in Command	1,570	Helicopter (Single Turbine)	96	BH-205/206B
Night	400	Fixed-Wing (Turboprop)	108	T-34C
Instrument	530	Fixed-Wing (Piston)	50	CE-152 and
Instructor Pilot	300			CE-172/RG

EXPERIENCE

June 2000–Present   U.S. Naval Air Training Command, Pensacola, Florida
                          3rd Marine Aircraft Wing, El Toro, California
                          1st Marine Aircraft Wing, Futenma, Japan
Designated a helicopter pilot upon completion of rotary-wing syllabus while assigned as student naval aviator at the Naval Air Training Command. Assigned **Squadron Pilot** (10/00) with Marine Light Helicopter Squadron 367, Camp Pendleton, California, and MLHS 165, Futenma, Japan. Performed the following duties in addition to acting as copilot of BH-205 and BH-206B helicopters and **Pilot in Command** of the BH-212:

Squadron Pilot

- Performed medical evacuation, search and rescue, troop transport, external lift, extractions, and ordnance delivery in offshore, mountainous, jungle, and desert environments.
- Operated in high-density traffic areas on both coasts of the United States with international experience in Japan, Korea, and the Philippines.
- Extensive night experience using nap-of-the-earth flying and night-vision goggle devices.

Pilot in Command

- Experienced in domestic and international all-weather flying. Over 800 cross-country flight hours.
- Designated flight leader of multiaircraft formations.

Instructor Pilot

- Coordinated, supervised, and instructed initial familiarization and advanced phases of tactical training for squadron pilots.
- Responsible for preparation of daily operational flight schedules for aircrews and aircraft.
- Supervisory and scheduling efforts resulted in the accomplishment of over 6,500 flight hours for 25 aircraft and over 400 initial training flights in one year.

Mark H. Rohrback, page 2

Maintenance Officer

- Supervised the quality-assurance program for maintenance operations. Ensured compliance with established procedures. Coordinated training of all personnel; maintained programs concerning fuel and oil analysis, maintenance safety, and aircraft weight and balance.
- Served as chief maintenance check pilot responsible for all training and designation of post-maintenance check pilots.
- Directed the efforts of 70 jet engine mechanics and aircraft crew chiefs.
- Established and directed the industrial and maintenance safety programs.

SPECIAL QUALIFICATIONS

Helicopter Aircraft Commander for BH-212
Graduate, Aviation Weapons and Tactics Instructor School
Distinguished International Pistol and Rifle Marksman

ELECTRONIC RESUME
EXAMPLE

Roger A. Wrenchturner
1525 Longacre Parkway
San Antonio, TX 78541
(210) 467-8922
rogerwrench@goodguys.com

Objective:
Seeking challenging management position in the field of logistics with a defense aerospace company or an overnight or overseas parcel express carrier.

Employment History:

2007–Present   Director, Aircraft Maintenance, San Antonio Air Logistics Center, TX

Direct 26-person staff in the execution of operational maintenance. Modernize and perform heavy-deport maintenance on entire fleet of C-5 heavy-cargo aircraft. Managed $20 million Depot Maintenance Industrial Fund.

2004–2007   Assistant Director, Depot Maintenance Production, Ogden Air Logistics Center, UT

Directed 23-member staff in execution of operational maintenance. Provided worldwide engineering logistics management for the F-16, representing the world's largest fleet of jet fighter aircraft. Responsible for logistics management and maintenance for Minuteman and Peacekeeper intercontinental ballistic missiles.

2001–2004   Special Logistics Manager, Warner Robins Air Logistics Center, Macon, GA

Provided logistics management, procurement, maintenance, and distribution support for the C-5, C-17, C-130, E-8, F-15, and UR tactical aircraft. Responsible for more than 200 electronic systems and programs and eight space systems and technology centers for VHS integrated circuits and fiber optics.

2000–Prior   U.S. Air Force

Served in various line and staff assignments of increased responsibility in the aircraft maintenance and logistics management fields. Completing service in the rank of Colonel.

Education:

MS in Logistics Management, USAF Institute of Technology, Wright-Patterson, OH
BS in Industrial Management, Boston University, Boston, MA, 1990

Computer Skills:

Computer literate in PC and MacOS10 operating systems and Windows 07, Excel, PowerPoint, Microsoft Office 08, and Microsoft Word software.

Associations:

Charter Member, Maintenance Officers Association
Council of Logistics Management
International Society of Logistics Engineers

OF 612 RESUME
EXAMPLE

David M. Bower

SSN: XXX-XX-XXXX
101 B Pine Court
Eglin AFB, FL 32542
(850) 613-6329
Dmbower1@cox.net
U.S. Citizen (Florida)

Vacancy DSSC-09-1303
General Supply Specialist, GS-2001-11/11

EXECUTIVE SUMMARY

Seasoned logistics and supply management professional with over 19 years of demonstrated success in the areas of supply chain management, inventory management, storage and warehousing, fuels distribution, and maintenance management. Accountable manager who drives organizational improvements and best solutions in uniquely challenging situations with demonstrated supply management competence. Seeking challenging inventory management specialist position that will best use my worldwide experience, logistics training, and proven capabilities.

WORK EXPERIENCE

11/2006–10/2007   Materiel Management Division (A4L), Directorate of Logistics, Headquarters Air Intelligence Agency, Lackland AFB, TX.

Supervisor: Colonel Rickey Kendle. Phone: (210) 946-2278
Title: Chief, Materiel Management Division

- Managed an $8 million acquisition and O&M financial program, developed wholesale logistics support policy and procedures for USAF cryptologic equipment, and managed Agency vehicle operations and transportation management.
- Cited as key member of the AIA logistics team charged with developing the materiel management policy for the transition of base operating support for Menwith Hill Station, United Kingdom. Ensured that $400 million worth of equipment at Menwith Hill Station was maintained at 100% accountability at all times.

Accomplishments:

- Led the Agency's (AIA) effort to revamp wholesale logistics and supply support for the multimillion dollar COBRA DANE radar system. Tireless research of organic support costs versus contractor costs saved the DOD over $11.5 million.

Awarded the Meritorious Service Medal   **Salary $XXK**

1/2003–11/2006   Supply and Transportation Division, Directorate of Logistics, Headquarters Air Intelligence Agency, Lackland AFB, TX.

Supervisor: Colonel John Orsino: (UNK)
Title: Chief, Supply and Transportation Division

- As Chief of the Supply and Transportation Division, developed and implemented Air Intelligence Agency (AIA) supply and transportation policies and provided surveillance over supplies, equipment, and vehicles valued at $200 million.
- Wrote Air Force Technical Applications Center supply chain management instruction, a first for AIA supply personnel.

Accomplishments:

- Directed Agency-wide review of more than 800 stock-numbered items worth $7.5 million—beat HQ Air Force directive by 30 days.
- Uncovered DOD asset accounting problems and led fix to ensure visibility of $50 million in classified/national assets.
- Developed Defense Property Accounting System implementation plan for Agency assets. Precise plan ensured $59 million in NSA property is put into DOD system.

David M. Bower, page 2

Awarded the Meritorious Service Medal   **Salary $XXK**

6/2001–1/2003   Supply Division, Directorate of Logistics, Headquarters U.S. Air Forces in Europe (USAFE), Ramstein AB, Germany.

Supervisor: Col. Gary Gaucho. Phone (591) 632-2640
Title: Chief, Fuels Management Branch

- Supervised 496 fuels distribution personnel at 7 main, 3 stand-by, and 16 collocated operating bases managing more than 1,400 fuel equipment assets and facilities valued at over $500 million. Determined distribution of 692 pieces of fuels mobility support equipment stored at three locations.
- Cited as Air Force fuels visionary providing $7 million solution to Rhein Main Air Base Transition Program fuels systems cost overruns.

Accomplishments:

- Averted operational catastrophe at start of Operation Enduring Freedom in Afghanistan when 3 inbound jet fuel tankers arrived in Theater with bad fuel. Worked nonstop with European Command, Defense Energy Supply Center, and the Turkish military. Reworked tanker schedule and brokered deal for 2 million gallons in Turkish Replacement-In-Kind fuel.
- Led fuels planning for Exercise VICTORY STRIKE II in Poland, saving USAFE $615,000 in Polish taxes.

Awarded the Meritorious Service Medal; Selected U.S. Air Forces Europe Staff
Fuels Officer of the Year   **Salary $XXK**

1/2000–6/2001   Supply Division, Directorate of Logistics, Headquarters U.S. Air Forces in Europe, Ramstein AB, Germany.

Supervisor: Colonel Jim Bennett. Phone (UNK)
Title: Chief, Weapon Systems Support Branch

- Managed the parts support for five Type/Model/Series aircraft flown throughout Europe worth over $185 million and over $110 million in communication spares.
- Worked with the Air Force Materiel Command, Defense Logistics Agency, and USAFE units to decrease mission capable parts grounding conditions and assure spare parts availability.

Accomplishments:

- Discovered Air Force Logistics Management Agency error when transferring critical demand data to home base. Supply system now better able to capture demand data for more realistic Mobility readiness Spares Packages (MRSP) computations.

Awarded the Meritorious Service Medal.   **Salary $XXK**

4/1999–1/2000   325th Fighter Wing, Tyndall AFB, FL

Supervisor: BGen Thomas Bowman Jr. Phone (813) 948-4580
Title: Wing Executive Officer

- Directly responsible to the Wing Commander (CEO) for formulating plans, policies, and administrative programs in 10 staff agencies, 4 groups, and over 4,000 military and civilian personnel.
- Managed and executed the entire Civilian Appraisal Program for more than 30 wing staff civilian employees.

David M. Bower, page 3

Accomplishments:

- Cited for improving the Wing Mission Brief by creating CD graphic database with photos of base and mission.
- Revised and managed the time-sensitive Air Force Outstanding Unit Award package, and disciplinary and personnel actions.

Awarded the Air Force Achievement Medal   **Salary $XXK**

12/1997–4/1999   325th Maintenance Squadron, 325th Fighter Wing, Tyndall AFB, FL

Supervisor: Colonel Armando Asante, Jr. Phone (UNK)
Title: Maintenance Supervisor

- Directed the maintenance production effort of 200 personnel and managed $90 million worth of support equipment, 33 maintenance facilities valued at $20 million and a munitions inventory of $250 million.
- Managed quality assurance oversight of a 5-year, $43 million Lockheed Martin Logistics Management maintenance support contract.

Accomplishments:

- Applied supply/maintenance knowledge to improve 2-Level Maintenance (2LM) production. Slashed repair times to one-half allowable Air Force standard. Saved 325th FW over $4 million through fault screening.
- Supercharged the avionics circuit card repair (CCR) element into the finest in the Air Education & Training Command with cost avoidance topping $350,000.

Awarded the Meritorious Service Medal.   **Salary $XXK**

2/1997–12/1997   607th Air Support Squadron, Air Component Command, Headquarters Seventh Air Force, Osan AB, Republic of Korea

Supervisor: Colonel James Yale. Phone (UNK)
Title: Seventh Air Force Deputy Chief of Supply

- As Deputy Chief of Supply for the 7th Air Force in Korea, managed three Mutual Logistics Support Agreements (MLSAs) and the programming of fuel facilities within the Korean theater of operations while working with the Defense Fuels Office Korea, 8th U.S. Army, the Combined Forces Command in Seoul, Pacific Air Forces in Hawaii, and the Korean Air Force.
- Provided effective supply and fuels support to two USAF main operating bases and five collocated operating bases with assets in excess of $50 million.

Accomplishments:

- Served as focal point for the thermal stability (JPTS) fuel conversion projects at Osan AB and Pohang Fuel Terminal in Korea, increasing peninsula JPTS fuel storage over 400% and saving $800,000 in annual transportation costs.
- Served as member of the U.S. negotiating team for petroleum pipeline support in Korea.

Selected 7th Air Force Logistics Group Company Grade Officer of the Year.
                                                            Salary $XXK

David M. Bower, page 4

EDUCATION

Formal

Newark Senior High School, Newark, OH, 1981
Bowling Green State University, Bowling Green, OH, B.A, Liberal Studies, 1987
Embry-Riddle Aeronautical University, St. Louis, MO, Master of Aeronautical Science, 30 hours

Specialized Training

Civilian Personnel Management Course, 2003; NATO Staff Officers Orientation Course, 2002; Air
  Command & Staff College (Correspondence), 2002; Advanced Logistics Officer Course
  (USAF), 2000; Base Level Quality Assurance Evaluation for Service Contracts, 1999; Air-
  craft Maintenance Officers Course, 1998; Squadron Officer School (USAF), 1992; Fuels Offi-
  cer Course
(USAF), 1990; Supply Officer Course (USAF), 1988; Information Assurance Training (Annually);
  Operation Security (OPSEC) Training (Annually)

OTHER QUALIFICATIONS

Security Clearance

Top Secret SCI Security Clearance (last updated May 2005)

Job-Related Awards

Meritorious Service Medal (with two Oak Leaf Clusters)
Joint Service Commendation Medal
Air Force Commendation Medal (with three Oak Leaf Clusters)
Air Force Achievement Medal (with two Oak Leaf Clusters)
Joint Meritorious Unit Award
Air Force Outstanding Unit Award (with five Oak Leaf Clusters)
National Defense Service Medal (with Bronze Star)
Southwest Asia Service Medal (with two Bronze Stars)
Humanitarian Service Medal
Global War on Terrorism Medal
Korean Defense Service Medal

Job-Related Skills

- Proficient in the use of Microsoft software applications to, including Windows VISTA/XP,
  Microsoft Suite, MS Word, Excel, Access, PowerPoint, and Outlook.
- Possess working knowledge of Military Standard Requisition and Issue Procedures (MIL-
  STRIP), Defense Logistics Management Standards (DLMS), and an in-depth knowledge of
  Military Standard Transaction Reporting and Accounting Procedures (MILSTRAP).

APPENDIX B

SAMPLE COVER LETTERS AND THANK-YOU LETTERS

It is important to include a cover letter when you send out your resume in response to a job opening. The purpose of the cover letter is actually twofold. First, it informs the reader of your interest in obtaining employment with his or her firm. Second, it acts as a letter of transmittal for your resume and, in some cases, may serve to amplify additional experience not covered in the resume.

This section contains three sample cover letters that are typical of the types of correspondence you may find useful in preparing your response to potential employment opportunities.

In addition, there is one sample thank-you letter that you may want to use in sending out your own thank-you letter following an interview with a prospective employer.

James J. Johnson
404 Ashton Road • Upper Marlboro, Maryland 20972
jjj@myisp.com

January 30, 2009

Name of Person
Name of Company
Address
City, State ZIP

Dear Whomever (Dear Employer if no name is given, or one cannot be obtained):

This letter is in response to your recent advertisement in *The Washington Post* (or wherever it was) for the position of (job description). After carefully reviewing the prerequisites for this position, I believe my background, experience, and education qualify me as a potential candidate for this job opening.

While my attached resume cites examples in many of the areas of the position opening, there are some additional specifics that serve to further amplify my overall qualifications. (Cite some additional factors and examples—briefly—that relate to specific bullets in the ad. If you do not have any additional information worth mentioning, leave this paragraph out. Should they ask for salary history or salary requirements, use one of the following statements: Salary history will be furnished at the time of interview; or Salary is negotiable based on the requirements of the job and the range of compensation being offered for the position.)

I look forward to hearing from you soon and welcome the opportunity to further discuss my qualifications and capabilities regarding the position you are attempting to fill. Should you desire additional information, you may reach me during the day at (202) 699-1695 or in the evening after 6 P.M. at (410) 630-1546.

Sincerely yours,

James J. Johnson

Enclosure

Robert B. Tubman
1643 Rancho Vista Drive • Aurora, Colorado 80012
tubman@tunafish.net

July 25, 2009

Mr. William Tungston
Vice President for Operations
Starflex Enterprises, Inc.
1462 Galaxy Drive, Suite 9000
Fremont, CA 94539

Dear Mr. Tungston:

In view of my upcoming plans to leave military service after twenty years, I am currently exploring potential job opportunities in the western part of the United States. Starflex Enterprises was mentioned by a number of friends and acquaintances as a company that is constantly on the lookout for top-notch military personnel with an engineering and information systems background (or whatever your background is). With this in mind, I have taken the liberty of sending you a resume for review in the event you may have any position openings in the near future where my background and experience would benefit your company.

A review of my resume will provide you with a synopsis of accomplishments in the various line and staff assignments I have held and also will point out a number of areas where my experience closely parallels work currently ongoing at Starflex Enterprises. In addition to the experience cited in my resume, I have also had responsibilities in the following areas: (use bulleted examples to show additional areas that may be of interest to the prospective employer).

I look forward to hearing from you in the near future and welcome the opportunity to meet with you to further discuss my qualifications and capabilities regarding any position you are attempting to fill in my area of expertise. Should you desire additional information, you may reach me during the day at (303) 823-4365 or in the evening after 6 P.M. at (303) 630-1546.

Sincerely,

Robert B. Tubman

Enclosure

Lawrence N. Grissom
6734 Redcoat Court • San Antonio, Texas 89014
lngriss@setsail.com

August 26, 2009

Mr. Todd Hanscom
Blake, Hanscom & Stovall
4 Rathman Place
San Diego, CA 92110

Dear Mr. Hanscom:

In reference to our recent conversation, I've enclosed a resume as requested. Not specifically mentioned in my resume is the fact that I've had additional responsibilities other than just the production of aircraft parts and accessories in three different organizations over the past ten years. These responsibilities included the following:

- Extensive personnel and financial management of midsize to large organizations
- Daily attention to industry-wide requirements such as EEO and labor relations
- Numerous public-speaking engagements

Industrial production management and leadership are my strongest suits, and these are the areas where my attention is primarily focused in my job search.

I referred to a "second career," and sometimes that has a negative connotation to someone who does not understand the military retirement process. Let me expand on this briefly. I retired with only twenty-four years of active service because I ran out of challenges. The decision to move to the civilian sector was strictly my own, and I'm not looking for another twenty years of security as a "second career" reference might imply.

On the subject of compensation, I don't want to appear evasive, but I'm more interested in gaining an understanding of where I might fit in the firm, and future growth opportunities, before I state a specific salary for the position opening.

I trust that this letter will provide you with the additional information you requested and will allow you to better evaluate my credentials as a candidate for the management position you are seeking to fill.

Sincerely,

Lawrence N. Grissom

Enclosure

Lawrence N. Grissom
6734 Redcoat Court • San Antonio, Texas 89014
lngriss@setsail.com

September 15, 2009
Mr. Todd Hanscom
Blake, Hanscom & Stovall
4 Rathman Place
San Diego, CA 92110

Dear Mr. Hanscom:

I want to thank you and the other members of Blake, Hanscom & Stovall for making my recent interview a most rewarding process. Special thanks go to Ms. Sandra Howard, the head of manufacturing design, for explaining the production and design parameters involved in manufacturing the BH&S widgets used in the Concorde Space Shuttle.

Based on my tour of the BH&S facilities, the in-depth briefings provided by your key supervisory personnel, and the potential for future defense and commercial contracts, I feel confident that my skills and talents would be a good match for the position opening in your production management department.

Should you require any additional information relative to our discussions, please feel free to call me at 210-953-1882 from 9 to 5, or 210-967-1998 after 6 P.M. I would welcome the opportunity to continue our dialogue concerning the position opening, and trust that you will consider my qualifications and interest in BH&S when making your final decision to hire.

Sincerely,

Lawrence N. Grissom

APPENDIX C

MILITARY SERVICE–RELATED ORGANIZATIONS

Note: Organizations marked with an asterisk (*) provide employment or career transition assistance.

Air Force Association (AFA)*
Membership Services
1501 Lee Highway
Arlington, VA 22209
(703) 247-5800
(800) 727-3337
www.afa.org

Air Force Sergeants Association
   (AFSA)
5211 Auth Rd.
Suitland, MD 20746
(301) 899-3500
(800) 638-0594
www.afsahq.org

AMVETS
4647 Forbes Blvd.
Lanham, MD 20706-4300
(301) 459-9600
(877) 726-8387
www.amvets.org

American Military Retirees
   Association (AMRA)*
5436 Peru St.
Plattsburgh, NY 12901
(800) 424-2969
www.amra1973.org

Armed Forces Communications
   and Electronics Association
   (AFCEA)
4400 Fair Lakes Ct.
Fairfax, VA 22033-3899
(703) 631-6100
(800) 336-4583
www.afcea.org

Army Aviation Association of
   America (AAAA)
755 Main St., Suite 4D
Monroe, CT 06468-2830
(203) 268-2450
www.quad-a.org

Association of Graduates of the
    U.S. Air Force Academy*
3116 Academy Dr.
USAF Academy, CO 80840-4475
(719) 472-0300
www.aog-usafa.org

Association of the United
    States Army (AUSA)*
2425 Wilson Blvd.
Arlington, VA 22201
(800) 336-4570
www.ausa.org

Disabled American Veterans
    (DAV)*
3725 Alexandria Ave.
Cold Spring, KY 41076
(859) 441-7300
www.dav.org

Fleet Reserve Association
    (FRA)
125 N. West St.
Alexandria, VA 22314-2754
(703) 683-1400
(800) FRA-1924
www.fra.org

Marine Corps Association
    (MCA)*
715 Broadway St.
Quantico, VA 22134
(703) 640-6161
(800) 336-0291
www.mca-marines.org

Marine Corps League
P.O. Box 3070
Merrifield, VA 22116
(703) 207-9588
(800) 625-1775
www.mcleague.org

Marine Executive Association
    (MEA)*
P.O. Box 9372
McLean, VA 22102-0372
(703) 734-7974
www.marinea.org

The Military Officers Associa-
    tion of America (MOAA)*
MOAA Officer Placement Ser-
    vice (TOPS)
201 N. Washington St.
Alexandria, VA 22314-2539
(703) 838-8117
(800) 245-8762
www.moaa.org

National Defense Transporta-
    tion Association (NDTA)*
50 S. Pickett St., Suite 220
Alexandria, VA 22304-7296
(703) 751-5011
www.ndtahq.com

National Guard Association of
    the United States
One Massachusetts Ave. NW
Washington, DC 20001
(202) 789-0031
www.ngaus.org

Non-Commissioned Officers
    Association (NCOA)*
10635 IH 35 N.
San Antonio, TX 78233
(210) 653-6161
www.ncoausa.org

Paralyzed Veterans of America*
801 18th St. NW
Washington, DC 20006-3517
(800) 555-9140
www.pva.org

U.S. Army Warrant Officers
    Association*
462 Herndon Pkwy., Suite 207
Herndon, VA 20170-5235
(703) 742-7727
(800) 587-2962
www.usawoa.org

U.S. Naval Academy Alumni
    Association
247 King George St.
Annapolis, MD 21402-5068
(410) 295-4000
www.usna.com

Veterans of Foreign Wars*
406 West 34th St.
Kansas City, MO 64111
(816) 756-3390
www.vfw.org

West Point Association of Grad-
    uates
698 Mills Rd.
West Point, NY 10996 (local
    societies throughout the
    United States)
(845) 446-1500
www.westpointaog.org

APPENDIX D

EXAMPLES OF COMPUTING SALARY REQUIREMENTS

The Department of Defense's Military Compensation website (*www.dod.mil/militarypay*) provides information on pay and allowances, retirement, benefits, survivor benefits, and other related compensation and benefits matters. Also available on the website are calculators for regular military compensation and retirement projects for the various retirements systems (e.g., High-3, CSB/REDUX). You are encouraged to use these tools in your salary research for career transition.

To compute the starting salary you will need to maintain your standard of living, obtain a current copy of your Leave and Earnings Statement (LES) and a copy of the federal income tax schedule for the tax year closest to your exit point. Using both the LES and the tax rate schedule, follow the steps provided for the example (A, B, or C) that most closely approximates your pay grade and time in service. The examples used in this appendix are based on the 2009 military pay scales and 2008 tax rate tables.

Computations used in these examples are based on combining your nontaxable allowances with your annual base pay in order to determine the tax bracket (15, 25, or 28 percent) this new gross income figure will place you in. Combining these numbers allows for taxes on income that no longer will be tax-free once you enter the civilian workplace. By following the example that is closest to your pay and allowance situation, you will see what the tax differential is in terms of real dollars for the loss of the nontaxable allowances. For the purposes of these examples, the following formula applies:

Additional taxes = nontaxable allowances × tax bracket
(15%, 25%, or 28%)

Tax differential = additional taxes ÷ [1 – tax bracket]

If you will be settling in an area with a state income tax, you can use the same formula to determine how these annual taxes will affect your pay picture. And finally, if you decide to go into business for yourself, don't forget that you will be responsible for accounting for the full F.I.C.A. withholding as well as your own estimated taxes, since you will be your own employer.

Example A—Army, USMC, USAF, Navy O-5 (LTC/Cdr)
(retiring in the Washington, D.C., area after twenty years' service)

Step 1 <u>Monthly Pay and Allowances Breakdown</u>

Base Pay (over twenty years)	$7,697.40
BAH (with dependents)	2,707.00*
BAS	223.04*
	$10,627.44

Step 2

Monthly pay and allowances × 12	=	$127,529.28
Annual retirement pay (High-3)	=	- 42,600.00
Pay differential after retirement		$84,929.28

Step 3 For the purpose of this example, let's assume you are married, with three dependents, and can claim $15,000 interest on your home and other itemized deductions. Using the federal tax guide for tax year 2008, take the rounded total income figure ($127,529) from step 2 and subtract your exemptions ($3,500 × 5) and your deductions ($15,000). We use the total income figure for our calculations in order to determine which tax bracket this income will place you in as a result of the loss of the nontaxable allowances (*). Subtracting the five exemptions and the itemized deductions gives you a taxable income figure of $95,029.

Step 4 Now take your taxable income figure ($95,029) from step 3 and, using Schedule Y-1 from the revised 2008 tax rate schedules, see where this figure falls in relation to the tax brackets shown. Since this number falls between the $56,800 and $114,650 figures, you are in the 25 percent tax bracket.

Step 5 In order to determine the tax differential figure, you will need to add to your total income figure to offset the loss of income from your nontaxable allowances, using the following formulas:

$$\text{Additional taxes} = \text{nontaxable allowances}$$
$$(12 \times \text{sum of monthly nontaxable allowances* [rounded], or}$$
$$\$35,160) \times \text{tax bracket (25\%)}$$
$$\text{Tax differential} = \text{additional taxes}$$
$$(\$8,790) \div (1 - \text{tax bracket}$$
$$[1.00 - .25, \text{ or } .75]) = \$11,720$$

Step 6 Now add the above tax differential of $11,720 to the rounded pay differential after retirement from step 2 ($84,929) and you will have a figure ($96,649) that, when added to your retired pay, should allow for a comparable standard of living. This number should be used as a baseline for all salary negotiations, with the idea of improving upon it whenever possible.

Example B—Navy Lieutenant O-3 (Naval Aviator) without Dependents
(separating on seven years' service in the Norfolk, Virginia, area)

Step 1 Monthly Pay and Allowances Breakdown

Base pay (over six years)	$4,948.80
Flight pay (over six years)	650.00
BAH (no dependents)	1,534.00*
BAS	223.04*
	$7,355.84

Step 2 Base pay and flight pay × 12   = $67,185.60
Nontaxable allowances (*) × 12   =   21,084.48
                                                                        $88,270.08

Step 3 Using the federal tax guide for tax year 2008, take the rounded total income figure ($88,270) from step 2 and subtract your one exemption ($3,500) and the standard deduction (unless your deductions exceed the $10,900 standard deduction figure). We use the total income figure for our calculations in order to determine which tax bracket this income will place you in as a result of the loss of the nontaxable allowances. Subtracting the one exemption and the standard deduction gives you a taxable income figure of $73,870.

Step 4 Now take your taxable income figure ($73,870) from step 3 and, using Schedule X from the revised 2008 tax schedules, see where this figure falls in relation to the tax brackets shown. Since this number falls between $32,550 and $78,850, you are in the 25 percent tax bracket.

Step 5 In order to determine the tax differential figure, you will need to add to your total income figure to offset the loss of income from your nontaxable allowances by using the following formulas:

Additional taxes = nontaxable allowances
                                ($21,084) × tax bracket (25%)
Tax differential   = additional taxes
                                ($5,271) ÷ (1 – tax bracket
                                [1.00 – .25, or .75]) = $7,028

Step 6 Now add the above tax differential of $7,028 to the rounded total of your base pay and allowances figure from step 2 ($88,270) and you will have a figure ($95,298) that represents in civilian dollars your current military pay after separation. This number should be used as a baseline for all salary negotiations, with the idea of improving upon it whenever possible.

Example C—Army, Navy, USMC, USAF E-7
(SFC/CPO/Gy SGT/MSGT)
(retiring in Tampa, Florida, after twenty years' service)

Step 1 Monthly Pay and Allowances Breakdown

Base pay (over twenty years)	$3,995.40
BAH (with dependents)	1,831.00*
BAS (messing separately)	326.87*
	$6,153.27

Step 2

Monthly pay and allowances × 12	=	$73,839.24
Annual retirement pay	=	$22,452.00
Pay differential after retirement		$51,387.24

Step 3 For the purpose of this example, let's assume you are married with two dependents, claim $14,000 ($3,500 × 4) in personal exemptions, and only have enough deductions to take the standard deduction ($10,900). Using the federal tax tables for tax year 2008, take the rounded total income figure ($73,839) from step 2 and subtract your exemptions and the standard deduction ($24,900). Use the total income figure for your calculations in order to determine which tax bracket this income will place you in as a result of the loss of the nontaxable allowances (*). Subtracting the four exemptions and the standard deduction gives a taxable income figure of $48,939.

Step 4 Now take your taxable income figure ($48,939) from step 3 and, using Schedule Y-1 from the revised 2008 tax rate schedule, see where this figure falls in relation to the tax brackets shown. Since this number falls between $16,050 and $65,100, you are in the 15 percent tax bracket.

Step 5 In order to determine the tax differential figure, you will need to add to your total income figure to offset the loss of income from your nontaxable allowance by using the following formula:

Additional taxes   = nontaxable allowances
                      (12 × sum of monthly nontaxable
                      allowances* [rounded], or
                      $25,894) × tax bracket (15%)

Tax differential   = additional taxes ($3,884) ÷
                      (1 – tax bracket [1.00 – .15, or
                      .85]) = $4,569

Step 6 Now add the above tax differential of $4,569 to the rounded
pay differential after retirement figure from step 2 ($51,387)
and you will have a figure ($55,956) that, when added to your
retirement pay, should allow for a comparable standard of living. This number should be used as a baseline for all salary
negotiations, with the idea of improving upon it whenever
possible.

APPENDIX E

RECOMMENDED READING

BOOKS

Beshara, Tony. *The Job Search Solution: The Ultimate System for Finding a Great Job Now.* AMACOM, 2006. "Deliberately challenges conventional job search wisdom, and in so doing, offers radical but inspired suggestions for success." Rated with four and a half stars (****1/2) on Amazon.com.

Doyle, Alison. *Internet Your Way to a New Job.* Happy About, Cupertino, CA, 2008. This compact guide contains straightforward information that is useful in all respects. The author advises you where to go, how to get there, and what to expect from Internet job searching. Also includes information on branding, blogging, and how to use Linkedin, JibberJobber, and other online job search management tools. The perfect companion to *Job Search* for answers to all your Internet job search questions. Five stars (*****) on Amazon.com.

Ferguson, et al. *The Encyclopedia of Careers and Vocational Guidance*, 14th edition, 5 volumes. Ferguson Publishing Company, New York, 2007. Volume 1 includes sixty-eight industries, covering such areas as general information, structure, career opportunities, industry outlook, and a list of organizations within each industry that can help the reader. Volumes 2 to 4 contain information on particular jobs and careers, including the top ten fastest growing careers through 2014. All five volumes are cross-referenced with either the *Occupational Outlook Handbook* or the *O*Net Dictionary of Occupational Titles 2006*. Excellent starting point for gaining insight into career fields of possible interest.

The Gale Group, editors. *Career Information Center*, 9th edition, 13 volumes. Macmillan Publishing Company, New York, 2006. Excellent companion to the *Occupational Outlook Handbook*. Covers all major occupational fields, from administration through transportation, with volume 13 containing the master index as well as essays on different aspects of employment. For each field, it discusses required education and training, salary ranges, and employment outlook. Occupational field titles match those in the *Occupational Outlook Handbook*.

Kennedy, James H. *The Directory of Executive Recruiters 2009–10*. Kennedy & Kennedy, Inc., Fitzwilliam, NH, 2009. A listing of more than 7,800 executive search firms, shown by occupational areas for both retainer and contingency recruiters. Contains a brief glossary of search-firm terminology, articles of interest for job changers, and advice for clients and executive search–firm candidates.

Levinson, Jay, and David Perry. *Guerrilla Marketing for Job Hunters: 400 Unconventional Tips, Tricks, and Tactics for Landing Your Dream Job*. John Wiley & Sons, Inc., Hoboken, NJ, 2005. This informative guide covers a wide range of job search topics, including using the Internet in a variety of ways, radically revising your resume, uncovering opportunities in the "Hidden Job Market," finding an identity for yourself that can be projected in your resume, and corresponding and interviewing with potential employers. Rated five stars (*****) on Amazon.com.

Oliver, Vicky. *301 Smart Answers to Tough Interview Questions*. Sourcebooks, Inc., Naperville, IL, 2005. This invaluable book explains how to handle difficult interview questions and prevent potential disqualifiers from previous jobs (military or civilian) from interfering with your quest for gainful employment. Amazon.com posts a rating of four and half stars (****$^1/_2$), but because it is so even-handed in assisting both male and female readers in fielding tricky and sensitive gender-related interview questions, I would give it five stars plus.

Whitcomb, Susan. *Resume Magic: Trade Secrets of a Professional Resume Writer*. JIST Publishing, St. Paul, MN, 2006. "Allows the reader to select a templated format based on own experience then write a draft using the building block approach." Also has two companion books titled *Cover Letter Magic* and *Interview Magic*. Rated five stars (*****) on Amazon.com.

Yate, Martin. *Knock 'em Dead 2009*. Adams Media Corporation, Cincinnati, OH, 2008. This book and its companion, *Resumes that Knock 'em Dead*, have both received high reviews from those who are in the job search process. Instructs the reader on identifying best job opportunities, crafting letters of introduction, and answering interview questions. Rated four and a half stars (****1/2) on Amazon.com and is billed as the best book for the interview process and the best overall book for getting a job.

OTHER REFERENCE SOURCES

The Kiplinger Washington Letter. The Kiplinger Washington Editors, 1729 H St. NW, Washington, D.C. A weekly newsletter that highlights areas of the economy that may have an effect on the average American, including issues such as Social Security, employment trends, real estate markets by areas of the United States, the stock market and investing, and pending legislation before Congress. Information of most significance to separating or retiring servicemembers would be the employment trends, forecasts, unemployment figures, and real estate and construction starts in the area where they might be planning on settling after they leave the service.

Marketing Yourself for a Second Career. The premier publication of the Military Officers Association of America (MOAA). It is a combination textbook and how-to guide for prospective job searchers preparing to embark on the second career job search. Generally updated every five or so years.

Occupational Outlook Handbook 2008–09. U.S. Department of Labor, 2008, Government Printing Office, Washington, D.C., 2002. Describes what workers do on each job, training and education needed, earnings, working conditions, and expected job prospects for 250 career occupations. In each biennial update, there is an introduction entitled "Tomorrow's Jobs" that provides statistics and information on the fastest-growing occupational fields, educational requirements for these fields, and the best jobs within a selected career field through 2010.

TOPS Job Bulletin Board. Put out by the Military Officers of America Association (MOAA). A daily listing of 1,500 job opportunities from across the United States that span the current and previous month's employment openings. This bulletin board is available to those members who participate in the TOPS Online Career Transition Assistance Program.

INDEX

aerospace and defense
  professionals, 39–40
Air Force
  Airman and Family Support
    Center, 46
  Transition Assistance
    Program 48–49
Air Force Association (AFA),
  53–55, 231
Air Force Sergeants
  Association (AFSA), 231
Air Force Times, 68, 71, 72, 74
Aircraft Maintenance
  Management resume,
  162–63
Airline/Air Cargo Pilot resume,
  216
Alliance International, job
  search website address,
  126
American Military Retirees
  Association (AMRA), 231
  job search website address,
  126
AMVETS, 231
annual reports, 79–80, 91
Architecture/Environmental
  Engineering resume,
  209–10

Armed Forces Communications
  and Electronics Association
  (AFCEA), 231
Army Aviation Association of
  America (AAAA), 231
Army Career and Alumni
  Program (ACAP), 46–48
  job fairs, 62
  as networking source, 59
Army Times, 68, 71, 72, 74
Association of Graduates of the
  U.S. Air Force Academy,
  232
Association of the United
  States Army (AUSA), 232
Aviation
  Operations/Information
  Operations/Resources
  Management resume,
  170–71
Aviation Week, 69, 79

benefits programs, 149–52, 157
  bonuses, 152, 157
  cafeteria plans, 152–53
  day care, 153
  dental plans, 150–51
  educational assistance, 153
  401(k) retirement plans,
    151–52

ABOUT THE AUTHOR

Since his retirement as a lieutenant colonel from the Marine Corps, David G. Henderson has provided career transition assistance services to over 4,000 officers and senior enlisted personnel from every branch of the armed forces. He has participated in career transition workshops and seminars for the Marine Corps Executive Association, the Society of Logistic Engineers, and the Association of Military Academy Graduates.

For the past nineteen years, he has provided resume preparation and critique services to the Air Force Association (AFA). His resumes have consistently received high accolades for their content and ability to portray career experience in a format best suited for the individual's qualifications and goals. In 2002, he signed on with The Destiny Group, a military job search assistance firm based in San Diego, California, to support their online FasTrac Resume Assistance program, a minimal fee–based service providing resume reviews and critiques of member resumes.

In addition to the four previous editions of *Job Search: Marketing Your Military Experience,* Mr. Henderson has written numerous articles on career transition, which have appeared in *Army, Navy.* and *Air Force Times*, the *U.S. Naval Institute Proceedings*, and the "Managing Your Career" supplement to the former *National Business Employment Weekly*, published by *The Wall Street Journal.*

STACKPOLE
BOOKS

Military Professional Reference Library

Air Force Officer's Guide
Airman's Guide
Armed Forces Guide to Personal Financial Planning
Army Dictionary and Desk Reference
Army Officer's Guide
Career Progression Guide for Soldiers
Combat Leader's Field Guide
Combat Service Support Guide
Enlisted Soldier's Guide
Guide to Effective Military Writing
Job Search: Marketing Your Military Experience
Military Money Guide
NCO Guide
Servicemember's Legal Guide
Servicemember's Guide to a College Degree
Soldier's Study Guide
Today's Military Wife
Veteran's Guide to Benefits

Professional Reading Library

Guardians of the Republic: A History of the NCO Corps
by Ernest F. Fisher

Looking for Trouble
by Ralph Peters

Wars of Blood and Faith: The Conflicts That Will
Shape the Twenty-First Century
by Ralph Peters

Roots of Strategy, Books 1, 2, 3, and 4

Stackpole Books are available at your Exchange Bookstore or
Military Clothing Sales Store or from Stackpole at
1-800-732-3669 *or* **www.stackpolebooks.com**